The Jews of Rhode Island

The Jews of

BRANDEIS UNIVERSITY PRESS

Waltham, Massachusetts

in Association with

Rhode Island Jewish Historical Association

Published by University Press of New England

Hanover and London

Rhode Island

GEORGE M. GOODWIN & ELLEN SMITH   EDITORS

Brandeis University Press
Published by University Press of New England,
Hanover, New Hampshire
University Press of New England,
One Court Street, Lebanon, NH 03766
In association with Rhode Island Jewish
Historical Association
www.upne.com
© 2004 by Brandeis University Press
Printed in the United States of America
5 4 3 2 1

Designed by Richard Hendel

Library of Congress
Cataloging-in-Publication Data

The Jews of Rhode Island / George M. Goodwin
& Ellen Smith, editors.
   p. cm. — (Brandeis series in American
Jewish history, culture, and life)
Includes bibliographical references and index.
ISBN 1-58465-424-4 (cloth : alk. paper)
1. Jews — Rhode Island — History.
2. Rhode Island — Ethnic relations.
I. Goodwin, George M.
II. Smith, Ellen.
III. Series.
F90.J5J49 2004
974.5′004924 — dc22   2004012149

CONTENTS

Few American Jewish communities have been studied as thoroughly as Rhode Island's. Beyond its colonial heritage, however, little about this community is widely known. *The Jews of Rhode Island* seeks to change all that. This volume celebrates the 50th anniversary of the journal that has presented and honored much of Rhode Island's Jewish past: *Rhode Island Jewish Historical Notes*.

First published in 1954 to celebrate the 300th anniversary of the arrival of Jews in North America, *The Notes* was the inspiration of David C. Adelman. Three years earlier, he and several colleagues founded the Rhode Island Jewish Historical Association to collect and preserve documents, photographs, and artifacts and to promote their study through lectures and publications. By establishing a journal, the founders built a lasting monument to the American Jewish tercentenary. They insured that knowledge of their own Jewish community would continue to grow.

For most of its first five years, authors kept up the breathless pace of generating enough material for two issues a year. As topics were examined in greater depth, the journal was published annually. Within Rhode Island, only *The Jewish Herald* and a few synagogue bulletins have a longer publishing history. Indeed, *The Notes* has become the longest-running publication by a state or local Jewish historical society in America.

Though most of the early contributors to *Rhode Island Jewish Historical Notes* were dedicated amateurs, they recognized both the necessity and urgency of their task. Unless they augmented the attention paid to colonial Newport, a comprehensive and livelier history of Rhode Island Jewry would be lost. Proud of their efforts, several writers were also remarkably successful. As a result, Rhode Island's Jewish community will be forever grateful to such patriarchs and matriarchs as David Adelman, Geraldine Foster, Seebert Goldowsky, Eleanor Horvitz, and Beryl Segal.

The Jewish community is also grateful to many Brown University professors and students for their contributions in recent decades. They have introduced new topics and methods as well as fresh perspectives. Researchers from additional colleges and universities have brought *The Notes* closer to the forefront of scholarly inquiry and debate.

The Jews of Rhode Island presents 17 from more than 300 previously published articles. These articles were selected for their high quality and also to suggest the rich variety of topics investigated over a half-century. The sampling of articles has been organized around four themes, representing demographic, economic, cultural, and personal dimensions of Rhode Island Jewish history. This arrangement is somewhat capricious, for many of the articles illustrate a combination of themes. While most articles have been shortened, none have been updated since their original date of publication.

There are also two new articles and other supporting materials. Three new photographic essays replace most of the photographs that once accompanied the articles.

Despite its fifty years in publication, *Rhode Island Jewish Historical Notes* has left significant gaps and omissions. For example, articles about faith and religious observance have been overlooked. Studies comparing Rhode Island's Jewish community to other Jewish communities and to other religious and ethnic communities within Rhode

Island are needed. More articles about newer Jewish immigrants to Rhode Island from the former Soviet Union, Israel, and South Africa would be appropriate. It is also time to examine the experiences of American-born generations, particularly in relation to Israel. There should be articles about Rhode Islanders who have studied, worked, fought, and settled in Israel.

As a matter of policy, *The Notes* shied away from articles about the eras in which it was created and through which it has evolved. For example, the topic of Jews in Rhode Island politics has been largely ignored. Though mentioned in many articles, the history of Jewish women needs a stronger assessment. There is an ongoing need to publish memoirs, letters, and distinctive photographs.

The Notes must no longer skirt controversy. It must take more risks to be both authoritative and timely. Nearly any topic, well researched and imaginatively written, will invigorate the journal.

Sooner or later the Rhode Island Jewish Historical Association will face a challenge not fully appreciated by its founders. Based on the sturdy foundation built by *The Notes*, the time is swiftly approaching when it will be necessary to erect a new structure. This will be a comprehensive history of Jews who have found and made a home in the Ocean State.

Providence and Boston   G.M.G. and E.S.
June 2003

ACKNOWLEDGMENTS

Through this anthology the Rhode Island Jewish Historical Association is delighted to celebrate the first half-century of its journal, *Rhode Island Jewish Historical Notes*. This celebration happily coincides with the 350th anniversary of the Jewish arrival in North America and the 150th anniversary of Sons of Israel and David, Providence's oldest Jewish congregation.

From its outset, *The Notes* has been an ambitious endeavor, but fundamentally a labor of love. Despite a meager budget, a small readership, and sparse recognition, the journal has nurtured a community of scholars, rabbis, teachers, students, genealogists, and history buffs. Jews and Gentiles, natives and newcomers, old and young have been surprised, challenged, and inspired by its pages.

On behalf of the Association, I proudly and humbly thank the scores of writers, editors, bibliographers, typists, proofreaders, and indexers who have contributed to the journal's success. For the creation of this anthology, I am deeply grateful to the Association's board of directors and its publications committee, especially chairman Stanley B. Abrams, who provided wise counsel and bounding optimism.

This volume would never have materialized without the encouragement and support of many friends and neighbors. The Association is deeply grateful to the trustees and staff of the Dorot Foundation for a magnificent grant. Thanks are also due to the leadership of the Jewish Federation of Rhode Island's Endowment Fund and the Rhode Island Foundation's ADDD Fund for their faith in this endeavor.

Additional financial support has been generously provided by: Sandra and Stanley Abrams, the Alperin/Hirsch Family Foundation, Beverly and Banice Bazar, Mitzi and Robert Berkelhammer, Susan and Stephen Brown, Rosalie and Norman Fain, Janice and Harold Gadon, Ira S. and Anna Galkin Charitable Trust, Maxine and Edward Goldin, Molly and Michael Goodwin, the Hassenfeld Foundation, the Koffler/Bornstein Families, Charlotte Penn, P. Susan Shindler, Jill and James Tobak, Arline and Eugene Weinberg, Harold Werner, the Yaraus Family Association, and Janet and Melvin Zurier.

Thanks to the following individuals for their ideas and high expectations: Michael Feldberg, director of the American Jewish Historical Society; Albert T. Klyberg and Bernard P. Fishman, the retired and current directors of the Rhode Island Historical Society; Professor Calvin Goldscheider of Brown University; and Naida Weisberg and Jane Civins of the Providence Jewelry Museum.

Most of the photographs reproduced in this volume came from the Association's vast collection. Eleanor F. Horvitz, our longtime librarian-archivist, deserves particular thanks for assembling and cataloguing these riches. Anne Sherman, the Association's office manager, has been helpful with photographs and in numerous other capacities.

Many archivists, curators, and librarians—too numerous to mention individually—have assisted in the search for additional photographs. The Association gratefully acknowledges the cooperation provided by the following institutions: The Detroit Institute of Arts, Narragansett Council of the Boy Scouts of America, Moses Brown School, Providence College, Providence Journal Company, Providence Public Library, Rhode Island

Historical Society, Slater Mill Historic Site, Temple Beth-El, Temple Emanu-El, Touro Synagogue, Trinity Repertory Company, and *Worcester Telegram & Gazette*. Several families and businesses also kindly lent photographs.

The Association is thankful for the advice and encouragement provided by Professor Jonathan D. Sarna of Brandeis University. The staff of the University Press of New England has been consistently helpful. Its executive editor, Phyllis Deutsch, has championed this volume. The Association and I also express our gratitude to my colleague, Ellen Smith, who strengthened many facets of this anthology.

In order to survive and flourish, the Rhode Island Jewish Historical Association must recruit new generations of readers, writers, editors, and benefactors. Please join us. Help us see our heritage in fresh, imaginative, and compelling ways.

George M. Goodwin
President

RHODE ISLAND JEWRY A PERSONAL PERSPECTIVE

George M. Goodwin

No doubt about it: Rhode Island is quirky. If named after Indian places like Connecticut and Massachusetts, this state should have been Aquidneck. Given a half-dozen islands in Narragansett Bay, including Prudence and Patience, we are named for one in the Aegean. Though founded as a haven of religious liberty, Rhode Island and Providence Plantations was home to New England's most successful slavers. Victory over Japan Day is still a legal holiday.

Rhode Island's mascot is a hen, and its official beverage is coffee-flavored milk. When a motorist stops for directions, a pedestrian usually remarks, "Turn where that fire station used to be." Indeed, in a capital city not untouched by skullduggery, some of the loveliest streets are Hope, Benefit, and Benevolent. Rhode Island's most famous Quaker was named Moses. The state's leading theater company, founded largely by Jews, is called Trinity Repertory.

Rhode Island may be America's smallest state, but Rhode Islanders consider it among the largest. Providence, North Providence, and East Providence are separate municipalities, as are Warwick and West Warwick. A favorite destination is South County, which does not actually exist. While proud of their thirty-nine cities and towns, Rhode Islanders can drive to any of them within an hour.

For more than three centuries, however, long distances and small scale nurtured Rhode Island Jewry. Indeed, an argument can be made that Newport's Jewish community reached its apogee during the eighteenth century, under British rule, when all of its members could gather in one building.

During the nineteenth century, when drawn to Providence or the state's next largest cities, Pawtucket and Woonsocket, Jews followed a familiar pattern. They consecrated cemeteries, established congregations, and created self-help organizations. Rather than feeling isolated or threatened, Jewish merchants often felt quite content. Such outposts as Bristol, Smithfield, and Westerly may have anchored Jewish families and farmers living in smaller crossroads.

At the turn of the twentieth century, when Providence was America's twentieth largest city and Rhode Island was fast becoming the first state with a Catholic majority, Jews were not confined to a single neighborhood. They were largely divided between South Providence (not a city) and the North End (not a terminus). Indeed, some Jews could differentiate between the enclaves of the North End and Smith Hill or argue over where the East Side began.

Quite happy on their home turfs, Jewish Rhode Islanders resisted repeated efforts to unify and consolidate. For decades, larger synagogues frequently splintered into smaller ones. Each neighborhood sprouted its own burial society, its own free loan association, or its own chapter of Hadassah. Not until 1945, a half-century after Boston established its Combined Jewish Philanthropies, did Providence succeed in forming its General Jewish Committee. The Jewish Federation of Rhode Island was not organized until 1970. And even today, despite the necessity of a central governing body, some individuals resent Federation's yearning for strength and order.

In addition to synagogues of every denomination and persuasion, Rhode Island's Jewish community has been able to create a remarkable system of educational and social service agencies. Needless to say, these agencies have served young and old, healthy and sick, prosperous and poor, natives and newcomers. In this sense, Rhode Island Jewry has been far from unique. Treasuring their heritage, most Jews here have worked hard to maintain and sustain it.

While some agencies were created in response to discrimination, anti-Semitism has only periodically clouded Narragansett Bay. By contrast, Native Americans and Blacks have suffered bitter ostracism. For most groups, however, Rhode Island endures as a safe haven. Its Baptist founders were exiles from Massachusetts, and Quakers and Jews became catalysts for trade and commerce. Waves of immigration brought Irish, Italians, French Canadians, Germans, Portuguese, Cape Verdians, Armenians, Greeks, Hispanics, Asians, and others to these rocky and windswept shores. Indeed, by the late twentieth century, most groups could claim minority status, including the disappearing Yankees.

While helping their own, Jews in Rhode Island have always shared some of their good fortune with the larger community. Since colonial times they have supported such institutions as Newport's Redwood Library and Brown University. In recent decades they have become major benefactors of artistic, musical, and theatrical organizations. Jews have also supported private schools, colleges, and universities as well as hospitals. After barriers were lowered, Jews helped govern the Rhode Island Foundation and led the United Way.

Jewish generosity was made possible by a keen entrepreneurial spirit, which both preceded and succeeded Rhode Island's golden age of manufacturing in the late-nineteenth and early-twentieth centuries. Jews were largely able to bypass jobs as factory workers to become peddlers, shopkeepers, and small manufacturers. Successful in discovering niches within the textile and jewelry industries, they also created new opportunities in such businesses as department stores, discount stores, mail order stores, tires, luggage, and toys. Given such ingenuity and competitiveness, is it surprising that they never established a Jewish Vocational Service?

For generations Jews also prospered in Rhode Island's public schools, which brought to life dead languages and helped bury Yiddish. Jewish kids excelled at many levels, and men and women found positions as teachers, administrators, and union leaders.

The Jewish presence at Brown University, a Baptist institution once requiring daily chapel attendance, has grown ever larger and stronger. Brown would gain renown not only for its program in Judaic studies but for Jewish faculty in numerous departments. Maurice Glicksman, a physicist, served as dean of the faculty and provost. Providence College, Rhode Island School of Design, Bryant College, and the University of Rhode Island, among others, also enrolled Jewish students and hired Jewish professors. U.R.I.'s Hillel foundation is housed in Christopher House.

For such postgraduate fields as law, medicine, and dentistry, however, Rhode Islanders have been required to study elsewhere. Harvard alumni are most eager to point this out. A large number of Jews have returned to establish practices here, and many have become prominent in their professions. For much of the twentieth century, Jews have also been appointed or elected to high judgeships.

Since the late nineteenth century, when Isaac Hahn was elected to the state legislature, many Jews have enjoyed the confidence and support of fellow Rhode Islanders. Perhaps inspired and emboldened by John O. Pastore, later the nation's first Italian American senator, two Jews have been elected governor. The Providence County Courthouse was named for Frank Licht; the passenger terminal at Green Airport for Bruce Sundlun. These public places sound better than "Jews Street," which became part of Bellevue Avenue in Newport.

As Democrats and Republicans, Jews have held nearly every office in state government. For example, Richard Israel, Julius Michaelson, and Jeffrey Pine served as attorneys general. Three Jewish women were elected to the legislature, though all were defeated in bids for higher office. Speaking of lost causes, Rabbi Baruch Korff, who tried to exonerate Richard Nixon, left his papers to Brown. At present, Providence has its first Jewish mayor, David Cicilline.

Generations of Jews have expressed their patriotism through military service. Numerous cemeteries and synagogue walls proudly bear the names of citizen soldiers. Leonard Holland's tenure as adjutant general and commander of the Rhode Island National Guard outlasted his counterparts in every state. Jews have also taught and studied at Newport's Naval War College and worked in weapons laboratories.

Some Jews in Rhode Island have expressed their patriotism in other ways. They have opposed bloodshed and resisted conscription. Milton Stanzler founded the state affiliate of the American Civil Liberties Union, and Richard Zacks became a national officer. Despite the tradition of religious liberty begun by Roger Williams, conflicts over the separation of church and state constantly erupt. Indeed, Daniel Weisman and his daughter, Deborah, won support from the United States Supreme Court for their opposition to a rabbi's prayer at a public school graduation.

The community is worldly in its support of the Jewish people and worldly in its concern for victims of injustice and misfortune. Ida Silverman spoke throughout Europe and North and South America for Israeli statehood. Max and Ruth Alperin built a regional college for Israeli Jews and Arabs. Sylvia Hassenfeld was national president of the Joint Distribution Committee, and Norman Tilles was national president of the Hebrew Immigrant Aid Society. Rabbis William Braude, Saul Leeman, and Nathan Rosen marched from Selma to Montgomery with the Reverend Martin Luther King. Lester Jacobs, most likely a Jew, sacrificed his life for democracy in the Spanish Civil War.

Since Aaron Lopez in the eighteenth century, Rhode Island Jewry has produced few figures of national or international stature. Two prominent newsmen, Irving R. Levine and Fred Friendly, grew up here, but no Jew associated with Rhode Island is chased by paparazzi or flickers in cyberspace. Yet, Jews from elsewhere have grabbed headlines here. During the 1950s and '60s, George Wein, from Massachusetts, created Newport's Jazz and Folk Festivals. Ben Cohen and Jerry Greenfield, the ice cream moguls from Vermont, revived some of those concerts. And Alan Dershowitz, from Cambridge, rode to the rescue of Claus von Bulow, when von Bulow was accused of murdering his wife Sunny in Newport.

Jews no longer reside in South Providence, and the North End no longer exists. We have become more scattered, more elderly, and more conditioned to intermarriage. Except for victims of intolerance and upheaval, Rhode Island no longer beckons Jewish immigrants.

Yet, a sense of continuity, particularly evident on Providence's East Side, may be the Jewish community's most precious asset. Generations of local marriages have produced a vast cousinhood or a never-ending high school reunion. Though seldom a springboard for professional advancement, Rhode Island has become home for numerous rabbis, cantors, teachers, and agency executives. Some have spent entire careers within one institution. Even while struggling to summon a *minyan*, many congregations have amazingly endured.

Ironically, no synagogue may face a more precarious future than Touro. As its stature grows as a symbol of religious liberty, it endeavors to survive as a house of worship. But a century and a half ago, such a celebrated visitor as Henry Wadsworth Longfellow could only look backward, never imagining a new Jewish community. Yes, a miracle.

Long after Rhode Island should have been annexed by Connecticut or Massachusetts or joined the Commonwealth of New England, this quirky state is still around. Perhaps its citizens are oblivious to change or seasoned by adversity. They know how briefly sunshine lasts and how little in their lives is ever foreseeable.

Who could have predicted that Jews, less than two percent of Rhode Island's population, would become so successful and admired? That in every era or circumstance, Jews would find freedom, opportunity, community, and purpose? Who would argue that their fate has been purely accidental? Many would declare that Rhode Island Jewry has been blessed, that its destiny has indeed been providential.

The Jews of Rhode Island

Introduction The Jews of Rhode Island

ELLEN SMITH & JONATHAN D. SARNA

What we know as Rhode Island began in 1636 when Roger Williams, an independent-minded "godly minister" banished from Massachusetts for propagating new and dangerous opinions, founded a new colony for himself and his followers on Narragansett Bay. He called it Providence. Two years later, another group of banished dissenters, led by the even more independent-minded Anne Hutchinson, bought the island of Aquidneck (Rhode Island) from the local natives and established Pocasset, renamed after a quarrel over governance, Portsmouth. This quarrel precipitated yet a third split, and in 1639 dissenters from Portsmouth moved to the southern end of the island and founded Newport. Still another group of dissenters founded the settlement of Warwick in 1643.

None of these headstrong founders were Jews, nor do we know for certain that any Jews lived in Rhode Island prior to 1678. But some of the ideas that underlay Rhode Island's creation would, in time, have dramatic impact on Jews. Roger Williams hinted at this in 1644 when, on a visit to England to obtain Rhode Island's original charter, he argued for according Jews liberty of conscience and sided with those who advocated their readmission into England. Subsequently, Rhode Island's 1663 charter became the first in North America that provided for religious liberty as part of a colony's organic law. (By contrast, Maryland's Act of Toleration of 1649 was only a legislative statute, and in any case only applied to those "professing to believe in Jesus Christ.") According to the Rhode Island charter, which continued in force until replaced by the state constitution of 1842: "Noe person within the sayd colonye at any tyme hereafter, shall bee any wise molested, punished, disquieted, or called in question, for any differences in opinione in matters of religion . . . all and everye person and persons may . . . at all tymes hereafter, freely and fullye have and enjoye his and theire owne judgments and consciences, in matter of religious concernments, throughout the tract of lande hereafter mentioned; they behaving themselves peaceablie and quietlie, and not using this libertie to lycentiousnesse and profanenesse, nor to the civill injurye or outward disturbeance of any others."[1]

New Netherland, though a far more heterogeneous colony than Rhode Island, espoused a quite different policy. In 1654, when a boatload of Jews landed in Dutch New Amsterdam and sought permission to settle, its governor, Peter Stuyvesant, attempted to keep them out. The Jews, he believed, were "deceitful," "very repugnant," and "hateful enemies and blasphemers of the name of Christ." He asked the directors of the Dutch West India Company to "require them in a friendly way to depart" lest they "infect and trouble this new colony." In a subsequent letter, he warned that "giving them liberty we cannot refuse the Lutherans and Papists." For pragmatic reasons, the Dutch West India Company overrode him. Influenced by Jews who owned stock in the Company, and realizing that Jewish traders could strengthen the colony's economic position, it granted Jews permission to live, travel, and trade in the colony "provided the poor among them shall not become a burden to the company or the community, but be supported by their own nation."[2] The colony did not, however, extend freedom of conscience to Jews; in fact, it denied them the right to public worship, and so did the British when they captured the colony and renamed it New York. At least on paper, seventeenth-century Rhode Island granted Jews many more liberties than did any of its surrounding colonies.

The arrival of Jews in Rhode Island put the colony to the test. Around 1677 a group of Sephardim (Jews of Iberian descent) from Barbados arrived in Newport, likely motivated by the burgeoning trade between these two communities. A year later, the Jews purchased a "piece of land for a burial place," a persuasive sign that they had decided to settle permanently.[3] In 1684, they even received legal protection. The Assembly assured them that "they may Expect as good Protection here, as any Strainger being not of Our Nation residing amongst us in this his Majesties Collony Ought to have, being Obedient to his Majesties laws."[4] Rhode Island had already provided a tolerant home for schismatic Seventh Day Baptists, who observed the Sabbath on the seventh day, as well as for large numbers of widely reviled Quakers. The Jews, however, were the first non-Christians to receive protection, albeit as strangers.

Shortly thereafter, the small community of Jews disbanded, for reasons that remain unclear but may have been related to their alleged violations of the English Navigation Acts.[5] Whatever the case, the first Newport Jewish community, short-lived as it was, established a precedent. It demonstrated that in the colony of Rhode Island Jews could differ from their neighbors in matters of religion, and still enjoy freedom of conscience.

Individual Jews turned up from time to time in Newport following the departure of the Barbados Jews, and an old map from 1712 discloses the existence of a "Jews Street" (now part of Bellevue Avenue) perpendicular to Griffin Street (now Touro Street), opposite the cemetery.[6] But while New York's Jewish community became well established in the early eighteenth century, and built a synagogue in 1730, the Jewish community of Newport only really took off in the 1740s. It was then that the community entered its pre-Revolutionary "golden age."

Trade and commerce fueled Newport's golden age. Growing economic ties with the West Indies, privateering, and the importation of slaves and contraband (especially sugar and molasses) brought new wealth to the community and resulted in a dramatic population increase—more than 40 percent in eighteen years. Jews were among those who immigrated at this time. At least nine New York Jewish merchants settled in Newport in the 1740s, most of them Sephardim and several of them former *conversos* who had practiced their faith underground in Spain and Portugal and returned to the practice of Judaism with their arrival on American soil. Thereafter, the community grew slowly. At its peak in the 1770s, it numbered about two hundred men, women and children, comprising roughly 2 percent of Newport's total population and about 10 percent of its substantial merchants.[7]

Jewish religious life in Newport developed as the community did. By 1756, a synagogue was formally organized. Three years later, fundraisers from Palestine began to include Newport on their itinerary—a sure sign that its Jewish community was gaining recognition. In 1759, the community began to build a synagogue of its own—only the second synagogue built by Jews in the American colonies. The synagogue was completed in 1763, and that same year Isaac Touro was appointed *hazan* (reader). For all intents and purposes, he served as the Jewish community's minister.

Newport's Jews enjoyed freedom of worship, abundant economic opportunities, and the right to live and work freely, but they continued to face political discrimination in such areas as voting and office holding. This imbalance was typical of most colonial American settings. But perhaps less typical was the response of Newport's Jews. In 1762, Newport Jewish merchants Aaron Lopez and Isaac Elizer applied to the Rhode Island general court for citizenship. Under the terms of the British Naturalization Act of 1740, those in residence for seven consecutive years in a British colony, regardless of religion, could become British citizens. Lopez and Elizer were in compliance with all terms of the Act. But the courts turned them down, claiming that the law applied only to underpopulated regions and that local law limited citizenship to believing Christians— dubious claims in both cases. Defeated but unbowed, Lopez crossed the border to be naturalized in Massachusetts and Elizer was naturalized in New York. In so doing, both men revealed their determination to fight, as Jews, for their rights.[8]

Moses Michael Hays likewise insisted that his status as a Jew be legally accommodated. In 1775, when asked with seventy-five other men to sign a declaration of loyalty to the American colonies, the merchant refused, objecting to having to sign the oath "upon the true faith of a Christian." He pressed his case until finally the offending phrase was removed, and only then did he append his name to the document. Years later his nephew, Abraham Touro, raised in his uncle's home, maintained this family tradition of pride in Jewish heritage. Presenting himself to the Boston selectmen in 1816, he requested that the town clerk "set forth in the records that he was of the Jewish faith and belonged to a synagogue."[9]

Proud as they were of their faith, Newport's colonial Jews were careful not to flaunt it. Centuries of diaspora experience had taught them to practice great discretion on the outside, not drawing excessive attention to themselves, while glorying in their faith on the inside, where tradition reigned supreme. In building their synagogue in 1763, that is just what they did. Designed by famed Newport architect Peter Harrison, the elegant synagogue was modeled in part after the Amsterdam and London Sephardic synagogues, but also after the classical models Harrison used and would use in his construction of Newport buildings like the Brick Market (1772) and the Redwood Library (1748). On the outside, it neither identified itself with any Jewish symbol nor did it challenge the preeminence of neighboring churches. It resembled in outer form the houses of worship of Protestant dissenters. Like Newport's Jews themselves, the synagogue blended with the neighborhood and the religious landscape but made its presence known.[10]

Inside, meanwhile, the synagogue provided worshipers with a warm feeling of tradition: the sanctuary resembled those of Sephardic synagogues in Europe and the West Indies. A central *bimah* (reader's platform) faced the *aron kodesh* (holy ark) that held the Torahs. Twelve columns with elaborate capitals supported the women's gallery on three sides above. Light-colored walls with contrasting trim, candelabrum, and the natural light let in by the clear arched windows provided a surprisingly bright space that enabled worship as sundown approached each day. Inside, Jewish symbols were elaborate and dominant. There was no quiet or hidden Jewish life here.

Similar approaches were taken by the Jews themselves. Newport's Jews dressed like other Newport citizens and occupied houses and workplaces among them. Only small details set them apart. A portrait of Billah Abigail Franks painted in New York, probably in the 1730s, depicts her as an aspiring English-style aristocrat, harkening to her family's English Askenazik roots. A portrait made of Sarah Rivera Lopez in the 1770s by Gilbert Stuart likewise has her looking like the colonial British matrons of her day. But there is a nod to her Sephardic background in the Portuguese lace she wears and, perhaps, in her dark complexion. Nevertheless, on the streets, one could not likely have distinguished a Jewish woman by her outward appearance. In their homes, meanwhile, women and men often did display the ritual objects of their faith. Colonial wills and inventories mention such family Jewish heirlooms as Torah scrolls, prayerbooks, candlesticks, kiddush cups and shofars. In addition, many Jews kept the Jewish dietary laws at home (maintaining a qualified ritual slaughterer and watching over imported food occupied much communal time and effort), and some, we know, scrupulously kept the Sabbath—none more scrupulously than Aaron Lopez, whose ships did not set sail on that day.[11]

Newport Jews lived among their Christian neighbors and worked alongside them. Indeed, Newport may well have been the most religiously integrated of all the colonies. Whereas New York Jews lived primarily in two districts and in close proximity to one another, Newport's Jews were more widely dispersed.[12] Newport's Jews also engaged in economic partnerships with their neighbors. The United Company of Spermaceti Chandlers, established in 1761 in an attempt to control the prices of whalehead matter, consisted of nine founding firms, two of which were Jewish, while another represented a Jewish-Christian partnership.[13] The Redwood Library also brought Jews and Christians together. As a rule, local Jews and Christians supported one another's causes, contributing mutually to the building of cultural and religious facilities.

This is not to say that religious prejudice was absent in Newport. The refusal to naturalize Lopez and Elizer, for example, clearly reflected anti-Jewish animus—so much so that Ezra Stiles, minister of Newport's Second Congregational Church and a friend of many local Jews, concluded sadly that "the Jews will never become incorporated with the p[eo]ple of America, any more than in Europe, Asia and Africa." Stiles himself, along with other local Christians, worked to convert the Jews, seeing this as a prerequisite to the coming of God's Kingdom. Rising tensions that accompanied the onset of the American Revolution led some local citizens to consider Jews as a group to be traitors, particularly since the Rev. Touro and various other local Jews supported the British. In sum, the relationship between Jews and their neighbors in Newport was characterized by a substantial degree of ambivalence. Fascination and close relations with individual Jews went hand in hand with suspicion and prejudice directed against Jews as a group.[14]

The American Revolution sounded the death knell for the Jewish community of Newport. The British invasion brought with it death and destruction. From Leicester, Massachusetts, where he had taken refuge, Aaron Lopez thanked God for giving him the fortitude to escape in time, and mourned that Jews less fortunate than himself were now unable to obtain kosher food and "were reduced to the alternative of leaving [living] upon chocolate and coffe[e]." He described a Newport dwelling that "sufer'd much," a former neighbor "found dead at his house," another neighbor whose wife "is crazy," and what he lamented most of all, "that the vertue of several of our reputable ladys has been attacked and sullied by our destructive enemys."[15] Though some Jews returned to Newport following the Revolution, its economy never recovered. By the mid 1790s, the Torah scrolls of the synagogue were sent to New York for safekeeping. Some old family members remained, but their numbers steadily dwindled. On October 5, 1822, according to a surviving diary, the last Jew left Newport for New York.[16]

Before then, however, Newport served as the locus of what may have been the most important exchange of letters in all of American Jewish history, between the "Hebrew Congregation in Newport" and President George Washington. The Newport congregation prepared its letter in the form of an address to be read out on the occasion of the

President's visit to the city on August 17, 1790, following Rhode Island's ratification of the Constitution. The address, drafted by Hazan Moses Seixas, paralleled other letters that Washington received from religious bodies of different denominations and followed a long established custom associated with the ascension of kings. Redolent with biblical and liturgical language, the address noted past discrimination against Jews, praised the new government for "generously affording to all liberty of conscience and immunities of citizenship," and thanked God "for all of the blessings of civil and religious liberty" that Jews now enjoyed under the Constitution. Washington, in his reply sent to the community after his return to New York, reassured the Jewish community about what he correctly saw as its central concern—religious liberty. Appropriating a phrase contained in the Hebrew congregation's original letter, he characterized the United States government as one that "gives to bigotry no sanction, to persecution no assistance." He described religious liberty, following Thomas Jefferson, as an inherent natural right, distinct from the indulgent religious "toleration" practiced by the British and much of enlightened Europe, where Jewish emancipation was so often linked with demands for Jewish "improvement." Finally, echoing the language of the prophet Micah (4:4), he hinted that America might itself prove something of a Promised Land for Jews, a place where they would "merit and enjoy the good will of the other inhabitants; while every one shall sit in safety under his own vine and fig tree and there shall be none to make him afraid." Jews rightly understood the President's letter as an explicit guarantee that freedoms spelled out broadly in the Constitution applied to them. The letter was frequently reprinted and is now read annually as part of a public commemoration in Newport.[17]

Even as the Jewish presence in Rhode Island came to a temporary end in the years following the Revolution, the synagogue survived. This was entirely due to the farsightedness of Abraham Touro of Boston and later his brother Judah Touro of New Orleans, sons of Hazan Isaac Touro, who had left Newport following the Revolution and died shortly thereafter. In 1822, just as Newport's last resident passed from the scene, Abraham financed a new brick wall for the Newport Jewish cemetery, securing its upkeep despite the absence of a Jewish community. With Abraham's untimely death later that year, his estate left five thousand dollars for the upkeep of the cemetery and street leading up to it, and ten thousand dollars in trust to the State of Rhode Island for the care and preservation of the synagogue. This may well have been the first bequest anywhere in America for the preservation of a vacant building. It marks the beginning of what we now call "historic preservation."[18] When Judah Touro died in New Orleans in 1854, he continued Abraham's efforts to preserve Newport's Jewish spaces. His ten thousand dollar bequest endowed a fund to support a religious leader for the synagogue and provided money to repair and embellish the cemetery. The present granite fence and archway resulted from his gift. Well into the nineteenth century, the legacy of colonial Jewish Newport—to keep Judaism visible and viable—persisted.

For half a century, as the Jewish population in the United States grew from about 3,000 in 1820 to about 200,000 in 1870, the Jewish community of Rhode Island languished. Immigrant Jews found greater opportunity elsewhere. Those Jews who did find their way to the state, moreover, settled in Providence, the capital and commercial center of the state, where Jews acquired a burial ground in 1849. Newport, having become a resort community, now only saw Jews in the summertime. By 1854, a sufficient number of Jews resided in Providence to form its first synagogue, B'nai Israel. The congregation, founded by Central European Jews, initially followed the Sephardic rite, perhaps in tribute to its Newport predecessor. But the resemblance ended there, for between 1850 and 1865, the number of Jewish names listed in Providence directories never exceeded twenty-two, most of them merchants, and the congregation did not have a building of its own. In 1871 a petition declared there to be "thirty-five male members of the Jewish Church, and of these only about twenty are Church members." During these years, neither the synagogue nor the Jewish community thrived.[19]

Rhode Island's Jewish population finally began to grow in the 1870s, thanks both to immigration and to increasing opportunities. In 1877, B'nai Israel transformed itself into a "Moderate Reform" congregation and saw its membership climb to nearly eighty families. A year later, the first official census of the American Jewish community estimated the state's Jewish population at one thousand.[20] As the state's industrial base broadened and its need for workers increased, Jews, like other immigrant groups, moved in and settled.

Rhode Island was the first state to industrialize in early America. In 1790 Samuel Slater, financed by Rhode Island merchant and industrialist Moses Brown, opened a textile mill along the Blackstone River. Rhode Island's proximity to granite to build factories and excellent water supply to power them, along with the introduction of power looms in 1817 and multiple navigable ports to move goods in and out, resulted in an explosion of factory building before the Civil War. Pawtucket and villages in the Blackstone Valley led the way. By the 1870s, Rhode Island's industries focused on textile and jewelry production and the auxiliary enterprises that supported them, including metalworking. Between the 1880s and the end of World War I, Rhode Island's textile and jewelry production would lead the nation.[21]

Beyond its physical resources, Rhode Island accommodated the people needed to run the factories and production lines. The state's location close to the immigrant entry-port of New York City made it a magnet for newcomers seeking work. As early as 1870, Rhode Island had the highest percentage of foreign-born residents in the country.[22] Its immigrant population and ethnic diversity would remain among the highest in the nation beyond World War II.

Rhode Island's industrial character provided opportunities as well as challenges to immigrants. When business was good, employment was generally plentiful. But work in the textile and jewelry industries was seasonal and subject to unpredictable fluctuation in demand. Much of the process could be done at home, and piece-work employment was common. The system could thus yield flexible employment patterns, enabling women and children, as well as men, to work. But whether in home or factory, wages remained low and uncertain. State census data from 1900 to 1915 shows that Providence textile, jewelry, machinist, and day workers had the "highest proportion of unemployment" of any sector.[23]

Jews experienced both the benefits and pitfalls of Rhode Island industry. As many as fifteen to twenty thousand Jewish immigrants settled in Rhode Island, part of the more than two million immigrants from Central and Eastern Europe who migrated to America from the 1870s to 1924, swelling the state's Jewish population to 25,000. Many of them went into the state's traditional industries.

Robert Posner's story is in many ways typical, though at the later end of the immigration.[24] He was born in Pforzheim, Germany, in 1909, where his family was in the jewelry business. His father and uncle manufactured "things like cigarette cases, compacts, bag frames for mesh bags" and wholesaled jewelry. Posner started in the business at age fifteen. His father died in 1933, one month before Hitler came to power, but Robert did not leave Germany until May 1938. In New York, Posner had trouble finding work until "an old Jewish man . . . said, 'You shouldn't be here, you should go to Providence.'" Posner did. He began by working for several other Jewish jewelry firms, left and opened his own business with minimal cash and a partner, dissolved the partnership, started again. He and his wife, Lottie, finally started Rolo (for Robert and Lottie) Manufacturing Company with a designer/partner who stayed for eighteen years. The firm manufactured necklaces, bracelets, pins, and earrings. Posner did all the selling for nearly two decades before hiring a salesman. The firm employed four or five people, several for thirty or more years. But Robert and Lottie continued to take work home.

Posner died in 1996. In the early 1990s, Rolo still employed 150 people and manufactured costume jewelry year-round. Clients included an international array of department stores (whose products often sold under a local brand name). Though Posner hoped to see a fourth generation in the family business, he knew that most small Jewish jewelry firms had already gone out of business. Many had not survived the Great Depression; others passed out of family hands when children went into other occupations.

Immigrant Jews' backgrounds in the rag and textile industries, in shoemaking, in small artisan crafts, and in peddling and shopkeeping translated well in the United States. Especially in New England, the national center for the textile and shoe industries, Jews found an excellent occupational match. Rhode Island was no exception. In 1900, according to the Providence city directory, the largest employment categories listed for Jews were peddling (311), jewelry (152), tailor (134), clerk (129), clothing (99), grocer (69), shoemaker (66), junk dealer (53), and laborers (53).[25] The 205 individuals employed in jewelry and as laborers made industrial employment the second-largest category of Jewish employment in Providence. The number was probably even higher if some Jews employed in "clothing" actually worked in the textile mills.[26] In only a few communities beyond the large industrial cities (like New York and Chicago) did such a high percentage of Jews labor with their hands in industrial settings.

Judith E. Smith, in her 1985 book *Family Connections: A History of Italian and Jewish Immigrant Lives in Providence Rhode Island, 1900—1940*, compared the Jewish households on Smith Hill (near Providence's North End, where 74 percent of the households were Jewish) and Italian households on Federal Hill (where 92 percent of the households were Italian). Looking at data from the 1900, 1915, and 1935 city directories, together with state census data, she traced a single generation of Jewish involvement in Rhode Island's industries. In the early twentieth century, 17 percent of Jewish men listed "laborer" or "factory operative" as their "first recorded job" (vs. 47 percent of Italian men). But by 1915, no Jewish men listed themselves as "laborer," and only 8 percent listed themselves as "factory operatives," a number that dropped to 4 percent of their "last recorded jobs." For Italian men, "laborer" and "factory operative" remained dominant: 33 percent in 1915 and 36 percent as a last recorded job. Jews, according to Smith's data, entered the labor pool upon arrival and left quickly thereafter, moving into the more traditional modes of Jewish employment, especially small shopkeeping.[27]

Women worked, too. For both Jewish and Italian wives, keeping boarders and "wage-earning relatives" served as their chief source of income. Twenty-nine percent of Italian women and 17 percent of Jewish women took in boarders between 1915 and 1935. During that same period, 4 percent of Italian women worked as shopkeepers, as did 11 percent of Jewish women. Overall, 59 percent of Italian women and 70 percent of Jewish women did not report wage-earning work, but that, of course, does not mean that they sat idle.[28] Official numbers rarely record services provided by women in family businesses, in the home, or even as community volunteers.

Finally, children worked, often in the same occupation as their fathers. In 1915, Smith records that 95 percent of sons over age 15 in Italian homes worked for wages, and 67 percent of sons in Jewish homes did as well. For daughters, 78 percent of those over 15 in Italian homes worked, as did 58 percent of daughters in Jewish homes. In 1935, 73 percent of Jewish sons and 70 percent of Jewish daughters age fifteen or over still worked (compared to 80 percent and 72 percent for Italian children).[29] That trend would persist until World War II.

Curiously, unlike New York and Chicago, a strong Jewish labor movement did not develop in Rhode Island, notwithstanding the comparatively large number of Jews who might have benefited from one. Paul Buhle, in this volume, suggests that the small size of the Jewish community was responsible. Rhode Island Jews met their social and communal needs instead in non-union socialist movements like the Workmen's Circle and labor Zionism. In any event, most Jews in Rhode Island did not remain laborers past the first immigrant generation. Like so many immigrant Jews, they were neither the sons of industrial laborers nor the fathers of industrial laborers. On the other hand, Rhode Island Jews did not move into the professional and managerial classes at the rate that other Jews did. In 1987, fully half of Rhode Island's Jewish adults were sales, clerical, or service workers, as compared to only a quarter of Jewish adults employed in Boston.[30]

If the economic history of Rhode Island's Jewish community was somewhat distinctive, so too were some of its residential patterns. The state's Jewish community never surpassed 30,000. Even at its peak, in 1937, it had fewer Jews than the city of Milwaukee. Today Rhode Island's Jewish population is estimated at 16,000 (1.5 percent of the entire state population), far fewer Jews than are found in the small Boston suburb of Newton. But it remains a community with several distinctive features. First, Rhode Island Jews are loyal: fully 83 percent, in a 1987 survey, had lived in the state for more than a decade. The comparable figure for Jews nationwide is 61 percent. In 1940, this trend was even more evident: only 2 percent of Providence's Jewish families reported that their nearest child lived in another city. Fifty-nine percent of the families studied had their closest (adult) child at the same address, and 86 percent reported their nearest adult child within ten blocks.[31] Rhode Island Jews also display stability in their family lives: the Jewish community's divorce rate is half that of New York's. The intermarriage rate among Jews is also at the low end of the spectrum, far below that of Seattle, Denver, New York, or Boston. Finally, Rhode Island Jews, since World War II, have tended to identify with their state, not just with their local community. While Jews in nearby cities (like Boston, Hartford, or New Haven), display local loyalties and view themselves as part of a local community, as evidenced even by their local Jewish history projects, Rhode Island Jews share a common Jewish federation, a common Jewish newspaper, and a common Jewish historical society.[32]

In many ways, indeed, the Rhode Island Jewish community retains the character of a traditional small town. Many Jewish Rhode Islanders know virtually every Jew in their community; many are related to one another by blood and marriage; many attended the same schools; and many belong to the same synagogues and organizations. The low rate of Jewish in-migration to Rhode Island, along with the relatively low rate of out-migration, reinforces these trends, creating a localism that has strengthened the bonds of community and the commitment of Jews to one another. The traditions of headstrong dissent that shaped Rhode Island's early history have given way, at least in the Jewish community, to an understanding of the need to work together.

NOTES

1. Reprinted in Bernard Schwartz, *The Roots of the Bill of Rights* (New York: Chelsea, 1971), 1:96-98.

2. Samuel Oppenheim, "The Early History of the Jews in New York, 1654-1664: Some New Matter on the Subject," *Publications of the American Jewish Historical Society* 18 (1909), 4-37.

3. Jacob Rader Marcus, *The Colonial American Jew* (Detroit: Wayne State University Press, 1970), 1:314-317. Marcus finds "no evidence" to substantiate claims of an earlier community.

4. Colony Records 2:111 as quoted in Sydney V. James, *The Colonial Metamorphoses in Rhode Island* (Hanover, N.H.: University Press of New England, 2000), 109.

5. The Huguenot (French Protestant) church also lasted only a short time. It was founded in 1686 and collapsed four years later; ibid., 110. For the court cases that may have frightened the Newport Jews away, see Morris A. Gutstein, *The Story of the Jews of Newport* (New York: Bloch, 1936), 40-44.

6. Gutstein, *The Story of the Jews of Newport*, opposite p. 19, 38, 49.

7. Marilyn Kaplan, "The Jewish Merchants of Newport, 1749-1790" in this volume.

8. Jonathan D. Sarna and David G. Dalin, *Religion and State in the American Jewish Experience* (Notre Dame: University of Notre Dame Press, 1997), 57-59.

9. Ellen Smith, "Strangers and Sojourners: The Jews of Colonial Boston," in *The Jews of Boston*, ed. Jonathan D. Sarna and Ellen Smith (Boston: Combined Jewish Philanthropies, 1995), 35-36, 41. The synagogue Touro referred to was probably Shearith Israel, to which he paid periodic dues.

10. Theodore Lewis, "Touro Synagogue, Newport, R.I." *Newport History* 48 (summer 1975), 281-320; Nancy H. Schless, "Peter Harrison, the Touro Synagogue, and the Wren City Church," *Winterthur Portfolio* 8 (1973), 187-200.

11. Ellen Smith, "Portraits of a Community: The Image and Experience of Early American Jews," in Richard Brilliant, *Facing the New World: Jewish Portraits in Colonial and Federal America* (New York: Jewish Museum, 1997), 9-21; Jonathan D. Sarna, "Colonial Judaism," in David L. Barquist *Myer Myers: Jewish Silversmith in Colonial New York* (New Haven: Yale University Press, 2001), 8-23.

12. Leo Hershkowitz, "Some Aspects of the New York Jewish Merchant and Community," *American Jewish Historical Quarterly* 66 (September 1976), 11.

13. Stanley F. Chyet, *Lopez of Newport* (Detroit: Wayne State University Press, 1980), 46.

14. Sarna and Dalin, *Religion and State in the American Jewish Experience*, 58; Arthur A. Chiel, "Ezra Stiles and the Jews: A Study in Ambivalence," *A Bicentennial Festschrift for Jacob Rader Marcus* (New York, Ktav, 1976), 63-76.

15. *American Jewish Archives* 27 (November 1975), 157-158; Chyet, *Lopez of Newport*, 161.

16. Gutstein, *The Story of the Jews of Newport*, 216, 225.

17. This paragraph is adapted from Sarna, *American Judaism*, ch. 2. For the correspondence, see Blau and Baron, *Jews of the U.S. Documentary History*, 8-11; Sarna and Dalin, *Religion and State*, 179-182. The editor of Jefferson's papers suggests that Jefferson may even have drafted Washington's reply to the Jews of Newport; see Julian P. Boyd, ed., *The Papers of Thomas Jefferson* (Princeton: Princeton University Press, 1974), vol. 19, 610n.

18. See the comments of Richard Moe, president of the National Trust for Historic Preservation, to the Jewish Historical Society of Greater Washington published in *The Record* 25 (2002), 16; the wills of both Touros are reprinted in Gutstein, *The Story of the Jews of Newport*, 291-295.

19. Seebert J. Goldowsky, *A Century and a Quarter of Spiritual Leadership: The Story of the Congregation of the Sons of Israel and David (Temple Beth-El), Providence, Rhode Island* (Providence: Congregation of the Sons of Israel and David, 1989), 1-13, 27.

20. Jacob. R. Marcus, *To Count a People: American Jewish Population Data, 1585-1984* (Lanham, Md., University Press of America, 1990), 200.

21. Naida D. Weisberg, ed., *Diamonds Are Forever, but Rhinestones Are for Everyone: An Oral History of the Costume Jewelry Industry of Rhode Island* (Providence: The Providence Jewelry Museum, 1999), 1-10. See Meckle in this volume.

22. Ibid.

23. Judith E. Smith, *Family Connections: A History of Jewish and Italian Immigrant Lives in Providence, Rhode Island, 1900–1940* (Albany: SUNY Press, 1985), 20.

24. See Posner oral history in Weisberg, *Diamonds Are Forever*, 130–133.

25. See chart in Marvin Pitterman, "Some Casual Observations," *Rhode Island Jewish Historical Notes* 3, no. 1 (November 1958), 44–54.

26. Ibid.

27. Smith, *Family Connections*, table 2–1, 37.

28. Ibid., chart, 46.

29. Ibid., charts, 59, 68, 74.

30. Ira. M. Sheskin, *How Jewish Communities Differ* (New York: North American Jewish Data Bank, 2001), 62.

31. Sheskin, *How Jewish Communities Differ*, 34; Smith, *Family Connections*, 108.

32. Sheskin, *How Jewish Communities Differ*, 57, 92.

Communities

America's Jews have lived predominantly in cities. While strongly associated with trade and commerce, they have endeavored to form cohesive religious and organizational bonds.

Since the mid-seventeenth century, Jews have settled in Rhode Island's largest ports, but they have also resided in smaller cities and towns. During the early and mid-twentieth century, some Jews also lived on farms. Having returned to towns that were abandoned by previous generations, Jews are once again dispersed throughout the state.

Despite cyclical patterns of mobility, Jews have remained in Rhode Island at higher rates than their counterparts in most other states. While this sense of stability nurtures close-knit communities, it also leads to relative isolation. A self-sufficient and wary lot, Rhode Islanders are known to look askance even at neighboring states.

Colonial Newport has been the topic most frequently studied in *The Notes*, and here are two articles with surprising insights. Marilyn Kaplan argues that Jews helped shape, but did not cause, Newport's "golden age" in the decades preceding the Revolution. Focusing on "hidden Jews," Holly Snyder reminds us that many community members never became erudite or successful merchants.

Through recollections and anecdotes, Eleanor Horvitz surveys the world of South Providence, where Jewish immigrants from Eastern Europe settled at the turn of the twentieth century. Like the city's North End, this was an overcrowded, bustling neighborhood, where adults and children struggled not only to survive but also to become Americanized. Success would lead to both neighborhoods' demise.

Steven Culbertson and Calvin Goldscheider profile the Jews of Bristol, a tiny community within a small town within a miniature state. By tracing the community's rise, decline, and resurgence, they suggest that most Jewish communities in Rhode Island are fragile and transitory. Through external and internal pressures, all communities are in perpetual flux.

Carrying the Torahs on Willard Avenue to Shaare Zedek's new home in South Providence, 1954.
Four small Orthodox congregations merged to purchase the former Temple Beth-El building at the
corner of Broad and Glenham Streets. Photograph by Fred Kelman.

The Jewish Merchants of Newport, 1749-1790

he rise and decline of the Jewish community in Newport coincided with fluctuations in that seaport's economy. From this fact filiopietistic historians have concluded that Jewish merchants were responsible for Newport's commercial growth. However, contrary evidence indicates that the Jews did not cause but responded to the changing economic situation. Newport's commercial growth preceded the mid-century arrival of the Jews. Jewish businessmen who came to Newport from 1740 to 1770 were attracted by the economic opportunities of a growing seaport. Many of them were energetic businessmen whose mercantile efforts were enhanced by the friendly cooperation of fellow coreligionists in other ports. Their successes contributed to Newport's commercial growth.

The American Revolution scattered the Jewish community and devastated Newport's commercial life. Those Jews who remained in Newport, or returned after the Revolution, worked to revive trade. It was only after it became apparent that Newport was destined to remain a second-rate port that the Jewish community dispersed. The departure of the Jews did not cause Newport's commercial decline. The Jewish community gradually disappeared as the older men died and the younger men left in quest of improved economic opportunities.

ARRIVAL OF JEWISH MERCHANTS IN NEWPORT

Existing evidence indicates that at least nine Jewish merchants came to live in Newport during the 1740s. Abraham and Naphtali Hart, Jacob Judah, Moses Lopez, Moses Levy, Isaac Seixas, Isaack Polock, and Jacob Rodriguez Rivera all came directly from New York. Initially they continued their affiliations with the Shearith Israel Synagogue in New York and maintained dual residence in New York and Newport.[1] These ambitious tradesmen regarded their move to Newport as an exploratory business venture. By the 1750s their faith in the commercial opportunities of this vigorous young port had been justified. All nine dropped their New York residencies and synagogue memberships as their Rhode Island businesses became more active. Proof of their confidence in Newport's future is the arrival of additional members of their families. In the 1750s Isaac, Benjamin, and Jacob Hart joined Abraham and Naphtali Hart. David and Aaron Lopez came directly from Portugal to join their brother Moses.[2]

Few ambitious merchants had been attracted to seventeenth-century Rhode Island. The opportunities were limited because there was no direct trade between England and Rhode Island and almost all English imports came to Rhode Island through the port of Boston. However, despite the colony's dependence on Massachusetts for the importation of most manufactured goods, Rhode Island did begin some direct trade with the West

Excerpted from *Rhode Island Jewish Historical Notes*, Volume 7, Number 1 (November 1975): 12–32.

Indies. In the seventeenth century Rhode Island's foreign trade was limited to the West Indies, and the West Indies trade remained light.[3] It was the growth of this West Indies trade that eventually brought prosperity to eighteenth-century Newport.

The stage was set for the great age of Newport commerce in the Middle Period from 1733 to 1756. During this period Rhode Island trade was "expanding and flourishing" mainly due to the trade with the French West Indies.[4] The prohibitive duties placed on sugar, non-English molasses, spirits, and rum by the Molasses Act of 1733 were not enforced. Colonists freely violated the act, and Newport continued to expand its trade with the French, Dutch, and Spanish West Indies. During King George's War with France (1744–1748), Newport became a center for privateering activity.[5] The newly arrived Jewish merchants joined in but did not initiate this profitable trade. Newport's shipping prospered during the war as most merchants became involved in privateering.

WEST INDIES TRADE

In the years of peace immediately following King George's War, Newport's trade with the West Indies and the Dutch colony of Surinam continued to grow and prosper. Rhode Island merchants continued to smuggle foreign sugar and molasses in violation of the loosely enforced Molasses Act. Newport's major exports to the Caribbean were horses, lumber, beef, pork, candles, cheese, and wool. Heavy imports of sugar and molasses were needed for the growing production of rum.[6] Newport's Jewish merchants possessed a special advantage in the Caribbean trade. Most of them had close and reliable contacts in the extensive Jewish mercantile communities of Jamaica, Curaçao, and Surinam. Later, when the Newport Jews were attempting to gather enough funds to build a synagogue, their Caribbean friends were most generous.[7]

With the outbreak of the French and Indian War in 1755, Newport's illicit trade once again became trade with the enemy. A parliamentary act of 1756 declared, to no avail, that "a trade closed in time of peace could not be opened in war."[8] In 1757 the Rhode Island legislature passed an act forbidding trade with the enemy. Nevertheless, Rhode Island merchants continued to trade with the French islands, and within one year the 1757 act was repealed.[9] Although most merchants supported the English cause, trade was their primary concern, and they needed French molasses, sugar, and rum. Consequently, Rhode Islanders continued to follow the same general course of trade as they had in peace, adjusting it somewhat to fit into a war situation. Merchants involved in the West Indies trade coveted French prisoners. Ships returning prisoners to French ports were entitled to fly the flags of truce, which enabled them easily to smuggle cargo in and out of the French West Indies.

By 1760 Newport had become a notable port, dispatching more ships than New York. Rhode Island's merchant marine, which was primarily centered in Newport, consisted of 184 vessels in addition to 342 small coasters.[10] The town had more than twenty distilleries, and more than half of the merchant marine was engaged in the triangular rum-slave trade. Commercial prosperity, accelerated by the French wars, is reflected in the port's population growth. In 1730 the population was estimated to be about 4,640. In 1748, at the end of King George's War, the population had grown by about 2,000 to 6,508. In the peaceful years that followed, the population was increased by only some 200 to 6,753 in 1755.[11] There was another spurt of population growth with the outbreak of the French and Indian War. By 1760 the population had grown to 7,500.[12]

A small part of the population increase is attributable to the Jewish businessmen attracted by Newport's booming shipping industry in the late 1750s and early 1760s. By 1760 there were about twelve Jewish families living in Newport. Ezra Stiles counted fifteen to twenty Jewish families living in Newport in 1764 and about twenty-five families in 1769.[13] The new arrivals in the 1760s were Isaac Elizer; Joshua and Moses Isaacks; Joseph Jacob, Hiam, Moses, and Benjamin Levy; Judah and Moses Michael Hays; Francis,

15
M. Kaplan
Jewish Merchants of Newport

Touro Synagogue, Newport, dedicated in 1763, as depicted in Harper's Monthly, 1874. The first published illustration of Touro shows the wooden fence of 1822, later replaced by the present one in iron and granite.

Jacob, and Issachar Polock; Abraham Mendes Pereira; and Isaac Touro. Most of these men were New York businessmen joining other members of their families or independently seeking improved economic opportunities.

In 1770 Stiles estimated the Jewish population at about thirty families.[14] The official census taken by order of the General Assembly on June 1, 1774 indicates that there were about twenty-five Jewish families, amounting to about 200 people in Newport.[15] Stiles's estimate is approximate, and census data are limited in value because the census counted only those who were actually at home at the time the census was taken,[16] and because some Jews declined to be counted for religious reasons.[17] Nevertheless, these figures clearly indicate that the Jewish population reached its peak and remained stable during the first half of the 1770s. At this time about 25 percent of the Jews in the colonies were living in New England, with virtually all the New England Jews settled in Newport.[18] These Jews constituted about 2 percent of Newport's total population but about 10 percent of Newport's substantial merchants."[19]

The New York Jews who came to Newport between 1740 and 1770 were a select group consisting principally of businessmen seeking improved economic opportunities in a developing young port. They also hoped to establish a New England foothold for the North American Jewish trading community. Newport was a more likely choice than Boston because opportunities were limited in the older, established port. Newport was also a likely choice because of its more liberal religious tradition. Newport's tolerant atmosphere attracted a community of Jews from Barbados as early as 1678. There is no indication that any religious difficulties precipitated the dispersal of this original community in 1685.

Although religious reasons may have entered into the decision to settle in Newport as opposed to Boston, it is clear that the Jews did not leave New York in search of religious freedom or improved political opportunities. Most of those who came to Newport had been naturalized in New York. They were freemen of the city, enjoying complete religious freedom and limited political recognition. In Newport the Jews, although free to worship as they chose, faced political restrictions. The Rhode Island courts denied naturalization to Aaron Lopez and Isaac Elizer in 1763. Lopez, one of Newport's most prominent citizens, temporarily established residence in Massachusetts in order to become a naturalized Englishman. Once naturalized, he returned to Rhode Island to pursue his business interests.

PRE-EMINENT FAMILIES

During the 1760s five Jewish families attained a position of pre-eminence in the Newport commercial community. They were the Lopez, Rivera, Levy, Hart, and Polock families. Aaron Lopez, who was to become the wealthiest and most successful of all the Jewish merchants, was involved in many new ventures during the 1760s. Although he was heavily in debt most of the time, his courage and ingenuity, combined with the patience and fortitude of his creditors, eventually led him to colossal success. Aaron worked closely with his brother Moses until 1767. After Moses's death, Aaron was frequently allied with his father-in-law, the prominent and powerful merchant, Jacob Rodriguez Rivera.

Isaac Hart was another prominent merchant and a major contributor to the construction of the synagogue. Hart, one of the more successful privateers, frequently combined with his brothers, particularly Naphtali. Naphtali realized a substantial profit selling clothing to the British army. Occasionally the Harts combined forces with Benjamin and Moses Levy, members of another successful family. Myer Polock, a prominent shipbuilder and trader, did not move from New York to Newport until the late 1760s. Polock's immediate success drew Moses Michael Hays from New York to join him in the shipbuilding industry. All of these men were leaders not only in the Jewish community, but also in the larger merchant community. All of them, but Lopez particularly, helped to create Newport's "Golden Age" of commerce, just prior to the Revolution.

Not all of the Jews who were drawn to Newport in the 1750s and 1760s received the financial rewards they expected. Bruce Bigelow claims that, despite the apparent boom atmosphere during the French and Indian War, privateering ventures were a failure for most Rhode Islanders. Newport vessels were frequently captured by English and French privateers and men of war. Merchants shared the risks of these voyages by providing insurance for each other. Eighteen assurers, including Issachar Polock, insured a voyage by Christopher Champlin in January of 1759. Those captains who succeeded in reaching French ports frequently found the markets glutted and had to sell their goods at a low price.[20] Newport's population and commerce had grown during the war years, but the profits were concentrated in the hands of a few of the more ingenious and venturesome traders.

The end of the war aggravated Rhode Island's economic problems. The colony had always been bothered by a shortage of hard money. Rhode Island's severely limited hinterland and lack of important staple products meant that the colony had few items to export for cash. One object of the West Indian trade was to obtain enough money to pay for English manufactured goods. The shortage of hard money made it almost impossible to maintain the value of paper money in the colony. In 1740 the Rhode Island legislature had attempted to correct the impossible inflation of its "Old Tenor" by issuing "New Tenor," lawful money which was to be issued sparingly to prevent depreciation. During the war the issue of "New Tenor" was greatly increased as the colony was forced to help finance the war. By the end of the war the colony was accumulating a debt and experiencing a further depreciation in value.[21] The courts made an attempt to stabilize the monetary situation by fixing the ratio of Old Tenor to lawful money, or New Tenor.[22] This Band-Aid measure did little to stem the tide of postwar inflation.

ECONOMIC DECLINE

The "Sugar" Act of 1764 was an additional blow to the postwar economy. This measure, which replaced the weakly enforced Molasses Act, lowered the duty on foreign molasses to an enforceable level. It also raised the tariff on refined sugar and put a tax on certain textiles, wines, coffee, and pimentos, unless these were shipped to the colonies via England. Serious attempts to enforce this new measure cut into the major source of supply for the molasses and sugar needed in the production of rum. There were more than twenty distilleries in Newport alone, and rum was one of New England's major exports. An angry and determined British ministry was making it virtually impossible for Rhode Island merchants to obtain the hard cash needed to purchase essential manufactured goods from England. The Rhode Island General Assembly in the Remonstrance of January 1764 informed the Board of Trade that the colony could not continue to exist without the foreign West Indian trade.[23] Meanwhile the large number of merchants petitioning for insolvency in 1764 bears witness to the unsettled state of the colony's economy.[24]

Myer Benjamin, a Hungarian who had arrived in New York about 1758 and in Newport about 1761, was the only Jew to declare bankruptcy during the difficult decade of the 1760s. It is probable that he arrived in Newport with very little capital, since in 1761, shortly after his arrival, he was employed as steward for the newly organized Jewish social club. After Benjamin's business failure, members of the Jewish community rallied to his support. In accordance with a long-standing Jewish concern for the needy in their own community, members of the congregation employed him as *shammos* (sexton) and *shohet* (ritual slaughterer) of the new synagogue.[25] All of the other Jewish merchants survived this difficult period financially, and some became quite successful.

AARON LOPEZ

Perhaps the best way to gain an understanding of the activities of the Jewish merchants in Newport of the 1760s is to take a closer look at the early career of Aaron Lopez, the most successful of them all. More is known about Lopez than most of the other Jews, not only because of his pre-eminence, but also because of the vast quantity of his business records that is still preserved in the vaults of the Newport Historical Society. Lopez brought his wife, daughter, and brother directly from Portugal to Newport in 1752. Aaron's brother Moses had emigrated to New York around 1730. After naturalization and some success as a New York merchant, Moses moved his family to Newport. By the time Aaron had arrived in Newport, Moses was a member of Newport's two-year-old Redwood Library Company, had been exempted from civil duties and personal taxes in recognition of his service translating Spanish documents for the colony's administration, and had been granted a ten-year monopoly in the manufacturing of potash.[26] Moses was in a position to help his twenty-one-year-old brother begin his business career.

The generosity of some Jewish merchants in New York enabled Aaron to establish himself in business as a shopkeeper almost immediately. Aaron received liberal credit for the purchase of goods for his local retail business. He quickly built his small local business into a large-scale retail and wholesale trade involving shipments throughout the colonies and abroad. His success entitled him to be recognized as a merchant, a man of consequence in eighteenth-century America. In order to earn the title of merchant a businessman had to be more than a retailer or small wholesaler. A merchant traded in bulk at a distance, and his business was regional, interprovincial, and even transatlantic. By 1755 Aaron Lopez was already an established merchant, buying and selling throughout Rhode Island and exchanging goods with agents in Boston and New York.

Lopez's trading interests were diverse, but he was particularly interested in the spermaceti candle trade. Spermaceti is the waxlike substance extracted from the headmatter of the sperm whale. Abraham Rodriguez Rivera supposedly brought the secrets of the manufacture of spermaceti candles from Portugal. The first colonial candle manufactory was built by a man named Benjamin Crabb in Rehoboth, Massachusetts. When the original building was destroyed by fire, Obadiah Brown of Providence built a new plant and hired Crabb as manager.[27] Brown's success inspired Aaron Lopez to establish a similar plant in Newport in 1756. By 1760 there were 12 similar factories in New England, although only three or four were needed to process all the spermaceti supplied by the whalemen. Demand for headmatter far exceeded the limited supply, and whalemen were able to command high prices for their product.

The Spermaceti Trust

In an attempt to exercise some control over the cost of the raw material, the spermaceti candle manufacturers formed one of America's first trusts. On November 5, 1761, the United Company of Spermaceti Chandlers was established to control the cost and distribution of headmatter.[28] Nine firms signed the agreement. Two of the first firms were completely Jewish (Naphtali Hart & Company and Aaron Lopez and Company) and one was a partnership of a Jew and a non-Jew (Collins and Rivera). The agreement was less than nine months old when the above-mentioned firms complained that some of the trust members had violated the articles of agreement by purchasing headmatter at excessive prices.

Despite their dissatisfaction with the functioning of the agreement, these critics joined in the renewal and expansion of the organization in April, 1764. The new agreement stipulated that every hundred barrels of North American headmatter was to be apportioned as follows: Nicholas Brown & Company, twenty barrels; Joseph Palmer & Company, fourteen; Thomas Robinson and Company, thirteen; Aaron Lopez, eleven; Jacob Rivera and Company, eleven; Isaac Stelle and Company, nine; Naphtali Hart and Company, nine; "the Philadelphians," seven; Edward Langdon and Son, four; and Moses Lopez, two. Jacob Rodriguez Rivera assumed a position of leadership in attempting to enforce the new agreement. In 1769, when it became apparent that the price agreement was being violated, Rodriguez wrote to William Rotch of Nantucket asking for Rotch's assistance in identifying the guilty purchaser. Rivera also wrote to Nicholas Brown in Providence proposing action against those who "have joined together, in order, if possible, to raise the price."[29] Rivera was a respected leader, but he could not force the association to maintain a ceiling on the price of headmatter. After 1769 the number of manufacturers more than doubled, placing an additional strain on the limited supply of headmatter. In 1774 there were twenty-four manufactories, thirteen in Newport alone.[30]

It is obvious from the 1763 allotment of headmatter that Aaron Lopez was a major manufacturer. Only three firms had larger allotments than Aaron's 11 percent proportion, and only Rivera was alloted as much. As a merchant seeking to expand his trade, Lopez was constantly in quest of goods for export. Until years later, when the market became glutted, candles were an excellent commodity for exchange. During the early and middle 1760s invoices for candles always appeared in the coastwise shipping to ports like Boston, New York, Philadelphia, and Charleston. His sales of spermaceti candles amounted to 3,150 pounds local (non-sterling) currency in the month of February 1763 alone. [31]

The Guinea Trade

Until about 1765 Lopez was primarily interested in coastal shipping to American ports and traded mainly in spermaceti. However, in 1763 he also became interested in transatlantic trade. Transatlantic ventures required greater capital investments than the young Lopez could afford. After Aaron's marriage to the daughter of Jacob Rodriguez Rivera in 1763, Lopez and Rivera frequently pooled their resources to finance long voyages. In the next few years they sent a ship to Lisbon, one to the Canary Islands, and several others to join in the African slave trade.[32] Lopez and Rivera were neither the first nor the only Newport Jews to engage in the slave trade. In October of 1762 Isaac Elizer and his partner Samuel Moses sent the sloop *Prince George* to Africa to pick up slaves for sale in the Bahamas.[33] Lopez and Rivera dispatched their first ship to Africa in the same year. The brigantine *Greyhound* brought 134 Negroes from the Guinea coast to Charleston, South Carolina. Two years later the sloop *Spry* exchanged a cargo consisting primarily of rum for a shipload of Negroes to be delivered to Jamaica. The following year two more of their vessels made the triangular trip from Newport to the Guinea coast and Jamaica. Lopez and Rivera had discovered a good source of bills of exchange on England. They continued to underwrite about two African voyages each year until 1776.

Although he explored new opportunities, Lopez was still primarily concerned with the colonial coastal trade in the early 1760s. The Sugar Act and the subsequent failure of merchants engaged in the West Indian trade discouraged his interest in the Caribbean trade. He made a few exploratory ventures in the transatlantic London trade, but feared becoming heavily indebted to a London mercantile firm. Then Lopez and Henry Cruger, a merchant in Bristol, England, concluded that American merchants were incurring debts because the London market was saturated with American goods and the prices the Americans received for their exports couldn't pay for their imports. Lopez and Cruger decided to tap the unexplored Bristol market, and Cruger agreed to furnish Lopez with the capital necessary to build this trade.

In 1765 Lopez began to construct new ships to be sold in England with their cargoes. Cruger agreed to obtain insurance for the vessels and to allow Lopez to draw bills of exchange on him even before the ships left Newport. He also arranged to provide Lopez with English goods on twelve months' credit.[34] According to Bruce Bigelow, sending five ventures to a new port at a time of postwar depression was one of the most daring plans Lopez ever followed.[35] This may be true, but it was a far more daring venture for Cruger, who was financing the entire adventure. Neither man anticipated the Stamp Act and the power of the Americans' threats of non-importation. As a result of the depression in England, the vessels and many of the goods sent to Bristol either remained unsold or sold for very low prices. The venture was a failure for Lopez and a disaster for Cruger. By 1767 Lopez owed Cruger more than 10,000 pounds sterling and was continuing to draw bills of exchange on him in accordance with their original agreement. Cruger plaintively wrote Lopez, "If I am not paid, how can I pay?"—but to no avail.

A less creative and persevering businessman might have succumbed to the burden of such a heavy debt. Instead, Lopez sought new markets where he could acquire the hard cash needed to pay off his debt. Anxious to recoup his losses, Cruger helped Lopez to establish himself in the West Indies trade. Unfortunately, Lopez initially sent his incompetent young son-in-law Abraham Mendes to act as his factor in Jamaica. It was only after Mendes had been replaced by a more reliable factor that Lopez's Jamaica trade began to realize a profit. Gradually Lopez extricated himself from his financial difficulties and emerged as one of the most successful merchants in Newport.

Financial Difficulties

The financial difficulties experienced by Aaron Lopez during the 1760s were typical of those suffered by the entire merchant community. His ability to survive the difficulties, recoup his losses, and prosper was unique. By 1772 a number of prominent Jewish merchants had failed. On September 30, 1771, Hays and Polock petitioned for insolvency. Their petition was granted on September 30, 1771.[36] Moses Michael Hays opened a small shop when he was released from debtors' prison.[37] In later years, after the Revolution, Hays re-established himself as a merchant in Boston.

The insolvency petition of Isaac Elizer was granted in December 1771[38] and that of Naphtali and Isaac Hart granted in January 1772.[39] The combined tax lists for 1772 and 1775 indicate that few Jewish merchants were prospering. Of the twenty-seven names listed, nineteen paid rates under £2, and three of them paid rates between £2 and £5. Moses Levy paid £6.18.3, Jacob Rodriguez Rivera £9.4.4, and Jacob Polock £10.3.0. The only Jewish merchant whose tax rate indicated true prosperity was Aaron Lopez, who paid £32.9.10, the highest tax rate in Newport.[40] However, his success was unique, and clearly this was not a Golden Age for everyone.

Bruce Bigelow called the period between the Peace of Paris (1763) and the opening of the American Revolution the "Golden Period" in Rhode Island trade. From 1764 to 1768 the commercial situation was seriously depressed, with most businessmen struggling for survival. Bigelow stated that after 1768 there was a definite boom in Newport's commercial activities, as evidenced by a considerable increase in shipping, new slave markets in the Carolinas and Virginia, a new West Indies frontier in Hispaniola, and the development of a Rhode Island whaling industry.[41] Undoubtedly, business conditions did improve after 1768, but many businessmen were still in serious financial difficulties. Even Aaron Lopez had not yet begun to extricate himself from his heavy debts. It is false and misleading to label the years prior to 1769 as "golden."

Economic conditions began to improve significantly in 1769. James B. Hedges, noted historian of the Brown family of Providence, observed that from 1769 to 1775, the Rhode Island economy experienced a "gradual recovery from the postwar depression of the sixties, from the stagnation which the Sugar Act had accentuated, and from the monetary stringency of the early years. The early seventies were years of relative political tranquility, and economic prosperity."[42] By the end of 1769 Newport's population had expanded to more than eleven thousand. The port had nearly two hundred vessels engaged in foreign commerce and some three hundred to four hundred craft engaged in domestic trade.[43] Most evidence supports Bigelow's contention that this was truly Newport's Golden Age. However, even in this apparently golden age the insolvency petitions continued to appear. Some businessmen never recovered from the postwar depression. Poverty and failure in the midst of prosperity and success argue against easy generalizations about this unstable prerevolutionary era.

Widespread Activities of Lopez

Aaron Lopez was one of the Newport merchants who enjoyed enormous prosperity during the early 1770s. By 1774 he had completely paid off his debt to Henry Cruger, although he still owed some money to his London agents, Hayley and Hopkins.[44] The secret of his success lay in the diversity of his activities. Although he became deeply involved in the West Indies trade, he continued to pursue the coastal trade and transatlantic voyages. His specialty was not whaling, candles, Caribbean traffic, or trans-oceanic commerce, but "business as a genre."[45] By 1772 he was becoming an industrialist as well as a shipper. As a manufacturer he produced spermaceti candles, ships, rum, freshly ground chocolate, and wooden barrels. In addition, he contracted for the production of textiles, clothing, shoes, hats, bottles, sulkies, and even prefabricated bungalows. By 1774 he had an interest in more than thirty vessels, and his commerce was sufficiently diversified so that a setback in one quarter did not mean complete failure.

Lopez and his fellow Newport merchants occasionally prospered at the expense of merchants in other colonies. In 1769 Rhode Island and New Hampshire were the only colonies that failed to use non-importation as a weapon in opposing British trade regulations. Even after a Providence town meeting pledged not to import or pur-chase British goods, the merchants of Newport remained indifferent. Newport reluc-tantly agreed to participate only after the Merchant's Committee at Philadelphia threat-ened to discontinue trade with the port. After the partial repeal of the Townshend duties, Newport prematurely repudiated the non-importation agreements and resumed trade with England. Angered by the Newport merchants' willingness to profit from the distress and self-sacrifice of their neighbors, eight provinces placed a temporary em-bargo upon Newport. This time Newport merchants reluctantly participated in non-importation until the total repeal of the Townshend Act of 1770.

The "Continental Association," organized in 1774 to prevent any kind of economic intercourse with England, forced compliance. Local committees in all the colonies sup-ported the Association and used every means of persuasion to enforce the boycott. The enforcement of the boycott drastically reduced Newport's trade. The Newport commit-tee wrote to Philadelphia in 1775: "So far as we can learn the Association hath been strictly adhered to by the merchants of this colony."[46] Undoubtedly, as the business papers of Aaron Lopez attest, there were some violations of the boycott.

BRITISH OCCUPATION

As Bruce Bigelow accurately observed, 1775 was the "beginning of the town's com-mercial death, as it was also the beginning of the end for many Newport merchant houses. . . . Business had come almost to a standstill, and money was tight in Newport, Jamaica, and London."[47] By October of 1775 the British fleet was moored in full view of Newport's harbor. Trade was devastated, and people lived in fear of imminent destruc-tion. Large-scale evacuation had begun, and in November the legislature appropriated £200 to help the poor people leave and to assist those who were forced to remain under adverse conditions.[48] By December 8, 1776, when the British troops landed in Newport with little opposition, most people loyal to the colonial cause had fled. The city's popu-lation dropped from 11,000 in 1775 to 5,299 in 1776[49] in anticipation of the occupation. Those who remained were indifferent, incapacitated, or Loyalist.

Aaron Lopez moved his business to Portsmouth, Rhode Island, early in 1776 and then to Providence after the occupation. In the summer of 1777 he again moved, this time to Boston, and then finally to Leicester, Massachusetts, to a spot, "where I could place my family secured from sudden allarms and the cruel ravages of an enraged enemy . . . (and move) in the same Sphere of Business I have been used to follow, which, altho much more contracted, it has fully answered my wishes. . . ."[50] The Lopez family was joined in Leicester by the families of Jacob Rodriguez Rivera and Abraham Mendes. Lopez set up a shop in Leicester and did some shipping from Salem and Boston. Much of his time was spent in traveling, trying to straighten out his tangled accounts and at-tempting to free those of his vessels that had been seized by American cruisers. Lopez's losses as a result of the war were monumental. Nevertheless, he persevered in his busi-ness. Had he not accidentally drowned in 1782, he undoubtedly would have returned to Newport and attempted to rebuild his trading empire.

The census of 1782 indicates the presence of only six Jewish families in Newport.[51] Those listed are Moses Isaacks, Abigail Polock, Moses Seixas, Moses Levy, Isaac Elizer, and Jacob Isaacks. The Lopez, Rivera, and Mendes families were still in Leicester. The Hart brothers remained in Newport during the British occupation but were forced to flee because of their Loyalist activities when the British withdrew in 1780. Isaac Hart was shot by Continental soldiers while seeking refuge on Long Island. Benjamin Meyer died in 1776, and his Loyalist wife fled to New York in 1780. Myer Polock was dead, but his widow Abigail remained on the census rolls. Moses Michael Hays fled to South Kingstown, Rhode Island, with the British occupation, returned briefly to Newport in 1780, and then settled in Boston.

POSTWAR DEPRESSION

The town rates for July 31, 1783, indicate the continuing presence of all of those Jews counted in the 1782 census, in addition to Abraham Mendes and the Lopez families. In spite of the postwar depression the most prominent merchant in Newport paid a tax of £4,000. The two most prosperous Jews were Moses Levy and Joseph Lopez, who each paid taxes of £15,000.[52] The state tax rate for June 1786 indicates that Jacob Rodriguez Rivera returned to Newport and was again in business. The firm of Rivera, Seixas and Company was assessed £2,500. The only other Jew paying substantial taxes was Joseph Lopez, who paid £2,800 as compared to Christopher Champlin's £3,000.[53]

Those merchants who attempted to restore Newport's commercial prosperity after the Revolution were severely handicapped. According to one observer, William Ellery, when the British left Newport five hundred buildings had been burned and considerable property carried off. Ellery estimated the damage at £124,798 and noted that in his absence "All the destructible property I had there was utterly destroyed."[54] Joseph Hadfield, a British visitor to Newport, observed in 1785 that as a result of the "devastations of war . . . the poverty of the inhabitants will be an insuperable barrier at least for some time."[55] Merchants attempting to restore trade were not only faced with the complete destruction of the Long Wharf, including most of their warehouses and stores, but also the loss of most of Newport's merchant fleet. Hadfield observed only twenty vessels in the foreign trade and thirty additional small vessels in the coastal trade. This fleet was smaller than those owned by each of the great merchants prior to the war. Hadfield noted: "The trade of Newport is not great. There are few persons of consequence in the mercantile line here."[56]

Merchants in post-revolutionary America were forced to realize that the nature of trade had changed. Those merchants who attempted to cling to the old trade routes and the old products failed. They found that much of the West Indian trade was closed to them by new British laws restricting foreign trade with their islands. Merchants who attempted to resume large importations of British manufactured goods soon found themselves heavily in debt to British mercantile firms. Foreign ships carried most of America's imports and exports. The future belonged to merchant families like the Browns of Providence, who realized that the way to prosperity involved increased American manufacturing. Manufactured goods were needed for domestic use and for export to help pay for imports. Merchants creative enough to find new markets such as China prospered. Before the old merchants learned to survive in this new economic world and won government protection for American trade, most of them suffered severely. The merchants and shipowners of Baltimore expressed a common grievance when in 1789 they complained that: "for want of national protection and encouragement, our shipping, that great source of strength and riches, has fallen into decay and involved thousands in the utmost distress."[57]

In the 1780s Newport merchants were suffering the effects of the postwar depression of trade while attempting to overcome the great property losses they had experienced during the British occupation. Newport's postwar recovery problems were aggravated by the increasing competition from Providence merchants. By 1775 the Browns of Providence had become the peers of the Newport businessmen and were beginning to overtake some areas of Newport's trade.[58] While Newport was suffering from the British occupation, the Providence merchants were able to solidify their control of Rhode Island commerce. Once Providence merchants gained commercial control of the Rhode Island hinterland, Newport was forever doomed to a secondary position in Rhode Island trade. Geographically, Newport, located on the tip of an island well removed from most of the mainland of Rhode Island, could never have remained a major trading post once overland trade routes were improved. However, the fact that Newport was destined to play a lesser role than Providence does not mean that the port was doomed to immediate and total eclipse.

Attempts were made to restore Newport's commerce. Christopher Champlin returned immediately after the war and revived his trade with London, Lisbon, Dunkirk, Dublin, and Amsterdam. Joseph Lopez and Jacob Rodriguez Rivera restored some of their transatlantic and West Indian trade, and Moses Seixas engaged in some trade with the West Indies. It is evident that there was a limited post-revolutionary resurgence of trade in Newport. A study of furniture shipments from Newport indicates that commerce resumed on a more limited basis after the war. Although there were a few transatlantic voyages and occasional trips to the West Indies, most of the trade was with domestic coastal ports. The bulk of the furniture was shipped to New York.[59] In the absence of sufficient studies of the problem, it appears that the revival of Newport's trade was hampered by the absence of the kind of creative, bold leadership exercised by Aaron Lopez in the 1770s.

One can only speculate upon the possibility that Aaron Lopez would have found new markets and expanded his manufacturing interests if he were in Newport in the 1780s. Although Lopez could not have reversed Newport's secondary position in the Rhode Island economy, he might have brought about a temporary resurgence of commercial prosperity. This was still the age of the individual entrepreneur. Lopez was largely responsible for Newport's prosperity in the 1770s, and the Browns were responsible for the ascent of Providence. Perhaps Aaron Lopez's presence in postwar Newport would have made a difference.

THE DECLINE OF NEWPORT

By the mid-1780s it was apparent, despite Newport's limited trade revival, that better business opportunities were available elsewhere. All of the younger, ambitious members of the Lopez family left Newport for New York and Boston before 1790. Jacob Rodriguez Rivera was old and tired. He continued to trade from Newport until his death in 1789. Gradually, the remaining Jews of the younger generation drifted off to New York, Boston, and Charleston, seeking new opportunities. The 1790 census list shows seven Jewish families remaining in Newport. These were the families of Abigail Polock, Jacob Isaacks, Sarah Lopez (Aaron's widow), Hillel Judah, Moses Seixas, and Isaac Elizer.[60] Jacob Isaacks died in Newport in 1798, Hillel Judah left in 1790, and Isaac Elizer left about the same time. Moses Seixas died in Newport in 1809. In 1822 Moses Lopez, the last remaining Jew in Newport, left for New York.

The Jews drawn to Newport in the middle of the eighteenth century were a select group lured by the prospects for economic expansion. Newport's commercial growth preceded their arrival. Although the Jewish community cannot be credited with Newport's prosperity, a few members of the community did help to accelerate the port's economic growth while fulfilling their own economic aspirations. The majority of the Jewish traders, however, met with only marginal success or failure.

After the Revolution, when it became apparent that Newport's economic opportunities had narrowed, the younger members of the Jewish community as well as many non-Jews scattered in search of greener pastures. The businessmen who left Newport were victims of the port's commercial decline. The absence of the Jewish merchant community was a very minor factor in the ultimate eclipse of Newport. However, no amount of individual entrepreneurial activity could have altered the fact that Newport would never again be a major seaport.

NOTES

1. Jacob R. Marcus, *The Colonial American Jews*, 3 vols. (Detroit: Wayne State University Press, 1970), p. 318.

2. Stanley F. Chyet, *Lopez of Newport: Colonial American Merchant Prince* (Detroit: Wayne State University Press, 1970), p. 16.

3. Bruce Bigelow, "The Commerce of Rhode Island With the West Indies Before the American Revolution" (Ph.D. diss., Brown University, 1930) Part I, Chapter III, pp. 2–18.

4. Bigelow, "The Commerce of Rhode Island," Part I, Chapter V, p. 4.

5. Carl Bridenbaugh, *Cities in Revolt: Urban Life in America, 1743–1776* (New York: Oxford University Press, 1955), pp. 65–66.

6. James B. Hedges, *The Browns of Providence Plantations: Colonial Years* (Cambridge, Mass.: Harvard University Press, 1952), p. xv.

7. Marcus, *Colonial American Jews*, p. 635.

8. Bigelow, "The Commerce of Rhode Island," Part I, Chapter VI, p. 24.

9. Bigelow, "The Commerce of Rhode Island," Part I, Chapter VI, pp. 25–27.

10. Chyet, *Lopez of Newport*, p. 67.

11. Bigelow, "The Commerce of Rhode Island," Part I, Chapter V, p. 5.

12. Bridenbaugh, *Cities in Revolt*, p. 216.

13. Ezra Stiles, *Literary Diary of Ezra Stiles*, ed. F.B. Dexter (New York, 1901), vol. I, pp. 6–11.

14. Stiles, *Literary Diary*, pp. 6–11.

15. *Census of the Inhabitants of the Colony of Rhode Island and Providence Plantations, Taken by the Order of the General Assembly in the Year 1774.* Arranged by John R. Bartlett (Providence: n.p., 1858).

16. Samuel Greene Arnold, *History of the State of Rhode Island* (New York: D. Appleton & Company, 1878), vol. II, p. 333, footnote 1.

17. Morris A. Gutstein, *The Story of the Jews of Newport* (New York: Bloch Publishing Company, 1936), p. 115.

18. Marcus, *Colonial American Jews*, p. 392.

19. Marcus, *Colonial American Jews*, p. 549.

20. Bigelow, "The Commerce of Rhode Island," Part I, Chapter VI, pp. 62–64.

21. Hedges, *The Browns*, p. 26.

22. Hedges, *The Browns*, p. 26.

23. Bigelow, "The Commerce of Rhode Island," Chapter VII, pp. 4–6.

24. Arnold, *History*, vol. II, p. 251.

25. Malcolm Stern, *Americans of Jewish Descent, A Compendium of Genealogy* (New York: Ktav Publishing House, Inc., 1971), p. 134.

26. Chyet, *Lopez of Newport*, pp. 21–22.

27. Hedges, *The Browns*, p. 89.

28. Chyet, *Lopez of Newport*, p. 44.

29. S. Broches, *Jews in New England: Six Monographs* (New York, 1942), p. 54.

30. Hedges, *The Browns*, p. 112.

31. Chyet, *Lopez of Newport*, p. 51.

32. Chyet, *Lopez of Newport*, p. 64.

33. Chyet, *Lopez of Newport*, p. 67.

34. Chyet, *Lopez of Newport*, pp. 84–85.

35. Bigelow, "The Commerce of Rhode Island," Part I, Chapter VII, p. 17.

36. *Newport Mercury*, September 30, 1771 and May 11, 1772.

37. Jacob R. Marcus. *Early American Jewry*, 2 vols. (Philadelphia: Jewish Publication Society, 1951 and 1953), p. 154.

38. *Newport Mercury*, May 11, 1772.

39. *Newport Mercury*, January 7, 1772.

40. Broches, *Jews in New England*, p. 75.

41. Bigelow, "The Commerce of Rhode Island," Part I, Chapter VII, p. 1.

42. Hedges, *The Browns*, p. 114.

43. Arnold, *History*, p. 300.

44. Chyet, *Lopez of Newport*, p. 122.

45. Chyet, *Lopez of Newport*, p. 128.

46. Arthur Meir Schlesinger, *The Colonial Merchants and the American Revolution 1763–1776* (New York: Facsimile Library, Inc, 1939), p. 485.

47. Bigelow, "The Commerce of Rhode Island," Part I, Chapter VII, p. 50.

48. Arnold, *History*, p. 360.

49. Bridenbaugh, *Cities in Revolt*, p. 216.

50. Aaron Lopez to Joseph Anthony, February 3, 1779, in *Commerce of Rhode Island*, vol. 2 (Boston: Massachusetts Historical Society, 1915), p. 51.

51. *Census Records of the State of Rhode Island for 1782*. Typed from original manuscript, Rhode Island Historical Society.

52. Newport taxes, town rate, July 31, 1783. Miscellaneous Manuscripts, Rhode Island Historical Society.

53. Newport taxes, town rate, June 1785.

54. William M. Fowler, Jr., *William Ellery: A Rhode Island Politico and Lord of Admiralty* (Metuchen: The Scarecrow Press, Inc., 1973), p. 131.

55. Douglas S. Robertson, *An Englishman in America 1785 Being the Diary of Joseph Hadfield* (Toronto: Hunter-Rose Co., 1933), p. 216.

56. Robertson, *An Englishman*, p. 217

57. Winthrop L. Marvin, *The American Merchant Marine* (New York: Charles Scribner's Sons, 1902), p. 37.

58. Hedges, *The Browns*, p. xviii.

59. Joseph K. Ott, "Rhode Island Furniture Exports: 1783–1795," in *Antiques Magazine*, May 1974.

60. *Heads of Families, First Census of the United States: 1790, State of Rhode Island*.

Reconstructing the Lives of Newport's Hidden Jews, 1740–1790

HOLLY SNYDER

When we think of the Jewish presence in colonial Rhode Island, the image that most readily springs to mind is of the prominent and well-to-do Sephardic merchant prince, who came to eighteenth-century Newport with little and proceeded to build a mercantile empire prior to the Revolution. And there is good reason why we remember the story of Aaron Lopez. The mercantile accounts and correspondence he left behind him, now dispersed among at least nine repositories in five states, is the single most significant cache of records of a Jewish merchant operating in colonial times. While Lopez has, for this reason, become the very symbol of Jewish enterprise in Newport, we are fortunate to have other records that reflect on eighteenth–century Jewish mercantile endeavors in colonial Rhode Island. Men such as Naphtali Hart, Jacob Rodriguez Rivera, Moses Seixas, and Moses Michael Hays have also left us their correspondence and mercantile accounts, through which we can track their activities and reconstruct their trading patterns.

These records, however, must be considered with a particular caveat, for there were many Jews in the Newport community who are not represented within them. Surviving mercantile accounts tell us little of the lives of Jews not heavily engaged in commerce. Jewish, and gentile, women, for example, make only sporadic appearances here, generally when they come to make household purchases. Others who are poorly represented include Jews who worked in the service of Jewish merchants, most likely in the position of a clerk. Poor Jews, who relied on the synagogue community and its Tzedakah (or charity fund) for their subsistence, as well as those who performed the routine functions necessary to preserve Jewish religious life, also do not appear. Mercantile accounts and correspondence thus tell us little of those at the very center of Newport's Jewish community—women, the poor and the unsuccessful, and those devoted to the religious welfare of the community. This silent lot have left few letters and no ledgers behind to document their lives. And, until recently, scholars in the field have perpetuated their silence by choosing to present the reading public with general communal histories that fail to flesh out the significant social and ethnic hierarchies that existed in colonial Jewish communities, or with biographies that focus attention on those Jews for whom the extant records provide extensive evidence.

Clearly, evidence from the intimate interiors of Jewish colonial Newport is not so easy to find. Apart from the 1677 deed for the cemetery and the legal proceedings initiated against eight Jewish merchants in 1684, we know little of the seventeenth-century founders of the community. Jewish births, deaths, and marriages were infrequently reported to colonial record-keeping authorities, and the town records for Newport—where most colonial Rhode Island Jews resided—were heavily damaged during the Revolution, thus destroying much evidence of Jewish wills, estate inventories,

Excerpted from *Rhode Island Jewish Historical Notes*, Volume 12, Number 4 (November 1998): 449–463.

and land holdings in the town. Nevertheless, the heretofore overlooked voiceless majority of the Jewish population in seventeenth- and eighteenth-century British America played a vital role in the formation of the fabric of community established by Jews in colonial America. Like their prominent and well-to-do co-religionists, they worked for a living, raised their families, interacted with their gentile neighbors, and expended their energies to promote and defend the interests of the Jewish community as a whole. Yet, because of their very lack of prominence, they may have carried out these activities in very different ways than the successful merchants who presented themselves as the public face of the Jewish community to the gentile world. It is, I believe, only through the study of these Jewish lives, at the margins of colonial society, that we can fully understand the complexity of the social world that the Jews who established their homes in colonial Newport inhabited.

This article will present three short cases that attempt to reconstruct lives of Newport's less notable Jews from existing documentary sources. Each case will highlight different types of archival or manuscript collections within which information about early Rhode Island Jews has been discovered, and each case attempts to raise different issues concerning the identification and description of Jews in early Rhode Island records, as well as to demonstrate the richness of existing records for documenting the cultural diversity of colonial Rhode Island. Through these case studies, I hope to shed illumination into the corners where it does not typically go, in order to suggest a more complete picture of Jewish communal life in eighteenth-century Newport.

SARAH RIVERA LOPEZ

Perhaps the best place to start discovering the overlooked is with the life of a woman who had every reason to be conspicuous, yet who remains largely invisible in the historical record. When Sarah Rivera Lopez died, she left little behind her. Though she led a privileged life and was not poorly educated, she never kept a diary and was apparently not an avid letter writer. The single remaining document that captures anything of her essence is the portrait of her as a young mother, painted by Gilbert Stuart, which hangs now in the Detroit Institute of Arts.[1] Stuart's painting shows a sedate and modest young woman, in a simply but elegantly appointed dress and lace cap. She is no great beauty, but nonetheless her portrait suggests a certain elfin charm, her dark eyes filled with merriment, the barest hint of a smile on her composed lips. Her right arm encompasses her small, grave son, who, unlike his mischievous mother, regards the viewer with a very adult solemnity. Sarah's image intrigues the viewer; we want to know her, but she has left us nothing to know her by.

Or has she? It is easy enough to reconstruct the bare details of her life. Born in New York to Jacob Rodrigues Rivera and his wife Hannah, she was raised largely in Newport and was married at age 16 to Aaron Lopez, a widower with six young children. The responsibilities of motherhood thus came to her early in life, and all indications are that Sarah took to the task readily. She would bear her husband another ten children between 1763 and 1782, of which only two did not survive infancy. In addition, after the death of his brother Moses in 1767, Aaron Lopez took on the support of the widow and her eight minor children. Since Rebecca Lopez was Sarah's aunt, this was probably not an infelicitous arrangement. Nevertheless, even with the benefit of servants, of which there were plenty, such a large household might have been nearly un-

manageable without someone of considerable talents to oversee the household operations. And, in the best tradition of the Jewish housewife, Sarah ran her ship with a warm and loving hand.

The Lopez household was well known among her husband's associates and friends for the warm and hospitable atmosphere that Sarah was largely responsible for creating. Letters to her husband regularly made note to deliver the regards of the correspondent to Aaron's "Worthy Spouse." During the Revolution, she provided sanctuary at the family residence in Leicester, Massachusetts, supplying her guests with whatever they might have needed to the best of her ability. Benjamin Seixas, noting that "my Parents & Sister flew to Your Hospitable roof for an Asylum from the British Mercanaries," begged Aaron Lopez to "Accept of my Sincere thanks for the friendly Civilities they received from You & Yours while at Liecester[.]" Sarah was particularly mentioned by Seixas for her generosity to his sister Grace, to whom she had given "some Linnen."² Aaron himself had a fair appreciation of his wife's instinctive nature on this score. Following a visit to Leicester by his friend Moses Seixas, Lopez wrote to Seixas that he "wish[ed]

Mrs Seixas had been able to Accompany you here as am Certain Mrs Lopez would have used her best endeavors to make her easy & as Comfortable as our situation would admit[.]"[3] He was also quick to invite his friend, Captain Joseph Anthony of Philadelphia, to bring his family for a summertime visit, knowing "you may at least be assured of a hearty and well come [inter]ruption" while entertained in "our humble habitation."[4] Sarah thus extended her gracious and generous reach to her friends and neighbors of all persuasions, to whom she might occasionally send the unsolicited gift of a "Pott of Pickles"[5] or a box of cookies.[6]

Sarah had all the household skills which we know, through the pioneering work of Laurel Thatcher Ulrich, were common to women of her time and social status. Though, like other privileged women, she had her clothes from a local dressmaker,[7] she had evidently had the same training in needlework as her equally polished contemporaries.[8] She had sufficient skill in the making of preserves to consider offering them for sale,[9] and knew how to render medicines from red sage and other herbs.[10] She nursed her family through various and sundry ailments, from chicken pox[11] to rheumatism,[12] and, even toward the end of her own life, managed to keep them together in the face of death and physical decline.[13] When Moses Lopez, her husband's nephew, became ill in 1822 and could no longer care for himself, she took him into the bosom of her own household as part of the family. Throughout her life, family was her first, and foremost, concern. Even the single surviving document in her hand—a narrative genealogy of the Lopez and Rivera families, which she prepared at the request of another family member—reflects Sarah's true *raison d'être*, both in its content and in the circumstances surrounding its creation.[14]

Sarah Lopez may have remained in the shadow of her father and her husband, but she was not altogether sheltered and unworldly. Though raised in Newport, she spent considerable time on the family's farm in nearby Portsmouth, resided in the country town of Leicester, Massachusetts, during the Revolution, and at the end of her life, moved her family to New York City. In 1780, she made a small "tour" of Boston and New England with her husband—a trip the devoted Aaron evidently designed to raise both her spirits and her flagging health.[15] While she left the pursuit of the family business interests to her father and her stepson Joseph following Aaron's death, she was not entirely unfamiliar with the concept of enterprise. In 1774, for example, Captain William English reported on an endeavor to sell some preserves and furniture she had sent with him to Africa and the West Indies for sale.[16] Although this effort was, sadly, not as successful as Sarah might have wished, the attempt itself reveals that Sarah understood the basics of mercantile trade and was willing to engage a modicum of risk. After her husband's death, she marshaled her small business skills to deal with those who performed the tasks of physical maintenance of her household. When George Nightingale, for example, served his account for services rendered in 1798, it was Sarah, and not her father or her stepson, to whom he addressed the bill.[17]

Those scattered details of the life of Sarah Rivera Lopez are derived primarily from letters of her husband and his associates, her nephew and her stepson, which are supplemented by information found in a few surviving household accounts. With the household as her center, Sarah Lopez manages to remain largely hidden from public view, even to the most discriminating of researchers. The merry eyes and enigmatic smile hang in the air before us like ghosts, inviting our approach but eluding our comprehension. For Sarah Lopez, as for other colonial Jewish women, being seen at all involves reading between the lines of other lives.

In looking backward to the eighteenth century, we tend to deem an individual as having social significance by his own merit. But our regard for the individual in society often shields us from his other, and more important, communal role as the connective tissue of an extended family group whose members wholly depend upon him for their support and sustenance. Such a figure was Israel Abrahams, who struggled, unsuccessfully, to meet the burdens of eighteenth-century family life and the demands of a difficult marketplace.

The Abrahams family first appears in the Newport town records on April 6, 1747, when the minutes of the Town Council record an order "That ye Town Sargeant Carry Israel Abrahams His Mother and all ye Rest of ye Family That Came from York out of Town to James Town and Deliver y^m To a Proper Officer There That They May Be Transported to York from Where They Came."[18] This instance of "warning out" is, to date, the only identified case of poor Jews living in a New England town. Who were these people, and what brought them to Newport from cosmopolitan New York? We know that Israel Abrahams found in Newport the prospects of home sometime in the early 1740s. He most likely believed his economic opportunities would improve with the change of venue. With his partner, Nathan Nathans, he seems to have engaged in a variety of mercantile activities in Rhode Island. But the partnership of Nathans & Abrahams, whatever efforts they may have made, achieved no success as merchant traders. Between 1744 and 1745, Israel Abrahams was imprisoned in the Newport jail, and the partners filed for protection under the "Act for the Relief of Poor and Insolvent Debtors" in October 1745.[19] Following the bankruptcy, Israel Abrahams apparently engaged in different attempts to make a living for his family; he appears, for instance, in the records of the Court of Vice Admiralty as a translator of Dutch and Spanish in 1746 and 1747,[20] and in August 1750 was identified as "a Jew Perriwigg Maker" in the records of the Newport Town Council.[21]

On May 1, 1749, Israel Abrahams appeared before the Town Council to render an Account of Estate for his brother Saul, who had recently died, and to claim administration of the estate as its principal creditor.[22] It is in the inventory of Saul Abrahams's estate that we find the clearest picture, in material terms, of what it might have meant to be both unsuccessful and Jewish in eighteenth-century Rhode Island. Saul Abrahams apparently owned, at the time of his death, little more than personal belongings. He died possessed of approximately six changes of clothes, almost all noted by the two town examiners as being "old." His two pairs of shoes were well-worn, and he had but one hat and one wig, as well as a single handkerchief and a silk *tallis* for use in prayer. Although his profession was "Merchant," he clearly had no inventory of merchantable goods. He had no cash, and owed money to Dr. Wigneron, Jacob Hasey, Elizabeth Clarke, Philip Wanton, and tailor Henry Sowle. The only items of real value that he owned were his silver shoe and waist band buckles, a few gold rings, and some gold buttons. Two chests, three razors, and a set of *Shochet*'s knives for the ritual slaughter of cattle completed his possessions.[23] The whole inventory, valued at just over £100, suggests a certain shabby gentility with a distinctively Jewish bent.

After the Abrahams family was warned out of town in 1747, they may indeed have gone back to New York. Nevertheless, their absence from Newport was only a temporary one, and they reappeared by January of 1749. The arrival, however, was not triumphant, for Israel Abrahams returned already indebted to creditors in town,[24] and with no collectible debts owed to him,[25] he was soon to become even further enmeshed in the spiraling cycle of debt. Francis Honyman (who presumably was in a position to know) would later claim that on January 5, 1749, Israel Abrahams was guilty of "illegally Entring into with force and arms & unjustly withholding" from his underage ward, William Martins, "the Possession of one certain Lot of Land situate . . . in Newport . . . with a Dwelling House thereon standing."[26] It is impossible to tell from the extant court records in this case how relations between the two men had started—whether Honyman had voluntarily agreed to lease the property to Abrahams, or Abrahams had indeed taken possession of the property without Honyman's knowledge or permission. By May of 1750, however, their relationship was clearly an embittered one, and with good reason. Though the language of the charges may well disguise a simple eviction proceeding, it is absolutely clear that Israel Abrahams was seriously in arrears with respect to the payment of his rent.[27] Abrahams, in any case, pleaded "Not Guilty" to the charge of trespass. But by then the damage to his reputation had already been done, and a few months later, in August 1750, he was called before the Town Council to "Give Bond" to ensure his future good behavior.[28] With such shameful proceedings in motion against him and no money to pay the judgments owed, Abrahams must have felt his fate in Newport was, by this, forever sealed. Before 1752, he had fled to Halifax, Nova Scotia, never to return.[29]

Between Newport's town government and its courts, Israel Abrahams had argued his case even when he must have known he had no chance of winning. His ongoing legal problems in the 1740s might suggest to some a troublesome personality. But, given the all of the evidence at hand, I rather think they were the result of desperation—of a man trying valiantly to avoid the consequences of impoverishment, and maintain some shred of dignity in a community where honor defined a member of civilized society. To look at either the town or the court records independently of each other is to miss an important part of his story. It is only when the two sets of records are read together that the whole twisted tale emerges.

HILLEL JUDAH

For women and poor Jews, there are, as I have shown above, bodies of records that may reveal significant details, if carefully read. But for the religious Jews of colonial Newport, the task becomes even more complicated. Ezra Stiles was pleased to note in his diary that he had known six rabbis during his residence in Newport;[30] these gentlemen, however, were only passing through on their travels. They were not responsible for meeting the day-to-day requirements of Jewish ritual life. The best source to get at those who dedicated themselves to providing for the Jewish community in this way is through synagogue records. Of these, however, nearly none have survived in Newport for the eighteenth century. With scant records to guide us, perhaps it is nonetheless possible to reconstruct one representative life which can inform our still incomplete portraits of other, similar lives.

Hillel Judah, born in New York to an Ashkenazic family, is one such life. He became a member (*Yachid*) of congregation Shearith Israel sometime prior to march 1759, and had served as *Hatan Bereshit* (Second Assistant) to the *Parnassim* in 1758.[31] In June 1759, he married Abigail Seixas, then 17. Abigail bore Hillel at least nine children between 1760 and 1779, one every two years.[32] With such a large family to support and little inclination for trade, Hillel Judah was never able to accumulate any assets to speak of. In 1780,

Benjamin Seixas was obliged to write to Aaron Lopez seeking the latter's assistance to aid Judah "in his Endeavours to procure a livelihood for his poor family" as he embarked for Newport. His brother-in-law, Seixas wrote from Philadelphia, would of course, "require a small Credit" to get started in the new location. But, wrote Seixas, "he is strictly Honest, & I dare answer will always strive to fulfill every engagement he enters into."[33]

His description of Judah's family as "poor" surely was not entirely sentimental. Indeed, the Rhode Island census of 1782 records that the Judah household consisted of five sons and two daughters under the age of 15 and one daughter over 15, in addition to Hillel and Abigail, but no servants of any description to assist in managing the household. Nor was this a temporary state of affairs for the Judah family. The federal census of 1790 reveals that the Judah household then consisted of two young sons and four daughters, but still no servants in addition to Hillel and Abigail; meanwhile Abigail's brother, Moses Seixas—who made a more respectable living as a merchant—had six slaves and one free servant to attend the needs of his family of eleven.[34] While the Judah household was not a wealthy one, it was also not entirely impoverished. Hillel Judah never had to file for protection as an insolvent debtor, and in all his years in Newport he was sued only once—over a book debt of £100.[35] Their house, on Thames Street at the corner of Fare, was in a grand and prominent location. Three of the Judah daughters reportedly grew to be great beauties, and were remembered by Newport residents long after the family had moved away.[36]

Though he may have had some small activity in trade, Hillel Judah found his principal employment as *Shochet* (ritual slaughterer, also recorded in eighteenth-century records as "Jew Butcher") for the Jewish community of Newport, for which he was paid a small salary. His name appears on an extant record of the congregation in this capacity in 1788.[37] Of Hillel, Moses Seixas noted that he had a "commendable conscience" in observing religious law with regard to the inspection of kosher meat. But Judah's strict interpretation of Halakah sometimes had deleterious consequences for his brother-in-law's business activities. On one occasion, Seixas noted that Judah's conscientious behavior had "prevented our having any chance as yet to make a beginning in procuring" kosher fat, thus preventing Seixas from providing a useful service to the Lopez household and himself the opportunity to ingratiate himself with his friend and business mentor.[38]

Hillel Judah's dedication to religious principle was absolute. He apparently circumcised his own sons, since none appear on the circumcision records of the known *Mohels* for New York and Newport (Abraham I. Abrahams and Moses Seixas, respectively). His high regard for Halakic standards in Jewish ritual practice sometimes brought him into conflict with the powers that be in the synagogue. In May 1768, for example, while living in New York, he was called before the *Parnassim*, along with Manuel Josephson and Uriah Hendricks, to answer for his behavior "in attempting to make Scandalous Offrings during Service," though "in contempt and defiance of the Good & Wholesome Resolve passed . . . for the Tranquility of the Synegouge."[39] In July of the following year, he and five other men were disciplined by the ruling body of Congregation Shearith Israel for having repeatedly, "for a Considerable time . . . Acted in Opposition, and tending to Subvert the Laws & Rules made for the Good order, and Support of our congregation," and warned to "make proper reasonable, and Satisfactory Concessions to the Parnasim & assistants" on pain of expulsion from the congregation.[40]

The nature of the "scandalous offerings" Judah and the others were alleged to have made in 1768 and 1769 is not described, but since all of those so disciplined were Ashkenazic Jews it is most likely that the conflict involved objections on their part to aspects of the congregation's form of service. Another clue to this incident is revealed in a letter of one of the co-conspirators, Manuel Josephson. Writing to Moses Seixas in February 1790, Josephson made reference to an earlier letter he had written to Hillel's wife, Abigail Judah, in which he "did point out some improprieties & recommended an alteration" in the practices of the Newport congregation. Moreover, Josephson declared, "I can't avoid to say a word in justification of Mr. Uriah Hendricks not attending publick worship when last at your place." Hendricks, he thought, had been right to have declined attendance "on the score of a religious principle," given the manner in which services were conducted in the Newport synagogue—by direction of the admittedly "capricious & whimsical disposition" of some of the regular members.[41] The 1768 refusal to submit to the prevailing regulations of the congregation by Hendricks, Josephson, and Judah thus reflected the protest of a small group of independent thinkers dedicated to a strict interpretation of religious law.

The evidence of other *Shochets'* lives suggests that Hillel Judah's approach to ritual life and to the spiritual welfare of the Newport Jewish community, if more rigorous than some, was not atypical. His immediate predecessor as *Shochet* had been Joseph Jacobs. In 1756, while living in New York, Jacobs had been a member of Shearith Israel, but was not well-to-do; in 1750, he subscribed to the seats in the second least expensive category.[42] When Jacobs arrived in Newport in the early 1770s, Myer Benjamin was serving as *Shochet* for the Newport congregation. Benjamin's untimely death in 1776, at age 43,[43] left a vacuum in communal practice that Jacobs was quickly tapped to fill—and, according to one recollection, "no man was more faithful to the ceremonial law." Jacobs, however, was an accomplished silversmith, who occupied the easternmost portion of a house owned by a Quaker lady, to whom he had "paid part of the rent in Silver Spoons" marked with his family monogram.[44] As ritual slaughtering was not his primary occupation, we may surmise that he was probably happy to surrender this obligation to someone as dedicated to religious observance as Hillel Judah.[45] Myer Benjamin, on the other hand, appears to have been as dedicated to Jewish religious life as Hillel Judah. Although he had brought his family to Newport in August 1761,[46] like Judah he never appears in any mercantile accounts and was sued only once.[47] His household details, revealed in the census of 1774, indicate that he followed the same family pattern as would the Judah household in later years—which is to say, that the Benjamin household consisted of Benjamin, his wife and eight young children, but no household slaves or servants.[48] He resided next to Davis's tavern "in a house near the court-house," where he rented a room to tailor Isaac Nunes Cardozo—a fact that undoubtedly reflected the need to generate extra income for the support of such a large family.[49]

This is the extent of what I have so far uncovered about Hillel Judah and the other eighteenth-century *Shochets* for Jewish Newport. Slight and inconsiderable as these three stories may seem, they tell us much about the structure of Jewish communal existence in colonial Newport and its dependence on those who quietly devoted their lives to its service. Moreover, the fact that I have been able to glean even this much information about them is a singular reflection on the research of one man—Jacques Judah Lyons, *Hazan* for Congregation Shearith Israel of New York between 1839 and 1877—who made it part of his life's work to collect documents and information pertaining to the early settlement of Jews in North America.[50] Jacques Judah Lyons made several trips to Newport to collect information firsthand, and met with elderly Newport residents, such as N. H. Gould, who had known and been friendly with members of the Jewish community. In addition to his superb collection of original documents, Lyons kept careful notes on the information he obtained from oral sources. The Lyons notebooks contain the record of these firsthand recollections, which otherwise would probably have been lost to posterity. Though Lyons died without having the opportunity to write the definitive history he had planned, his research collections document nearly every important aspect of Jewish religious life in colonial times, from synagogue minutes to circumcisions. If we know anything of Jewish religious life in this period, it is largely due to his efforts to preserve these private records that had been heretofore kept in the attics of the recordkeepers' descendants.

Merchants such as Aaron Lopez certainly played an important role in colonial Jewish Newport. In the end, however, they were merely the most public facet of the broader, complex, and interdependent network that constituted Jewish communal life in the eighteenth-century town. To the extent that we neglect to look behind the mercantile façade, we will necessarily miss seeing the body of the iceberg under the surface of the water. And so, I would like to close this brief presentation with passages from two letters written by Providence resident David Lopez, Jr., during the hard winter of 1780, which provide us with an unusual insight into the day-to-day lives of ordinary Jewish Rhode Islanders of the eighteenth century. Writing to his uncle Aaron in Leicester, Massachusetts, in late January of that year, Lopez could hardly help making note of "the large quantities of Snow, which has so effectually blocked up the road as to impeed the Travelling on every side." Since he was thus unable to make his way to Leicester for a visit, he reported that he now had "deliberated on attempting a retreat to Provid[en]ce on snow shoes, in Company with a Young Gent n who setts off from hear early in the morning." Nine days later, he was able to "have now the sattisfaction to advise you my safe return here after a very fatigueing journey, on foot. [T]he roads not being passable for a Horse, was forced to take snow shoes, & they being machines I did not perfectly understand the use of, made our Journey two days long[. W]e however reached here without any other inconveinency than my feet Terribly Blisterd."[51]

Now, I submit to you that here, in this brief but very personal account, we can find a central metaphor for the kind of work undertaken by the historian writing about marginal Jews in early Rhode Island. Just like the snowed-in route from Uxbridge to Providence in January 1780, the way is not easily traversed. So, like the intrepid Mr. Lopez, we must strap on intellectual snow shoes to tread impassable routes through the wilderness of damaged, dispersed, and inconsistent records, slogging persistently until, blistered to the point of exhaustion, we have finally reached our goal.

NOTES

1. This portrait has been reproduced in Jacob Rader Marcus, *The Colonial American Jew, 1492–1776.* Detroit: Wayne State University Press, 1970, Vol. II, facing p. 493. Chyet states that the portrait has been dated to 1773, when Sarah would have been 25 or 26 years old. See Stanley F. Chyet, *Lopez of Newport: Colonial American Merchant Prince,* Detroit: Wayne State University Press, 1970, p. 206, n.1.

2. Benjamin Seixas & Co. to Aaron Lopez, 21 Jan. 1780 [addendum in the hand of Benjamin Seixas]. G. W. Haight Collection of Aaron Lopez Papers, Box 169, folder 2, Collections of the Newport Historical Society.

3. Aaron Lopez to Moses Seixas, November 4, 1781. Aaron Lopez letterbook, Houghton Library, Harvard University.

4. Aaron Lopez to Joseph Anthony, April 3, 1782. Aaron Lopez letterbook, Houghton Library, Harvard University.

5. Aaron Lopez to Moses Seixas, November 4, 1781. Aaron Lopez letterbook, Houghton Library, Harvard University.

6. Moses Lopez to Stephen Gould, December 27, 1825. Lopez Collection, Rare Documents file, Collections of the American Jewish Archives.

7. See, e.g., Account of Sarah Bissell, 1764, Papers of Aaron Lopez, Box 12, folder 7, Collections of the American Jewish Historical Society.

8. On January 13, 1775, Sarah appeared at her husband's warehouse to take 3 1/2 yards black flowered Satin and 3/8 of a yard black persian, which was charged to the account of her father, Jacob Rodriguez Rivera. Store blotter Dec. 1774–Mar. 1775, Papers of Aaron Lopez, folder 2, Collections of the Rhode Island Historical Society.

9. See William English to Aaron Lopez, January 10, 1774. G. W. Haight Collection of Aaron Lopez Papers, Box 168, folder 7, Collections of the Newport Historical Society. In this letter, English wrote to Lopez from St. Nicholas Mole in Haiti: "I am Sorry itt Did Not Ly in my power to turn Mrs Lopez's adventure out more advantageous as the preserves was for a Gentleman that Thought the first Cost in america to much to pay for them on the Coast[.]"

10. Moses Lopez to Stephen Gould, December 12, 1822, January 26, 1823. July 24, 1823, April 24, 1824, January 28, 1825, September 24, 1827, October 10, 1828; Lopez collection, Rare Documents file, Collections of the American Jewish Archives.

11. David Lopez, Jr., to Aaron Lopez, November 16, 1780, G. W. Haight Collection of Aaron Lopez Papers, Box 169, folder 3, Collection of the Newport Historical Society.

12. Joseph Lopez to Stephen Gould, July 15, 1822. Lopez Collection, Rare Documents file, Collections of the American Jewish Archives.

13. Moses Lopez to Stephen Gould, December 12, 1822 (on death of stepson Joseph Lopez), January 26, 1823 (on death of Sarah's brother, Abraham Rivera). Lopez Collection, Rare Documents file, Collections of the American Jewish Archives.

14. "The Genealogy of the Lopez Family, Presented by Sarah Lopez to her Friend, Mrs. Priscilla Lopez, of Charleston, by her Request," in Chyet, ibid., pp. 197–199; reprinted from *Publications of the American Jewish Historical Society*, vol. 2 (1894), pp. 103–106.

15. David Lopez, Jr., to Aaron Lopez, June 12, June 18, and June 28, 1780. G. W. Haight Collection of Aaron Lopez Papers, Box 168, folder 7, Collections of the Newport Historical Society.

16. William English to Aaron Lopez, January 10, 1774. G. W. Haight Collection of Aaron Lopez Papers, Box 168, folder 7. Collections of the Newport Historical Society.

17. Account of George Nightingale to Sarah Lopez, 27 Aug. 1798, Box 52, Folder 3. Collections of the Newport Historical Society. The account covered the following labor, performed between November 1797 and August 1798: milking the cow for seven weeks, digging a well and a drain, chopping 11 cords of firewood, and cleaning a cellar.

18. Newport Town Council Minutes, vol. X, folio 149. Collections of the Newport Historical Society.

19. *Isaac Beauchamp v. Israel Abrahams*, Newport Court of Common Pleas, November 1744, CCP Book B, folio 590, Collections of the Rhode Island Supreme Court Judicial Records Center (noting that Abrahams "is in the Custody of the Sheriff (by Virtue of a Writt by the said Isaac Sued out agst him the said Israel"; the writ included Nathans, "who coud not be found by the said Sheriff or his Dep^t in the County of Newport"); Public Notary Records, vol. 5, Collections of the Rhode Island State Archives, published in Jacob Rader Marcus (ed.), *American Jewry—Documents, Eighteenth Century: Primarily Hitherto Unpublished Manuscripts*, Cincinnati: The Hebrew Union College Press, 1959, no. 119, pp. 325–326. Among the creditors who sued Abrahams and his partner before 1746 were not only Isaac Beauchamp of Boston, to whom the pair owed £250 on a Note of Hand, but also Samuel Webb of Newport (book debt of £80), Jacob Franks of New York (£1500 by Bond), and Moses Levy of Newport (book debt of £500). See, e.g., Newport Court of Common Pleas, CCP Book B, folios 534, 590, 592, 595, Collections of the Rhode Island Supreme Court Judicial Records Center.

20. Lee Max Friedman, "Notes: Jews in the Vice-Admiralty Court of Rhode Island," *Publications of the American Jewish Historical Society*, vol. 37 (1947), pp. 392.

21. Newport Town Council Minutes, vol. IX, folio 373, Collections of the Newport Historical Society.

22. Ibid., folios 380, 382.

23. Ibid., vol. X, folio 204.

24. In November 1747, Israel Abrahams was sued by Newport merchant John Bannister over a book debt of £700, on which he had defaulted after paying £200; that same session, the widow

Rebecca Allen sued him for a book debt of £200 owed to her late husband, Joseph Allen. *John Bannister v. Israel Abrahams, Rebecca Allen v. Israel Abrahams*, Newport Court of Common Pleas, November 1747, CCP Book C, folios 127, 151, Collections of the Rhode Island Supreme Court Judicial Records Center. In May 1748, merchant Patrick Grant sued Abrahams over default of a Bond for £600, and Newport distiller John Brown sued Abrahams in an action of Covenant for performance of promise, claiming £800 in damages, and Abrahams countersued for performance under the Articles of Agreement he and Brown had signed, with a claim for £1,000 in damages; the parties agreed to arbitrate their differences. *Patrick Grant v. Israel Abrahams, John Brown v. Israel Abrahams*, Newport Court of Common Pleas, May 1748, CCP Book C, folios 202, 222, Collections of the Rhode Island Supreme Court Judicial Records Center. In November 1748, blacksmith Joseph Cleveland of Norwich, Connecticut, sued Abrahams over his default on a note of hand for £80. *Joseph Cleveland v. Israel Abrahams*, Newport Court of Common Pleas, November 1748, CCP Book C, folio 256, Collections of the Rhode Island Supreme Court Judicial Records Center. In each of these cases, the Court eventually found in favor of the Plaintiffs. Abrahams appealed the Bannister and Grant decisions, but apparently failed to prosecute his appeals—a tacit indication that he perhaps knew he had no viable case to make.

25. Between November 1747 and May 1749, Abrahams filed suits for debts allegedly owed to him by Newport mariners John Rouse (book debt of £450), Bartholomew Smith (Note of Hand for £140), Joshua Lyon (book debt of £500), and mariner David Gardner of Nantucket (book debt of £50). *Israel Abrahams v. John Rouse, Israel Abrahams v. Bartholomew Smith, Israel Abrahams v. Joshua Lyon, Israel Abrahams v. David Gardner*, Newport Court of Common Pleas, CCP Book C, folios 164, 170, 251, 344. Collections of the Rhode Island Supreme Court Judicial Records Center. See also the countersuit by Israel Abrahams against distiller John Brown, cited in Note 24, above. In at least three of these cases (Brown, Lyon, Gardner), the suits were clearly filed as a desperate ploy by Abrahams to find the wherewithal to pay his debts, as the Court repeatedly found nothing owed by the respective defendants. Indeed, in the Lyon case, the appointed referees determined that Abrahams, in fact, owed Lyon some £400, and awarded court costs to the defendant. *Joshua Lyon v. Israel Abrahams, Israel Abrahams v. Joshua Lyons*, Newport Court of Common Pleas, November 1748, CCP Book C, folio 272, Collections of the Rhode Island Supreme Court Judicial Records Center. In the Gardner case, after Abrahams appealed the jury verdict, in favor of the defendant, to the Superior Court of Judicature, a panel of appointed arbitrators confirmed "that having examined the Appellants Accounts against the Appellee they find to the Appellant nothing due," and awarded costs to Gardner. Newport Superior Court of Judicature, March 1750, SCJ Book D, folio 164; appealed from Newport Court of Common Pleas, May 1749, CCP Book C, folio 344, Collections of the Rhode Island Supreme Court Judicial Records Center.

26. *William Martin v. Israel Abrahams*, Newport Court of Common Pleas, May 1750, CCP Book C, folio 519, Collections of the Rhode Island Supreme Court Judicial Records Center.

27. *William Martins v. Israel Abrahams*, case file, Newport Court of Common Pleas, May term 1750, Collections of the Rhode Island Supreme Court Judicial Records Center. In addition to the former suit, for trespass and ejectment brought in the name of his ward and for which he sought £5,000 in damages, Honyman brought the latter suit in order to recover £440 for rent. Though the court ruled against him in both cases, Abrahams appealed only the suit for trespass—a fact that suggests that he acknowledged the debt for overdue rent. See, e.g., *William Martins v. Israel Abrahams and Francis Honyman v. Israel Abrahams*, CCP Book C, folios 519–520; *Martins v. Abrahams*, Newport Superior Court of Judicature, Book D, folio 216, Collections of the Rhode Island Supreme Court Judicial Records Center.

28. Newport Town Council Minutes, vol. IX, folio 373.

29. Marcus, *American Jewry—Documents*, no. 121A, pp. 331–332. In Halifax, Abrahams attempted to set himself up as a manufacturer of potash. However, having no more capital in Halifax than he had in Newport, he this time threw himself on the mercy of the Lords of Trade and Plantations by casting himself as a benefactor to the Nova Scotia colony.

30. By 1783, Stiles recollected that he had known six different rabbis during his years in Newport, between 1759 and 1775. Franklin B. Dexter (ed.), *The Literary Diary of Ezra Stiles, D.D., LL.D., President of Yale College*, New York: Charles Scribner's Sons, 1901, Vol. III, pp. 77–78.

31. The Lyons Collection, Volume I, *Publications of the American Jewish Historical Society*, vol. 21 (1913), p. 79. Originals of the items published here and in the Lyons Collection, Volume II (*PAJHS* vol. 27), are located in the collections of the American Jewish Historical Society.

32. The Lyons Collection, Volume II, *Publications of the American Jewish Historical Society*, vol. 27 (1920), pp. 161, 170.

33. Benjamin Seixas to Aaron Lopez, 02 May 1780, G. W. Haight Collection of Aaron Lopez Papers, Box 169, folder 2, Collections of the Newport Historical Society.

34. John Mack Holbrook, *Rhode Island 1782 Census*, Oxford, Mass.: Holbrook Research Institute, 1979, RIA 782:11.

35. In 1788, Hillel Judah was sued by Newport hatter Jacob Barney over a book debt of £100. Although Judah is listed in the proceedings of this suit as a "trader," there is no evidence (including newspaper advertisements of goods or other suits for debt), that either suggests or would support any extensive activity in trade on his part. See *Jacob Barney v. Hillel Judah*, Newport Court of Common Pleas, November 1788, CCP Book J, folio 501, Collections of the Rhode Island Supreme Court Judicial Records Center.

36. Lyons Collection, Volume II, p. 213. This information was collected by Jacques Judah Lyons on his 1872 visit to Newport, and appears to have come from his principal contact, N. H. Gould. Gould thought the names of the three daughters were Naomi, Grace, and Huldah. Seixas family records, however, show only daughters named Sarah, Rachel, and Rebekah. See Lyons Collection, Volume II, pp. 76, 170. Lyons himself believed that Gould had simply got the names wrong.

37. Lyons Collection, Volume II, P. 185.

38. Moses Seixas to Aaron Lopez, July 9, 1781, printed in *Commerce of Rhode Island, 1726–1800*, Massachusetts Historical Society Collections, 7th Series, vols. IX–X, Boston, Massachusetts Historical Society, 1914–1915, Volume II, pp. 139–140.

39. Excisions from the Minutes of Congregation Shearith Israel, Rosh Hodes Yiar 5528 [May 1768]. The Lyons Collections, Collection of the American Jewish Historical Society. This document does not appear in the published compilation of the Lyons Collection.

40. Lyons Collection, Volume I, pp. 103–104. The other members so disciplined were Solomon Hays, Manuel Josephson, Moses Judah (brother of Hillel), Barrak Hays, and Andrew Hays.

41. Manuel Josephson to Moses Seixas, February 4, 1790, Lyons Collection, Volume II, pp. 185–190.

42. Lyons Collection, Volume I, p. 63. The general distribution of seats breaks down as follows:

Rate	Number
£4	10
£2.9.0	10
£1.16.6	8
£1.6.0	9
£0.15.0	24
Synagogue Seat Assignments, 1750.	

Source: Minutes of Cong. Shearith Israel

Jacobs was still living in New York in 1771, as he appears in Shearith Israel's minutes for that year. See Lyons Collection, Volume I, p. 111.

43. Lyons Collection, Volume II, p. 198.

44. Lyons Collection, Volume II, p. 211. As JBJ stood for Joseph and Bilhah Jacobs, these were probably spoons that he had made for his own family.

45. List of Members of the Gemilut Hasadim, 1786–1790; Lyons Collection, Volume II, p. 253.

46. Newport Administration Bonds, vol. 3, folio 229, Collections of the Newport Historical Society. On August 3, 1761, Moses Levy and Jacob Isaacks posted bond of £10,000 each for the good behavior of Nathan Hart and Myer Benjamin and their families.

47. Myer Benjamin appears only once in the judicial records, when he was sued by Judah Hays of New York for failure to perform a promise in 1762. *Judah Hays v. Myer Benjamin*, Newport Court of Common Pleas, November 1762, CCP Book F, folio 665, Collections of the Rhode Island Supreme Court Judicial Records Center.

48. John Russell Bartlett (arr.), *Census of the Inhabitants of the Colony of Rhode Island and Providence Plantations in New England, 1774*, Providence: Unpublished Ms., 1858, Collections of the Rhode Island State Archives.

49. Irwin S. Rhodes, *References to Jews in the Newport Mercury, 1758–1786*, Monographs of the American Jewish Archives no. III, Cincinnati: American Jewish Archives, 1961, no. 166, p. 14; George

Champlin Mason, *Newport: Historical and Social Reminiscences of Ye Olden Times with More than 550 Illustrations...*, 6 Volumes with original illustrations, Newport: 1892, Volume I, p. 61, Collections of the Rhode Island Historical Society.

50. See "Jacques Judah Lyons" [Biographical Sketch], Lyons Collection, Volume I, pp. xxiii–xxviii.

51. David Lopez, Jr., to Aaron Lopez, January 22 and January 31, 1780, G. W. Haight Collection, Newport Historical Society, Box 169, folder 3, Collections of the Newport Historical Society.

Old Bottles, Rags, Junk! The Story of the Jews of South Providence

ELEANOR F. HORVITZ

Who were the immigrant Jews who became junk peddlers, who opened small grocery and variety stores, who were employed by the jewelry manufacturers in the vicinity of South Providence? Where did they come from and why did they leave?

The families of the majority of those interviewed had emigrated from Russia. While several families came from Austria and Galicia, a smaller number left homes in Poland, Romania, Hungary, and Czechoslovakia.

Some of the men met their wives in this country and married here. Others, already married, came to America and South Providence alone to make a living and establish themselves. Eventually their wives and children were sent steamship tickets to join their husbands.

My father's and mother's house used to be Ellis Island. Everybody who was a *landsman*, when they had to come from Europe, my mother used to go out and collect goods for them. She used to sew sheets, get aprons, get all ready for them. They used to land where? The Zellermayers. In the four rooms with the four daughters. The men used to come first and then, when the wife was supposed to come, my mother used to see that they had an apartment, to see that they had it furnished with what they needed to set up housekeeping.[1]

The reasons for leaving Eastern Europe were in most cases similar—to escape compulsory military training, to escape persecution, and to improve one's economic lot. An opportunity to better oneself in the United States, that was the common dream.

What was this area known as South Providence, which these Eastern European families chose for their home in the new land? Willard Avenue was the focal point. Either on this street or in its immediate vicinity the majority of Jewish-owned businesses were located. Street numbers on Willard commenced at Eddy Street and ended at Broad Street with No. 368. A house directory for 1909 listed no Jewish-sounding names below No. 132, at which address lived Marcus Fried, a machinist. At 134 Willard lived the following tenants: David Korn, a coal dealer; Jacob Tennenbaum, a clerk; and Carl Fischman, a jeweler. Within those relatively few blocks—Willard Avenue and the streets that either crossed it or were adjacent to it—160 Jewish-owned businesses or Jewish residents were listed. This contrasts to 1878, when the Providence city directory lists no Jewish families on Willard.

The house directory of 1909 enumerated 172 occupants on Robinson Street, a short street between Taylor Street and Gay Street. Of this number 102 had Jewish-sounding names; the following occupations were listed: 9 grocers, 14 jewelers, 8 tailors, 17 peddlers, 4 shoemakers; two each in dry goods, plumbing, and carpentry; and one listing

Excerpted from *Rhode Island Jewish Historical Notes*, Volume 7, Number 2 (November 1976): 189–257.

each for variety store owner, laundryman, harnessmaker, soapmaker, fish dealer, teacher, and junk dealer. Among those with Irish-sounding names, many were employed as machinists, painters, electricians, drivers, masons, gardeners, and laborers, occupations not commonly listed for Jewish immigrants in this neighborhood.

Other streets that were primarily associated with the South Providence Jews, their businesses, the various shops where they purchased their food, the schools their children attended, their synagogues, and the halls that accommodated their weddings, dances, and meetings were the following: Taylor Street, Prairie Avenue, Hilton Street, Staniford Street, Plain Street, Robinson Street, Paca Place, Ash Street, Chester Avenue, Gay Street, Dudley Street, and Blackstone Street. As a family became more affluent, it might move to a higher rent district, such as Somerset Street, Public Street, or Reynolds Avenue. Only an occasional Jewish family lived on other South Providence streets. Where Willard Avenue crossed Plain Street was the dividing line between the quarters occupied by Irish and Jewish families. That part of Willard Avenue extending eastward toward Eddy Street was the Jewish section.

> The neighborhood in those days presented a very poor appearance. The main business street, Willard Avenue, had no sidewalks, and in the rainy seasons people had to jump over muddy puddles to get across from one side of the street to the other. In wintertime the snow would be piled up in the middle of the street, and people would slide up and down snowy mounds.[2]

Winter Street and Warner's Lane were often mentioned in the interviews, but these lay outside of the Willard Avenue section. Many immigrants lived there before moving to South Providence.

THEY ESTABLISH A HOME

Because so much has been written about Jews in New York, there is a tendency to think of this early period in South Providence as being overcrowded, undesirable, and having a slum character. Interviews with those who lived there dispel this image. Despite the absence of electricity, perhaps housing on the whole was more than adequate. In the vicinity of Willard Avenue, most dwellings were tenements or flats rather than single-family cottages. Generally a tenement contained four or six apartments, consisting of three to six rooms each.

> I went into some very poor Jewish homes. They would have little furniture, using orange crates for chairs.[3]

This would be an example of a very poor family. Sadie Jacobs gives a different picture in describing her family's home:

> People would congregate at our house before daily services. It was because we had a big seven room house, whereas so many had only three rooms. We owned the house at 205 Willard Avenue. It was a large six tenement house, and my family occupied the middle floor. They had broken through so that they actually used two apartments. For those days we had lots of land.

The Zellermayer family had gas lights, and their bathroom had a tub. They lived at the corner of Gay Street and Willard in a house with four rooms, built by Abraham Bazar. As newly weds, Sarah Rosen and Frank Scoliard rented a house, then built a house at 221 Plain Street at the corner of Willard Avenue. It was the first house in the neighborhood to have electricity. Scoliard's plumbing shop (Guarantee Plumbing & Heating) adjoined the property at 219 Plain Street. Early in his career, Doctor Ilie Berger's dental office and home were located at the same address, 164 Prairie Avenue.

Many tenements contained no bathing facilities. Public baths were erected by the city, which owned and operated them.

> An hour or two before twilight, if you lived in the neighborhood of Gay Street, you saw many of the women who had hurried that morning to Willard Avenue (for their shopping) rushing along with white towels under their arms. From Plain Street they came, and Prairie Avenue and Robinson, Dudley and Blackstone Streets, from all the neighborhood homes to the little red brick building on Gay Street. It was a public bath house, and Friday was the busiest day. There were two entrances, one for men and one for women. And each side was subdivided, the front half for children and the back half for adults. Privacy was undreamed of, and doors unknown either on the dressing stalls or the showers across from them. The housewives came and found themselves a dressing stall and unrolled their towels. Inside would be a comb, a face-cloth, and a piece of soap. Sometimes they carried a change of underwear. You could tell the housewives who mopped their floors from those who scrubbed, for the scrubbers would have darkened, reddened knees and streaks of dirt on their legs. The women undressed wearily, removing their mended, soiled underthings with tired aching arms, but hurrying, naked, they walked across the wet tile floor to the showers, adjusted the water to as hot as they could stand it, and stepped into the needle-like downpour. Soon the weariness was washed away, and you heard them talk with their neighbors. Clouds of steam rose and the walls perspired, and voices of the women blended and vied with the beat of the water against the slate sides of the shower and the tile floors. Thin women with droopy breasts dried themselves vigorously until their bodies were red, and fat women with wobbling thighs paddled to the shower and back to their stalls, dripping wet. And above it all, one sometimes would hear the strong rich baritone of a male voice from the other side where a father cleaned himself for the Sabbath and sang happily in the shower.[4]

Between visits to the public baths, one would heat water on top of the coal stove and pour kettles of this hot water into a large portable tub for bathing. Even those families with indoor plumbing and tubs had to heat the water to mix with the cold water from the faucet. Hot water plumbing was to come later.

It is difficult now to imagine the large number of persons who shared a tenement's three or four rooms. Boarders and relatives often lived with a family. The privacy of a separate room for each person was unimagined.

> There were at least four to a bedroom, ten in our house. In addition there were always one or two strangers in the house who had just come to the country, and you had to take them in.[5]
>
> We took a house of three rooms, a living room, bedroom, and kitchen. Ettie slept in the bedroom with her kids. My father and mother slept in the living room, and my brothers, Dave and Harry, slept on a couch. I slept in the kitchen. It was very cold in the living room where my parents slept. Finally I had a bedroom (we moved about five times in two years), but a cousin came and again I had to sleep in the kitchen. Whoever

had to get up early woke me up when they would eat breakfast. I remember we first had kerosene lamps for lighting and then used gas and finally electricity. The tub in which we bathed was kept in the kitchen, and water for it was heated on the stove.[6]

The ice wagon was a familiar sight on Willard Avenue and neighboring streets. There were no icehouses in the immediate neighborhood, however. Ice was harvested from outlying ponds and stored in icehouses, where it was packed in sawdust for protection. The iceman loaded his wagon at the icehouse for delivery in the neighborhoods.

Joseph Jagolinzer described the procedure of lighting gas mantles:

They would first be lit and the smoke would go up from them. After they got started, there would be the first flash of light. It was then usable as a light. Since everybody lived in a tenement house, any noise from upstairs could distort and break up these delicate mantles, and only carbon would then be left. One would have to start all over again to light them.

THEY EARN A LIVING

Peddling was a common means of earning a living. Other options often required a better use of English. Children, regardless of age, helped out by bringing in whatever pennies they could earn to augment the family outcome.

A story was related by Benjamin Brier, who arrived with his family just before the turn of the century. His family—eleven in all—included half-brothers and half-sisters. His father, who could not find work, spent his time in the synagogue.

We all went to work very early, selling newspapers at the age of eight on. It was pretty much the case with everyone we knew. I worked also as an errand boy and floor sweeper in jewelry shops, where I began to learn the fundamentals of manufacturing. With my brothers, Harry and Charlie, we started in the jewelry business with a few in help, and then it grew. My sister had married a man from Boston in the wholesale jewelry business, and he gave us our start. In those days many immigrants who worked in the jewelry business brought home work from the factories, which was done by those not able to leave home.

Many families operated grocery and variety stores. Often a husband peddled fruits and vegetables "on the road" while his wife tended the store.

Some women, in addition to toiling as mothers, ran their own businesses. Mrs. Louis Grant opened a millinery shop on Prairie Avenue, Mrs. Wolf Semonoff ran a dry goods store in her living room, and Mrs. Benjamin Kane worked as a pharmacist in her husband's drugstore.

What made these few streets in South Providence such a center of activity? Judging from street and city directories between 1900 and 1912, an amazing number of stores and services were crammed into this relatively small area. Businesses thrived in the midst of residences, synagogues, and schools. Delicatessen, grocery, and variety stores abounded. One could get the best 10-cent corned beef sandwich at Ackerman's Delicatessen at 190 Willard Avenue. Sarah Webber remembered the fact that the Ackermans had a pet monkey! Later Lightman and Diwinsky were to open delicatessens in this vicinity. Joseph Jagolinzer's description of Golemba's Grocery Store at 83 Gay Street, where he worked, goes into mouth-watering detail:

Everything in the grocery store in those days was loose. Butter was cut from the tub; vinegar had to be drawn from a barrel. Any kind of groats, chickpeas, came in sacks, which were lined up. Even the cane sugar and the cubes of sugar came loose in a barrel. Prunes were pressed in a box. One had to dig them up with a fork. The herring was in small barrels. Nothing was probably sanitary, but I do not know if anyone got sick. The herrings were laid beautifully—first laid along the edges, then filled in— the line and rhythm of the barrel being followed by the herrings. Jewish people were great herring eaters. You could buy a herring for 5 to 7 cents. One always had herring in the house, and with bread and boiled potatoes it made quite a meal. The herring came with two fillings, one with milt and one with roe. [Milt is the sperm and roe the eggs.] Most of the women wanted the milt. They would use it pickled, and give it color. Also we sold *halvah*.

Samuel Altman describes a typical variety store:

On the corner of Willard and Gay was a variety store that was the popular gathering place for the neighborhood. A man would go in to buy a newspaper, a package of cigarettes, or a glass of soda and remain for a discussion that lasted for hours. Everything was discussed on that corner, and the owner of the store would also join in, neglecting the customers. The crowd would block the entrance to the store, but no one cared.[7]

Kosher bakers and butchers did a thriving business. One would pick a live chicken, and the *shochet* would kill it. Mrs. Abraham Zellermayer's daughters recall their mother's story of how Archibald Silverman drove her to the North End to buy chickens and meat before Willard Avenue had such stores.

And there were the fish markets, with fresh-looking fish displayed on top of ice in long open cases.

My earliest memories are of Friday shopping trips on Willard Avenue, the Jewish marketplace. The street, from Prairie Avenue to Plain Street, bustled with activity from early morning. I remember the bearded, long-frocked rabbinical butchers hustling to their chicken stores, the windows of fish stores full of glassy-eyed mackerel, perch, and whitefish glistening on their beds of ice, and the proprietor of the egg store separating the brown shell from the white shell eggs, which, for some unaccountable reason were priced differently. Willard Avenue was a street of smells, many of them unpleasant, but on Friday the air was rich with the hot, delicious odor of freshly-baked bread, the challah which every housewife carried home.

Friday shopping had to be a hurried-up affair. You bought your chicken and took it home to clean it out, and you bought your favorite fish for gefilte (stuffed) fish, and perhaps you stopped at a pushcart at the sidewalk's edge to buy some prunes for dessert, and a few soup greens for the chicken soup.[8]

Dry goods stores carried dishes, pots, pans, and utensils of all sorts, as well as towels and linens. Before Passover it was "murder to go down there," according to Joseph Jagolinzer, who described women's frantic activity.

Jagolinzer remembered a dealer on Gay Street, Mendel Ladashinsky, who had various ways of disposing of the merchandise that peddlers brought him. He had a big barn in back of his house filled with chairs, lamps, and clothing. Sometimes the stockings didn't even match.

In those days of horses, blacksmiths were a necessity. Samuel Goldenberg was at 238 Willard, and Fishel Jagolinzer had his shop on Gay Street. Both Sam Greenberg and Michael Gold were at 136 Willard.

A very important business for the South Providence neighborhood was David Korn's hay and grain business at 195 Willard Avenue, which sold feed for horses. In an earlier period hay and grain had been sold from pushcarts.

There were many more businesses. Joseph Jagolinzer remembers a tailor named Miller, who made a suit for $25. One off the rack cost $10. The well-known Troy Laundry was at the corner of Gay and Blackstone Streets. Here, it was said, boys stood to pitch pennies and cards. Weinbaum's and Smira's vied for the brisk bottling and seltzer business. And then there was the cigarmaker, Charles Becker, at 252 Prairie Avenue.

The modest origin of Max Siegal's famous City Hall Hardware Store was recalled by several people. While Siegal worked as a stonesetter in a jewelry factory, his wife, Rebecca, stayed in their little hardware store on Prairie Avenue. When business improved in the hardware store, Siegel brought his work from the jewelry factory and worked in the back of the store. "City Hall" came when the store moved to Washington Street, across from City Hall.

Providence was not without its bank; yet another of Abraham Bazar's enterprises was on Willard Avenue. Jews and other immigrants could borrow money to bring over members of their families who had remained in Europe.[9]

Besides the smaller merchants and storekeepers were the manufacturing companies, which employed many of the residents in the South Providence neighborhood. Most manufacturers were in the jewelry industry. One of the largest was Silverman Brothers, founded in 1897 by Archibald and Charles. Both Cutler Jewelry and Henry Lederer and Brother were located on Eddy Street. Another of Abraham Bazar's interests was the Mounted Combs at 165 Willard.

One person called Ash Street "the Wall Street of Willard Avenue." Fortunes were built from junk businesses. Some of the dealers were Abraham Bazar, Max Silverman, Abraham Zellermayer, and Harry Zusman. On Sundays the junkyards were the site of crap games—cheap and expensive ones. And all those men who sat around the barber shops on weekdays were out shooting craps on Sunday.

IT WAS NOT ALL WORK

Sundays were for drives in the country and for picnics—a release from the pressures of earning a living during the week.

Came Sunday, who could afford to go out anyplace? Berman, the butcher, had a horse and buggy and would pile in the family and go to Roger Williams Park. If the horse was in good trim, they might go as far as Toby's farm or Palace Gardens (in Warwick). That is where the picnic was held. Palace Gardens had more pines and a baseball field. Most people did not have a buggy, so they went with a man named Ehrenkrantz, a mover, who had a long moving van (horse-drawn) with seats on both sides.

He would load up the van with a couple of barrels of beer. Everyone would take their own food. On Sunday mornings around 10 o'clock off they would go to Palace Gardens to spend the day! Whole families. That was fun! It was really something to see on Sunday morning. The few Jewish families who did own horses and buggies would hitch up and go off for the day.[10]

Ethel Scoliard remembers that her father, Frank, used his plumber's torch to roast frankfurters.[11]

Two sisters recalled trips to Rocky Point amusement park:

Father had a horse and buggy—a real "surrey with a fringe on the top." Every Sunday Mr. Steiner used to get his horse ready, hitch it up, and bring it to our home. That buggy just shone! And we four girls would wait, all starched up, wearing crinoline under our dresses, and holding our baskets of lunch. We would go to Rocky Point with a group of three or four other buggies, all lined up in a procession.[12]

Nat Fishman wondered how his father managed in his buggy (driven by a horse called Charlie). "Where did he put the eight kids?" he asked. "Perhaps there were four kids in four laps."

Dancing was a popular form of recreation. Lillian Berger Rubinstein said "Jew night was Friday night at Rhodes [on the Pawtuxet]. Families took their children with them while they danced." One daughter remembered her father's opposition:

I wanted to dance, and go to dances, but my father was against it. My mother was more liberal and gave me the money to go, although it was actually my own money for I had to turn over my pay envelope to my father.[13]

Maurice Bazar enjoyed many dance halls.

For younger people the big social life was at Rhodes on the Pawtuxet. We would take the Broad Street trolley there for the weekend dancing. It was the meeting place for girls and boys. Sometimes we would go dancing at Hunt's Mills (near Rumford in East Providence) and Vanity Fair.[14]

Samuel Tatz was a dancing teacher in South Providence. He held classes for adults and children. Jack Leichter described Tatz as "a fairly short man, who wore high heels and drove around on a motorcycle." Tatz and Sam Bander were orchestra leaders for Jewish weddings and parties. Benjamin Brier described Tatz as "the Arthur Fiedler of South Providence."

Bazar's Hall, located at 61 Willard Avenue, was used for a variety of purposes, including weddings, dances, lectures, and meetings. Maurice Bazar described his father's building:

The hall was upstairs, and stores were downstairs. Maurice Robinson (the lawyer and later judge) had his first office in that building. My folks even had a jewelry business in that hall, where we used to make those combs with celluloid. This building burned down in 1907, but my father put up another hall. The new one was of brick and was erected in 1908.

Friday night was movie night—10 cents admission. It could hold one to two hundred people. We would put up chairs for the movies, and my sister played the piano for the silent movies. An operator would come in every Friday night to operate the movies. There was always a lot of noise from the movable chairs. There was a detective, Jack

Bafia, who used to be at the movies. He would walk around with a big stick to keep order. Eventually bowling alleys and pool tables replaced the movies in the hall.[15]

OUTDOOR ACTIVITIES

The boys of South Providence engaged in the usual sand lot activities, often in a vacant lot near the Chester Avenue School. A favorite hill for sliding and tobogganing was the incline of Blackstone Street. Kids would start at the top of Blackstone Street, near Prairie Avenue, and slide all the way down to Plain Street. Abraham Bloom recalled that the grounds of the Rhode Island Hospital were good for sliding. Others spoke of skating at Roger Williams Park and bathing at Kirwin's Beach. Jack Leichter also remembered such games as "hit the wicket," "peggy," "duck the ducket" and, of course, baseball—all played in the street.

Joseph Jagolinzer was often drawn to the fire station to hear bells ring and watch men train with their horses. An annual ritual brought excitement and danger, he recalled: "There was always a bonfire at the corner of Willard Avenue and Gay Streets the night before the 4th of July. The material for the bonfire began by fences being ripped. Nobody's fence was safe. A loose chair, anything that would burn, were all for the fire. In my father's blacksmith shop there would be wheels—they would steal the wheels, the shafts, etc. They would heap it up. Once the bonfire got going the Fire Department would have to come around as the fire was so close to the buildings."[16]

It was apparent, however, that the so-called social life for the most part centered about the home.

THEY PRAY

For the first families who settled in South Providence, there were no synagogues. Sadie Jacobs spoke of her family having to travel to What Cheer Hall on North Main Street for the High Holidays. For morning and evening *davening*, her father gathered a group at his house. By 1890 Reform Jews of the Congregation of the Sons of Israel and David had built their own structure at Friendship Street and Foster Street.[17] The Orthodox did not wish to worship with Reform Jews, however.

One of the first synagogues established south of downtown (1898) was located at 201 Willard Avenue. Chartered on January 30, 1901, it was known as the South Providence Hebrew Congregation, also known as the "big Shul," the "Russian Shul," and *"die Rusishe Shul."*[18]

Many other synagogues bore names of the founders' origins. For example, Tifereth Israel (Glory of Israel), was the "Romanian shul." Chartered in 1910, it was located at 225 Willard Avenue.[19]

Chevrah Beth Yisroel Anshe Austria (House of Israel, Men of Austria) built a synagogue on Robinson Street in 1906.[20] It was commonly known as the "Robinson Street Shul."

There were other synagogues. A small congregation, Lenard Azedeck (Merciful Care of the Sick), was chartered in 1896. It was known for its strict observance of the Sabbath.[21] Machzeka Hadas (Supporters of Faith) was incorporated eleven years later.

Temple Beth Israel, the first Conservative congregation, was established in 1921. It borrowed one of the Torah scrolls from Anshe Austria for its first service.

Congregation Beth Israel Anshe Austria ("The Robinson Street Shul") located at 53 Robinson Street in South Providence. When erected early in the twentieth century, this stately structure represented a marriage of historical imagery and modern utility. The building was torn down in 1954.

The last congregation, Shaare Zedek, was not chartered until 1954. It purchased the building on Broad Street when Congregation Sons of Israel and David moved to the East Side of Providence. Shaare Zedek resulted from the merger of four smaller synagogues: Lenard Azedeck, the South Providence Hebrew, the Machzeka Hadas, and the Congregation Beth Yisrael.[22] The factors leading to the merger were the decrease in the local Jewish population and the razing of the synagogue buildings by the South Providence redevelopment project.

Sarah Webber has vivid memories of an Orthodox service to which she was taken by her grandfather when she was a very small child. The High Holiday service was held in the upstairs rooms of the What Cheer Hall.

My grandfather was one of the oldest present. There were great big tall candles, taller than I was, very large in circumference, and they would be stuck in sand. My grandfather would be the head reader at the lectern, and he would be wearing a white wool kittel that covered him from head to foot, and he would wear white wool stockings and no shoes. The smell of camphor intermingled with the smell of spice and citron which the women carried, because they were fasting, and they kept it handy in case they might faint. The women were at the end of the room near the door at a long table. The kids were stuck in another room and would raise cain. They had carpeting, and we would take long runs and slide so that clouds of dust would come up. We would come out of there black as coal. The mothers would often have cold chicken stashed away, which they would surreptitiously slip to their children.[23]

There was evidence, however, that synagogue attendance was not a universal practice:

On Friday evening Willard Avenue was the haven for only the very pious, the stooped, bearded old men carrying their velvet covered prayer books as they hurried to shul. After they had recited their prayers and left for home for the Sabbath meal, Willard Avenue was a deserted street.[24]

In summer, a *mikveh* located on Staniford Street often attracted visitors and fundraisers from Eastern European yeshivas or from orphanages and charities in Palestine. These men were easily remembered:

On Friday afternoon they would come out of the Staniford Street *mikveh*, water dripping from their long beards and side curls, clean and ready for the day of the Sabbath. They walked in their long black *kapotes*, and wide hats keeping close to the walls of the houses so as not to rub elbows with passing women. People would stop to look at these visitors from another world, and they regarded them with respect.[25]

THEY ENCOUNTER ANTI-SEMITISM

How did Jews who settled in South Providence get along with Gentile neighbors? Was anti-Semitism rampant as in Eastern Europe during the late nineteenth century and early twentieth centuries? Benjamin Brier made these observations: "There was the Jewish and the Gentile sections of Willard Avenue with Plain Street the dividing line. My family did not have trouble renting where they wanted, for they never tried to live beyond the Jewish neighborhood. Those boys who would torment the Jew with the beard did it out of ignorance. The conflicts were street fights, not real anti-Semitism."

Brier felt that discrimination prevented a young Jewish man from getting a good job. Open to him would be such jobs as foot-press operator in a jewelry shop, which was the lowest in the trade, or work as a janitor or a newsboy.

Others referred to fights between young Jews and Gentiles. Joseph Jagolinzer commented, "[Irish] boys would come up to the Jewish section and fight. There were some real fights—great animosity was created between these kids. Some big men came up to take revenge for their children. We had our men too who could defend the neighborhood, if someone were looking for trouble."

But it would be a mistake to think that all Gentiles in South Providence were hostile to the Jews. Many Jews and Gentiles lived next to each other as good neighbors, worked together, and did business with one another.

THEY PURSUE AN EDUCATION

While most children learned Yiddish at home, they had no difficulty learning English at school.

There were several public schools in South Providence. Willard Avenue, Chester Avenue, and Beacon Avenue Schools were primary schools (kindergarten through grade 2). Point Street and Peace Street were grammar schools (grades 3 through 8). High schools included Classical, English, and Commercial. Very few children were fortunate enough to go on to college.

Many children attended the Chester Avenue Talmud Torah, which was chartered in 1911 as the South Providence Hebrew School.[26]

Fannie Krasnow Horvitz, a teenaged immigrant who worked long hours in a jewelry factory, was determined to master English so she went to the public library and read authors whose work she had been familiar with in Russia. Another kind of library was found next to Bazar's Bank:

> It was a meeting and lecture hall where people gathered to read newspapers and magazines and to discuss all kinds of social and political problems. It was considered the center for all radicals and socialists of the day. Here was the home of the Workmen's Circle, Branch 110, to which every young man of progressive ideas belonged.[27]

Several clubs were also formed for mutual self-education. These included the Hebrew Literary and Dramatic Club, the New Idea Social Club, and the 20th Century Elite Club.[28]

Some men and women attended night classes, but many could not. There were neither time nor energy to concentrate on learning to read and write English. It was easy to read Yiddish newspapers from New York. According to Bessie Edith Bloom, around 1908 about six hundred copies of the Jewish *Tageblatt* (Jewish Daily News) came into the city every day.[29] There were also copies of the *Forward* and the *Wahrheit*.

LEGAL AND MEDICAL ATTENTION

The Robinson family lived at the corner of Eddy Street and Willard Avenue. Two sons, Charles and Maurice, were among the first Jewish lawyers in Providence. There were some half-dozen Jewish lawyers. Benjamin Brier remarked, "Needless to say, they had a Jewish clientele—all poor people."

Home remedies and self-doctoring were mentioned when the subject of medical care was discussed in my interviews. Home deliveries by midwives were customary. Joseph Jagolinzer said his mother was "a saintly woman and catered to anybody, anytime, day or not. She delivered more babies than anyone in South Providence in those days. Who spent money to go to an emergency room of a hospital? [She] never took any money. This was her way of life.[30]

Emergencies, however, were treated in the accident rooms of either St. Joseph's Hospital or Rhode Island Hospital, which were closest to South Providence. Among the Jewish doctors who took care of many South Providence residents were Louis J. Pobirs of 167 Prairie Avenue, Mark H. Plainfield of 172 Prairie Avenue, and Samuel Starr of 522 Broad Street.[31]

Angell's Drug Store, which was owned by Louis D. Angell, was located on the corner of Prairie Avenue and Willard Avenue. Angell's telephone was used by many neighbors. David Ettleman owned a drug store at 244 Willard Avenue, and Frank Markensohn owned a store at 183 Prairie Avenue.

Benjamin Kane purchased a drugstore from his brother-in-law, Frank Markensohn, in about 1911. It was located at 183 Prairie Avenue, at the corner of Blackstone Street. Kane's wife, Esther, was the first woman to graduate from the Rhode Island College of Pharmacy. She completed her schooling while continuing to work in the store and care for her family and home.

To bring food to a sick neighbor, to nurse him, was part of one's daily life. There were many examples of women who, faced with the many pressures of a full and busy life, helped the less fortunate. Ethel Scoliard recalled her mother's charitable impulse:

> She would go to the St. Joseph's and Rhode Island Hospitals to interpret for the doctors and nurses who could not understand the Jewish patients who often spoke mostly Yiddish. And these patients would not eat the food. She started cooking chickens in tremendous pans—this was done in her small area on a two-burner stove behind her millinery shop—and the woman whose day it was would go with the chickens to serve the Jewish patients. The Miriam Lodge got money to allow two Jewish patients in each hospital. The patient had to have my mother's signature and was not questioned by hospital authorities.[32]

THEY FACE POLITICAL ALTERNATIVES

Many immigrant Jews were slow to enter politics. They had come from countries where they had had little or no part in politics. Some commented that most political activity took place in the synagogue. Frank Scoliard, active as a Democrat in the 11th ward for many years, eventually served twelve years as a city councilman. Two famous Jewish politicians were Jacob A. Eaton and Harry Cutler. Eaton made no bones about the fact that he was a Jewish politician, and that he wanted to advance Jewish causes and help deserving Jews become established. Harry Cutler, president of Cutler Jewelry, was a state representative from 1910 to 1913.[33]

There was a fairly active branch of the Socialist party in South Providence. It was organized for Yiddish-speaking people by Joseph Shore and Jacob Pavlow. Its purpose was to educate Jewish workers about political and economic problems. There were frequent lectures and forums, both in Yiddish and in English, to hear such great names as Abraham Kahn, B. Vladek, B. Feigenbaum, Myer London, S. Yanofsky, and S. Zametkin—all giants of the American Socialist movement. They attracted enormous crowds at Bazar's Hall.[34]

Another aspect of the political scene was Zionism. An outstanding leader was Alter Boyman, who lived on Reynolds Avenue in South Providence. Jack Leichter observed that Boyman, Sonya Silverman, and Jack Rabinowitz spent all of their spare time working for this movement. Doctor Ilie Berger, the first president of the Rhode Island Zionist Region, held that office for ten years.

THEY ARE THEIR BROTHERS' KEEPERS

There were no Social Security or welfare programs when the first Jewish settlers established their homes and businesses in South Providence. Neighbor took care of neighbor. Concerned men and women would get together to form an organization to meet the community's growing needs. One such group was the South Providence Hebrew Free Loan Association, which began in 1906.

Every evening the market peddlers would stop in front of the office with their push-carts or horse and wagons to pay old debts and to make new loans, free of interest. A $25 loan was a large sum. . . . More often it was only a $10 or $5 dollar loan to buy goods for the next day's business. People in better circumstances paid annual dues of one dollar, half a dollar, and even a quarter. Collectors would go from house to house to collect the dues in installments. No donation was too small. All the business of the office was done by volunteers.[35]

Joseph Jagolinzer considered Hebrew Free Loan one of the most important organizations. "Here poor people could go to borrow, pay no interest and paying back as little as $1 per week. Was that a busy place! Just like a bank. The hard part was finding someone who would guarantee the loan, but eventually he would find someone who had enough faith in him to be a guarantor."

Women also led organizations. For example, Mary Grant was the founder and first president of the South Providence Ladies Aid Society, which began in 1902 and made loans to men and women. Raffles were a source of fund-raising, as were coffee socials, where a cup of coffee and a piece of cake cost ten cents. Another of Mary Grant's interests was the orphanage that was built in the rear of the Machzeka Hadas Synagogue at the corner of Willard and Prairie Avenues.

The Jewish neighborhood of South Providence was not without its problems of juvenile delinquency. References were made to girls and women who became prostitutes. A few of the more notorious characters went to jail for stealing or embezzlement. Most offenses were for truancy.

They Leave South Providence

South Providence became a haven for Jewish immigrants. Here they met *landsleit* and relatives, raised their children, and earned their living. Here they pursued their intellectual, religious, and social interests. As Jews became "Americanized" and shed their old world customs, however, they moved beyond South Providence.

Much of the community left before World War II, the balance soon after. Few traces of Jewish life remain in South Providence. Fortunately, many memories survive through documentation, but mostly among the very elderly and their adult children who once resided there.

NOTES

1. Interview with Mrs. Joseph Field and Mrs. George Silverman, August 23, 1976.

2. Samuel Altman, "Fifty Years in South Providence," (written in Yiddish), trans. Beryl Segal, *The Jewish Herald* (Providence, Rhode Island), July 13 [no year listed].

3. Interview with Mrs. Joseph Webber, July 19, 1976.

4. Beatrice Levin, "The Old Neighborhood," *Providence Sunday Journal*, January 25, 1948.

5. Interview with Mr. and Mrs. Benjamin Brier, August 5, 1976.

6. Interview with Mrs. Jacob Horvitz, June 25, 1976.

7. Altman, "Fifty Years," July 13.

8. Levin, "The Old Neighborhood."

9. Altman, "Fifty Years," July 13.

10. Interview with Joseph Jagolinzer, July 20, 1976.

11. Interview with Ethel Scoliard, August 3, 1976.

12. Interview with Mrs. Joseph Field and Mrs. George Silverman, August 23, 1976.

13. Interview with Mrs. Jacob Horvitz, June 25, 1976.

14. Interview with Maurice Bazar, July 29, 1976.

15. Interview with Maurice Bazar, July 29, 1976.

16. Jagolinzer interview.

17. *Rhode Island Jewish Historical Notes*, Volume 5, No. 1 (November 1967), p. 120.

18. RIJHN, Volume 2, No. 1 (June 1956), p. 34.

19. RIJHN, Volume 2, No. 1 (June 1956), p. 50.

20. RIJNH, Vol. 2, No. 1 (June 1956) p. 45.

21. RIJHN, Vol. 2, No. 1 (June 1956) p. 28.

22. RIJHN, Vol. 2, No. 1 (June 1956) p. 85.

23. Webber interview.

24. Levin, "The Old Neighborhood."

25. Altman, "Fifty Years," July 20.

26. RIJHN, Vol. 2, No. 1 (June 1956), p. 54.

27. Altman, "Fifty Years," July 13.

28. RIJHN, Vol. 2, No. 1 (June 1956), pp. 47, 48, 54.

29. RIJHN, Vol. 5, No. 4 (November 1970), pp. 406–407.

30. Jagolinzer interview.

31. Seebert J. Goldowsky, "Jews in Medicine in Rhode Island," RIJHN, Vol. 2, No. 3 (December 1957), pp. 151–191.

32. Scoliard interview.

33. RIJHN, Vol.4, No. 3 (November 1965), p. 294.

34. Altman, "Fifty Years," July 13.

35. Altman, "Fifty Years," July 6.

United Brothers, Bowling and Bagels in Bristol
A Study of the Changing Jewish Community in Bristol, Rhode Island

STEVEN CULBERTSON & CALVIN GOLDSCHEIDER

This paper is a study of the emergence, decline, and re-establishment of the Jewish community in Bristol, Rhode Island. We examine the community through the changing character of its major institution, the synagogue, and through it broader changes in the community. Bristol may be an unlikely place for a synagogue; yet here in the midst of a predominately Catholic town on Narragansett Bay stands one of the older synagogues in Rhode Island. Chartered on June 11, 1900, United Brothers Synagogue, Chevra Agudas Achim, provides the focus for understanding the migration of a predominately Eastern European Jewish community from Long Island to Rhode Island around the turn of the twentieth century and its transformation to an Americanized third- and fourth-generation community. This study illuminates the acculturation process of Eastern European Jews into American society and documents the historical foundations of a changing small Jewish community in Rhode Island.

Several aspects of the Bristol Jewish community are investigated, including the relation of the location of Bristol to the economic growth of the community, the interaction of the Jewish community with the surrounding community, and the changing religiosity of the community. We show that the earlier semi-isolated location of Bristol, specifically its distance from Providence, influenced the development of unique features of the community. The model for Eastern European Jewish acculturation in America traditionally follows the emergence of the community in a metropolitan context. It is the progressive and political reality of urban life that allowed Jews the opportunity to become a part of American culture and society relatively quickly. In Bristol, a different set of values, those of a small American town, guided its development. Many of the changes we document—from factory positions in the National India Rubber Company to real estate dealerships, from religious ecumenicism to competition, from orthodoxy to reform-liberalism—symbolize the impact of "small town American" ideals and suburban lifestyles on Jewish religious practice. The history of Bristol's Jews is linked therefore to other Jewish communities, where the small size of the population and limited economic opportunity are critical constraints on communal expansion or stability.

The small-town emphasis on personal economic success, rather than a cosmopolitan emphasis on education as a means to upward mobility, provides a key insight into the development of Bristol's Jewish community. As with other Jewish communities in America, Bristol's also maintained a strong identity, even as the content and expressions of that Jewishness changed.

The Bristol Jewish community was influenced by major historical changes in American society. Mass culture with its opportunity for communication and interaction among communities certainly diminished the former isolation of small communities in the nineteenth century. Technology and transportation changes linked Jews into a

Excerpted from *Rhode Island Jewish Historical Notes*, Volume 9, Number 4 (November 1986): 283–297.

broader network of communal relationships. Bristol changed from a small isolated town to a distant suburb of Providence, forging new metropolitan ties and changing the nature of Bristol's religious institutions. World War II transformed the life of the Bristol Jewish community. Sustained contact with the cosmopolitan world brought about by the war changed the religious and ethnic identities of Bristol Jews and their pathway to upward mobility. Suburbanization, educational opportunity, and religious freedom lured the Bristol Jews away from their stable, perhaps provincial, community.

THE FORMATION OF THE EARLY COMMUNITY

The development of the early Jewish community in Bristol centers on four major events: the formation of the Young Men's Hebrew Association (YMHA), the chartering of the United Brothers Synagogue, the move of the National India Rubber Company from Long Island to Rhode Island, and the building of the synagogue in 1908. Location played a role in all four events. The distance of Bristol from the city of Providence motivated Bristol Jews to form their own YMHA and then to establish United Brothers Synagogue. The Jewish families of Bristol "realized that to remain in Bristol they had to form their own synagogue, since they were, at that time, an uncomfortable distance from the city."[1] The location of Bristol, between Providence and Newport on Narragansett Bay, attracted the National India Rubber Company to Rhode Island. The building of the synagogue reveals the desire of Jews to remain and to develop institutional roots.

Bristol's Jewish community was founded by Eastern European immigrants, some of whom arrived in the last decade of the nineteenth century. They founded a Young Men's Hebrew Association in 1896[2] "for social and benevolent purposes," in a place where no synagogue existed.[3] The concept of a YMHA is a very American one, which appears anomalous as the starting point of a new Jewish community of European origins in a small American town. Yet, it points to the early influence of "Bristol" culture rather than to Eastern European traditions as the motivating ideology in the formation of the new Jewish community. United Brothers Synagogue grew from the seed of the Bristol YMHA.

The synagogue was organized according to Eastern European Orthodox tradition. The congregation met in the homes of members throughout the early part of the twentieth century; in 1908 a house on John Street was purchased and then moved to a site on Richmond Street. The present synagogue building on High Street was built in 1916. The influx of a large number of new Jews from Long Island transformed the community and led to the formation of a more traditional form of Jewish organization than the YMHA.

A sisterhood also was formed. Since men officially ran the synagogue and organized the prayers, women assumed a supportive role within the synagogue as charity and service providers to the Jewish community in Bristol. The "Sunshine" committee, which persisted until the mid-1950s, organized visits to sick Jews and helped elderly Jews of the community stay in touch with the synagogue. The synagogue became the gathering point for the small community.

Many of the communities formed by Eastern European Jews in the early twentieth century began as Jewish burial societies. By contrast, the formation of a Young Men's Hebrew Association in Bristol, with ideals of Jewish brotherhood, led to the formation of the Chevra Agudas Achim, the Fellowship of United Brothers, in 1900. It appears that the group from Long Island brought with them a more traditional view of community. Thus, a strong Jewish community emerged in Bristol based on a combination of ideas from Eastern Europe and on new ideas from the American YMHA.

The two communities of Jews that combined to form the United Brothers Synagogue came from different economic strata. The founders of the synagogue lived in Bristol prior to the arrival of the National India Rubber Company. These men and women had already become part of the Bristol economy in the sales professions in the late nineteenth century. Among the founders were also rubber workers in the National India Rubber Company, which moved from Long Island to Rhode Island between 1897 and 1907. They had come as blue-collar workers, but soon after moving to Bristol many of the Jewish men who stayed in the community changed employment. They became grocers, furniture salesmen, and jewelers, revealing prior knowledge of and connections to such occupations.

Economic growth during the first two decades of the twentieth century provided the opportunity for the newer Jewish immigrants to move into the sales positions. A major factor was the expansion of the National India Rubber company during World War I. Rubber was needed for the war effort, and it came from Bristol. As the plant expanded, new immigrants, the Italians, were brought to Bristol. It was the location of Bristol, relatively far from other towns and cities, combined with the expansion of the economy and the help of fellow Jews already in services and sales, that provided an early opportunity for first generational upward mobility.

The interaction of Bristol Jews with the surrounding community provides an interesting example of religious ecumenicism and economic opportunity at the turn of the century. The founders of the Chevra Agudas Achim, having formed the YMHA in the late nineteenth century "to build the morality of young people," interacted with the historic YMCA in Bristol that had been formed in 1863.[4] This ecumenicism among the various religious groups of Bristol represents a liberal trend that began in American religion during the Progressive era and was maintained until the Second World War.

The Jews of Bristol were also treated with kindness by the congregations of several churches in the Bristol area. St. Mary's Church (Catholic) donated the pews to the United Brothers Synagogue. The founders of the synagogue were aided in their search for a building by Dr. George Lyman Locke, rector of St. Michael's Episcopal Church, who also donated his services in teaching Hebrew.[5] Religion served to unite the Jews in their interactions with the community.

The interaction between Jews and non-Jews was much more widespread in Bristol than in metropolitan areas, simply because there was less of a chance for Bristol Jews to remain isolated within their own community. Jews lived close to the synagogue on High, John, Wood, and Catherine streets, but not all in one place. Only about forty Jewish families were members of the synagogue at one time.

Yet, the Jewish community in Bristol was very stable from just after the emigration from Long Island until the years after World War II. What was it about Bristol that allowed Jews to form a community and maintain that community for close to forty years when most American Jews were highly mobile? The answer in part relates to the range of local economic opportunities available; perhaps the continuing orthodoxy of Bristol Jews also played a role when many Jews elsewhere were moving away from orthodoxy. Bristol Jews continued to maintain the synagogue as the center of their community throughout the first half of the twentieth century. An absence of anti-Semitism was noted often in conversations with members of the Bristol Jewish community and was repeated in the minutes of the Chevra Agudas Achim. This receptive behavior of the Bristol community to Jews was also an important factor in their stability.

On the other hand, the community had to contend with the limitations of a small town. There was no rabbi; they had to send to Providence for kosher meat, sabbath candles, and bagels.[6]

Economic mobility, religious flexibility, and Jewish institution building characterized the early development of the Bristol Jewish community. The rapid mobility of both the first settlers and the migrant National India Rubber Company workers provided a firm economic base for the community to thrive and grow. Ecumenicism and women seated on the main floor of the Orthodox synagogue provide evidence of religious flexibility. The establishment of the YMHA and the United Brother Synagogue aided the formation of a small, yet vital, Jewish community. Finally, the building of the present synagogue in 1916 firmly rooted the community in Bristol.

NEW INSTITUTIONS, NEW CHALLENGES

During the 1930s, United Brothers Congregation attempted to maintain regular Sabbath services and developed a Sunday School for religious instruction. In the course of the 1930s, two new institutions were formed. The first was a bowling league, which eventually was transformed into the Bristol Jewish Community Center. The other was the Young Judea Sunday School. Second and third generation Jews faced the option of either transforming the community or leaving for greater economic, social, and educational opportunities elsewhere.

The formation of the Young Judea, a Sunday School for Jewish children, in the 1930s marked another step in the institutional development of the Bristol Jewish community. The children of the original founders of the synagogue were the members of the Young

The *"Cranston Tigers" of the Rhode Island Jewish Bowling Congress, 1962. Left to right: Mike Miller, Shep Kauffman, Edwin Cohen, Mel Shanfield, and Lester Silverman.*

Judea. The "Bristol Jewish Community Center" had been the original name of the "club," Young Judea, first formed in 1934. The motto of the club, "American Jew," was formally selected on Sunday, November 18, 1934. Young Judea in 1935 held a debate on whether to associate with Gentiles. The Bristol Sunday School children thus were interested in questions and ideas that many older Jews hesitated to ask or discuss openly. The debate was a foreshadowing of what was to come in the life of the Bristol Jewish community.

The children who formed Young Judea were second- and third-generation Jews of Bristol. They were no longer identified as ethnically Eastern European. They were American, and they were Jewish. Their choice of slogans for their club reveals their desire to integrate the beliefs of their parents with their national identity. This tension between Americanness and Jewishness was at the heart of their identities throughout their lives. The education that these young Jews received provided the impetus for change within the Bristol Jewish community.

The Jewish Community Center and the Young Judea movements were particularly American forms of Jewish communal expression, broader than the traditional synagogue. They provided the space and the resources for Jewish cultural events, for Jewish education, and for other forms of Jewish expression.

BAGELS . . . AND THE BRISTOL JEWISH COMMUNITY CENTER

In the period following World War II the Bristol Jewish community was transformed in two ways. First, new ideas and opportunities were generated by greater contact with other Jews and with non-Jews during the war. Second, there was an increase in the geographic mobility of all Americans following the war. There was a significant out-migration of Jews from Bristol in search of greater economic, social, and educational opportunities elsewhere in the United States. At the same time, there was a small immigration of Jews to Bristol during the late 1940s to the 1960s as part of the suburbanization of the Providence Jewish community. These changes resulted in the development of a new institution, the Bristol Jewish Community Center, and the reformation of Chevra Agudas Achim.

In 1947, the writing of the Bristol Jewish Community Center's constitution marked a transition of leadership. Men who had returned from the war with new insights about their religion reshaped Judaism in Bristol.

The concept of a community center appeared in the thirties, with the formation of a Sunday school for the children of the original immigrants to Bristol. It also served as a bowling league in the late 1930s, but was not constituted as an organization until 1946. The Bristol Jewish Community Center, formed as a parallel organization to Chevra Agudas Achim, became a social center of the Jewish community. Prior to the war, Jews in Bristol saw the synagogue as the focal point of Jewish life. This shift resulted from the ascendancy of the second generation of Jews in Bristol. The constitution of the Bristol Jewish Community Center written in 1946 reflects the change.

PREAMBLE OF THE CONSTITUTION
BRISTOL JEWISH COMMUNITY CENTER

We, the peoples of Jewish faith of Bristol County, in order that we may be of greater service to our community and to each other, do hereby unite to establish a permanent organization.

Article I Section II
This organization is to be a religious, social, civilian, and nonpolitical group.

Article I Section III
Objects of the Organization
The objects of the organization shall be:

1. To unite socially all peoples, male and female of Jewish parentage and of good moral character.

2. To give all moral and material aid in its power to its members and those dependent upon them. Also to assist the widows and orphans of deceased members.

3. To assist Chevra Agudas Achim in the promulgation of its program in-so-far as it may be consistent with its rules and regulations.

4. To work toward and strive for increased interest in the synagogue and all things Jewish.

5. To elevate the moral and social standings of its members.

The formation of the Community Center implies that the synagogue was not meeting all of the needs of the Jewish residents of Bristol. The terminology of the Constitution is distinctly "American" rather than traditionally "Jewish." Jewish war veterans stressed the moral, not the ritual, dimension of Judaism. They wanted to integrate their heightened sense of American morality, which was formed in the service of their country, with their Jewish heritage. The appearance of a "chaplain" position in the Community Center hearkens to the experience of returned Jewish veterans, as does the stated purpose of the Jewish Community Center: "This organization is to be a religious, social, civilian, and nonpolitical group."

Discussions about Palestine, letters to Congress about international issues, buying Israel Bonds, and Jewish education classes for adults and children during the early years of the Community Center represent a successful attempt at integration of Jewish religious and moral values with American social institutions. The Bristol Jewish Community Center became the institutional symbol of the suburbanization of a small town, close to a large city. The Bristol Jewish Community Center took on the functions of the "sisterhood" of the previous generation. Building improvements were undertaken by the Community Center rather than by the synagogue. The "Sunshine" committee became a part of the Community Center, as did the Sunday School, fundraising, and moral education.

In the late 1940s and 1950s, Judaism had become less of a lifestyle difference and more of a different system of cultural and social symbols within an American lifestyle. The repetition of a Jewish morality theme in the constitution of the Jewish Community Center symbolizes the transformation of Judaism in Bristol. Women gained positions of leadership in the center, and men who had formed the center moved into positions of leadership in the synagogue.

The out-migration of Bristol Jews also had a major impact on the community. Members of the Bristol Jewish Community Center attempted to reshape the community and stop the decline of the once stable community. The absence of second- and third-generation families among the center's membership, however, indicates that many left Bristol to find greater economic, social, and educational opportunities elsewhere. The G.I. Bill was a major cause of the flight of young families. Jews could not climb any higher in Bristol's economic structure. Interviews with older members of the community further revealed that there were only so many women. Marriage to Jews from beyond Bristol and intermarriage with non-Jews within Bristol resulted in the out-migration of young men and women. The departure of Jews resulted in the closing of the synagogue in the early 1960s.

The Bristol Jewish Community Center lasted just over ten years. This period marked the ascendancy, not only of the second generation, but of a distinctly "American" outlook. Many families abandoned Orthodox Judaism for the Conservative movement, a pattern that paralleled national trends[7] as well as those in metropolitan Providence.[8] Women assumed positions of leadership and more English was used in High Holiday services.

Bristol's Jewish future meant greater competition with Providence suburbs. Ultimately, the Bristol Jewish Community Center and the remnant of United Brothers Synagogue could not prevail over the Barrington Jewish Center, also located in the East Bay, or Conservative synagogues emerging in Cranston and Warwick, in the West Bay.

THE BREAKDOWN AND RENEWAL OF THE BRISTOL JEWISH COMMUNITY

The Bristol Jewish community became too small to maintain its synagogue. Several attempts in the 1950s to attract new members failed. There was some discussion of starting a Hebrew school in Bristol, but the response was inadequate. The United Brothers Synagogue ceased to exist sometime between 1962 and 1965.

The Levitan sisters, natives of Bristol, became caretakers of the Synagogue. Though some day-care services were provided in the building, no religious services were held for over a decade. This did not mean the end of Bristol's Jewish community, however. Beginning in 1975, a new group of Jews sought to restore United Brothers Synagogue and rebuild the Jewish community. The majority of new members of the Bristol community were not relatives of former residents, but were newcomers to the small seaside town. The new United Brothers Synagogue can be understood as completely distinct from the old Chevra Agudas Achim. As a "liberal-reform" synagogue, it represented the formation of a completely new institution.

Efforts to rebuild United Brothers Synagogue did not come to fruition until Nancy Hillman and the Brody family became involved. With the aid of a youth group from the Barrington Jewish Center and a local Scout troop, the restoration of United Brothers got underway in 1975. St. Michael's Episcopal Church and St. Mary's Catholic Church assisted in the restoration. An organ, paneling, and light fixtures were also donated anonymously to the Synagogue. The reopening party in 1975 brought back many former members from all over the United States. Though still without a rabbi, the new "historic" United Brothers Synagogue is a transformed institution.

Bristol has remained a small American town, where Jews can maintain their own identity while interacting comfortably with the surrounding community. Thus, the values that attracted Jews to Bristol in 1900 remain valid today.

NOTES

1. Arline Suzman, *A History of the United Brothers Synagogue*, Souvenir Booklet, The 275th Anniversary of Bristol, 1984, p. 1.

2. Geraldine Foster, *The Jews of Rhode Island: A Brief History* (Providence: Rhode Island Heritage Foundation and the Rhode Island Publications Society, 1985), p. 32.

3. Foster, *The Jews of Rhode Island*, p. 32.

4. Suzman, *A History*.

5. Douglas Allen, "Judaism is Alive and Well in Bristol," *The Evening Bulletin*, Providence, April 3, 1975.

6. Foster, *The Jews of Rhode Island*, p. 33.

7. Marshall Sklare, *Conservative Judaism* (New York: The Free Press, 1955).

8. Sidney Goldstein and Calvin Goldscheider, *Jewish Americans* (Englewood Cliffs, New Jersey: Prentice-Hall, Inc., 1968).

The Colonial Period through World War I

Congregation Jeshuat Israel/Touro Synagogue, Newport. Dedicated in 1763, it is the oldest surviving synagogue building in North America. Designed by famed Newport architect Peter Harrison, the structure was preserved through bequests from Abraham and Judah Touro, sons of Isaac Touro, the synagogue's colonial hazan. Shuttered for much of the nineteenth century, the building sheltered a new congregation at the beginning of the twentieth century. In 1946 Touro was designated a National Historic Site by the Department of the Interior. Photograph by George M. Goodwin.

Newport's Jewish cemetery showing the gravesites of Moses Seixas and Judah Touro. Seixas, who penned the 1790 letter to the newly elected President George Washington, included the phrase the president later used, "a government which to bigotry gives no sanction, to persecution no assistance."

Congregation Sons of Israel and David ("The Friendship Street Synagogue") was dedicated at Friendship and Foster Streets in downtown Providence in 1890.

The synagogue was the first constructed in Providence and only the second in Rhode Island. In 1909 it was sold to the First Swedish Baptist Church.

The structure was demolished in 1959 to make way for Interstate 95. Providence Journal Company.

The Confirmation Class of 1905,
Congregation Sons of Israel and
David. The first Confirmation was
held in 1886. In 1910 Rabbi
Henry Englander (back center) left
to become a professor at Hebrew
Union College in Cincinnati.

The Epstein-Feinberg family
Sabbath, Providence, probably
1920s.

The New Idea Store, Pawtucket, 1886. Founded by Jacob Shartenberg (center) in 1882, the dry goods business became a landmark on Main Street. Providence Public Library.

Shartenberg's Department Store, 260 Main Street, Pawtucket, 1916. Anonymous. Main St. Looking West from the Slater Trust Co. Pawtucket, RI. 1916. PHOTOGRAPH. RHi X3 510. Courtesy of the Rhode Island Historical Society.

Harry Cutler (far right) was president of Temple Beth-El when former President William Howard Taft and his wife, Helen, visited Providence in 1915. President Taft came to Beth-El to deliver a Passover address. Cutler, a jewelry manufacturer, was also a state representative, a founder of the American Jewish Committee, national president of the Jewish Welfare Board, and a delegate to the Versailles Peace Conference. Temple Beth-El.

Decoration Day (later renamed Memorial Day) parade, Main Street, Woonsocket, ca. 1930. Simon Israel, who fought in Cuba in 1898 during the Spanish-American War, carries the American flag. Harris Fellman's and Samuel Kameroff's jewelry stores were long-standing Woonsocket establishments. Worcester Telegram & Gazette.

Hyman Goldsmith, a former shoemaker and probably Providence's first Jewish policeman, ca. 1900. Having joined the force in 1896, he served for many years in South Providence.

Sadwin Brothers' dry goods shop, 139 South Main Street, Woonsocket, 1914. Like many Jewish retailers, Louis and Morris Sadwin served French Canadian immigrants, the town's dominant ethnic group. Though they learned to conduct some business in French, they relied on employees who were native speakers.

The Outlet Company, 168–176 Weybosset Street, Providence, May, 1914. Founded in 1894 by brothers Joseph and Leon Samuels, the business expanded west to occupy the entire city block, becoming Rhode Island's largest department store. Providence Public Library.

Interior of The Arcade, 65 Weybosset Street, Providence. Constructed in 1828, The Arcade was one of the earliest examples of an enclosed, multi-level commercial space in America. By 1910 it housed several Jewish businesses, including the shop of A. Axelrod, Violin Maker. Berger Bros. Providence, RI, Printers. Interior of the Arcade, Providence, RI. Providence, RI. n.d. Color Lithograph. POSTCARD. Postcards-Providence-Buildings-Arcade. RHi X3 7604. Courtesy of the Rhode Island Historical Society.

Orphans and staff of the Machzeka Hadas Home for Jewish Orphans, South Providence, 1908 or 1909, probably the Fourth of July. In 1910 Machzeka Hadas merged with the Rhode Island Home for Jewish Orphans to become the Jewish Orphanage of Rhode Island (JORI). In 1924 it moved from North Main Street to Summit Avenue on the East Side.

Samuel H. Zucker & Co., Delicatessen and Gentleman's Lunch, 48 Broad Street, Pawtucket. Zucker also sold "Pure Wines and Liquors for Family and Medicinal Use" at his store at 21–23 Railroad Avenue, corner of Mason Street.

The Class of 1919 of the Thomas A. Doyle Grammar School, 83 Doyle Avenue, Providence. Numerous Jewish children attended this school on the East Side. Nathan G. "Pop" Kingsley (back row with hat) served as principal from 1895 to 1935.

Phi Epsilon Pi Fraternity, Brown University, 1916–1917. The first Jewish fraternity on campus, it disbanded in 1919, after only three years. Back row, left to right: Maurice Bazar '19, Arthur Levy '19, Samuel Silverman '18, Charles Bolotow '19, George Lubinsky '19, Walter Adler '18, Joseph Cohen '19. Front row, left to right: David Robinson '19, Abraham Burt '16, Isaac Olch '17, Herman Feinstein '16, Jacob Risenberg '16, Maurice Adelman '16, Herman Davis '16.

Business and Labor

Beginning in the late eighteenth century, Rhode Island pioneered America's industrial revolution. Until the mid-twentieth century, the state remained an industrial giant. Immigrants from many lands powered Rhode Island's mills and factories, which attained world renown.

Erwin Strasmich provides an overview of Jewish involvement in the mighty textile industry, listing owners, locations, and specialties of numerous companies. Richard Meckel describes the parallel history of Rhode Island's jewelry industry, leading to its dominance in costume jewelry production. He explains how Jews, like many ethnic groups, sought careers as entrepreneurs.

In his study of Russian Jewish immigrants, Joel Perlmann compares business opportunities in Providence to those in many larger cities. Through highly resourceful methods, he reveals that Jews in Providence were exceptionally motivated and competitive. While looking at a wider sampling of Jews from Eastern Europe, Paul Buhle explores the idealism and determination in Rhode Island's labor movement. He shows that small number of individuals, strengthened by socialist and Zionist organizations, exerted a large influence.

Bypassing epic conflicts between industrialists and workers, Eleanor Horvitz and Geraldine Foster go down to the farm. They identify a cadre of Jewish agriculturalists who raised chickens and cows, grew vegetables, tended orchards, and rented rooms to city dwellers. While some of these farmers prospered, most eked out a living. This is of course the larger story of Rhode Island's rising and falling economy.

American Tourister luggage factory on North Main Street (Highway 114), Warren, ca. 1960. Many Jewish entrepreneurs built manufacturing plants in former textile mills. American Tourister, which eventually operated five factories in Rhode Island, employed generations of immigrants who walked to work from nearby tenements. The Koffler/Bornstein Families.

Jews and the Textile Industry in Rhode Island

ERWIN STRASMICH

INTRODUCTION

Textile mills, once flourishing and prosperous in Massachusetts and Rhode Island, are now mainly historical remnants. The booming and bustling factories of the 1930s have become deserted and decrepit buildings. This paper is an attempt to recreate the fascinating life of early mills in this area and to present an informative discussion of their owners, many of whom were successful Jewish entrepreneurs.

Moses Brown of Providence, who was identified with the East India trade, began cotton manufacturing in Rhode Island in 1788. Brown financed Samuel Slater, who then built a mill in Pawtucket with new machines. This simple beginning created an industry that grew uninterruptedly for 135 years. The introduction of English machinery and the invention in 1793 of the cotton gin (through which a thousand pounds of cotton were cleaned in the time formerly taken to clean five or six pounds) gave an immediate impetus to the cotton industry. Local men, guided by Samuel Slater, began their own plants.

Early workers were mostly Irish immigrants, but by 1929 (according to the *New England Cotton Textile Industry* by J. Hubert Burgy) nationalities represented in various Blackstone Valley Mills were: French Canadian 28.8 percent; Portuguese 2.5 percent; Polish 5.2 percent; English 22.4 percent; Hebrew .15 percent, and Russian .04 percent.

The textile industry (woolen and cotton) spread with an uninterrupted growth throughout New England, New York, and Pennsylvania during the nineteenth century. It expanded rapidly until World War I. Growth was encouraged by the federal and state governments, which provided capital and legislation to protect the infant industry against foreign competition.

In 1812 there were thirty-three factories in Rhode Island with approximately thirty thousand spindles and twenty factories in Massachusetts with over seventeen thousand spindles. The cotton base was firmly established, and the woolen industry also entered the area. At the time of Slater's death in 1835 the textile industry was solidly established. By 1909 Providence produced thirty-seven million dollars worth of textile materials; Woonsocket, twenty million dollars; Fall River, Massachusetts, fifty-six million dollars. These figures were enormous when one considers that no industry existed until Slater established his mill in 1788.

Early bold investors had choice locations for water power and selected sites at the junction of rivers and at falls. Physical descriptions of most mills were similar: granite, quarried from ledges within a few hundred yards of the building sites, was used to construct four- or five-story high factories.

Textile manufacturing encompasses broad woven cloth (woolens, cottons, rayons, sateens, nylons), carpets, cordage, twine, sewing thread, jute linens, commercial fishing nets and seines, curtains, cotton smallwares, dyeing and finishing, hosiery, knit

Excerpted from *Rhode Island Jewish Historical Notes*, Volume 6, Number 2 (November 1972): 249–299.

Stanley Steiner (bootblack and newsboy, 10 years old) and Jacob Botvin (newsboy, 13 years old) in South Providence, November 24, 1912. This photograph, taken at one o'clock in the morning by famed photographer Lewis Hine, was part of his series documenting the perils of child labor in Rhode Island. Photograph courtesy of Slater Mill Historic Site, Pawtucket, Rhode Island.

goods, suit manufacturers, woolen and worsted manufacturing, wool felt goods, and hats. Other facets of textiles include allied and auxiliary items such as braiding (elastic, candle wicking, oval rugs, sleeving wire, hose, cables, tapes); rope, twine, and cordage; webbings, shoe lacing and embroidery; and vinyl coated and plastic fabrics backed with textile items (cloth, rugs and carpeting, weaving, and braiding).

In the 1930s the territory within a thirty-mile radius of Providence was the greatest textile center in America. The textile industry, in value of output, was second only to the food industry.

Most Jews in the late 1800s and early 1900s, rather than invade the factory, chose, at first, to work independently. Yet, amazingly, by the 1950s a large segment of the cotton and woolen industries was controlled by Jews, a newly arrived immigrant group. They accomplished this remarkable feat through first buying and selling items manufactured by the concerns they later controlled, and by purchasing used equipment from mills and revitalizing it for their own use. These early efforts were incredibly strenuous, but determination and fortitude prevailed. It is remarkable that in just thirty years the control in each of the aforementioned industries in this area had been acquired by Jews, either by direct control of assets or by the purchase of mill properties.

Unfortunately, following their initial spectacular success, mills in the southeastern area of New England began to decline after World War I. They continued to leave the area during the 1930s, and, in spite of a surge of prosperity during World War II, the pattern of movement of textile mills from New England to the South increased in the 1950s. By 1960 there were few cotton mills left in the entire area. This exodus was the result of competition from the South, where labor was much cheaper, cheap foreign imports from Japan and Hong Kong, and uneconomical operational methods on the part of the mills themselves. The remaining manufacturers, now chiefly Jewish, made specialized items which, while competitive, were also unique.

During the 1920s and 1930s, while mills closed and ceased operations, the abundance of available floor space and willing laborers was exploited by the garment industry. Shops from New York, besieged by labor problems, and desiring to acquire low-priced manufacturing space and an available supply of relatively low-priced, unskilled labor, moved to this area. Jewish entrepreneurs purchased the granite and brick mills and leased, subdivided, or sold them to apparel or needle trades industries.

Industries utilizing mills in the area included clothing, curtains, braiding, dyeing and finishing, automobile tires, battery cases, retail outlets, abrasive wheels, yarn spinning, candy, boxes, lamps, plastics, luggage, plating, file folders, potato chips, rubber thread, disposal cans, webbing, and electronics. The industrial diversity filling the empty mills enormously helped the economy of the area, since it no longer depended on one or two industries with low wages and limited economic power.

NARROW FABRICS

We have assembled the story of this specialized branch of the textile industry as a separate section of this history of Jews in the textile industry in Rhode Island. This story had its beginning in the latter part of the nineteenth century with the establishment of the National Tubing company in Providence.

National Tubing Company: Isaac Hahn established National Tubing, located on Sabin Street, prior to 1885. It engaged in the manufacture of flexible tubing for illuminating gas appliances. The business was an outgrowth of an earlier enterprise that fabricated silk, worsted, and mohair braids.

I. Miller & Sons: Another pioneer in the field is I. Miller & Sons, formerly the Pawtucket Vienna Braid Company, established in 1908. It manufactures elastic braids for the apparel industry.

Growth of the Industry

The narrow fabrics industry required less capital than weaving wide goods. An investment of fifty thousand dollars would sustain a mill of fifty to one hundred employees.

Narrow fabrics are classified as cotton small wares. They comprised only 7 percent of the total value of New England cotton manufactures in 1925, but total output of the region represented over 60 percent of the national output. Small wares are considered narrow, woven, or braided fabrics, such as webbing, tapes and cords, elastic and non-elastic, and mill banding, ruffling, edging, figure labels, flat and round braids, cords, and shoe and corset laces.

This industry was concentrated in southern New England. Rhode Island with sixty-six establishments contributed 40 percent of the New England output in 1925. The greatest production occurred in the Providence-Pawtucket district, where an abundance of skilled labor, proximity to finishing plants and markets, and availability of raw materials from local mills favored greater output.

Braided rugs were an important factor in the narrow fabrics industry. Abraham Percelay and his brothers Jacob and Joseph began the manufacturing of braided rugs in 1918. The rugs were braided from odd lots of yarns and sewing threads.

The complexity of the story, and the constant shifting of company ownership, the short duration of some businesses, and the difficulty at times of establishing the Jewish identity of owners make it inevitable that some Jewish textile enterprises will have been missed or overlooked. The possible omission of individuals or businesses from this roster is inadvertent and is in no way a measure of their importance or their contributions to the industry. In this essay I have been able only to sketch the uniqueness of Jewish participation in Rhode Island textiles.*

Adler Brothers: A braiding company operated by Bernhard and Morris Adler of New York and Arthur M. Radlauer. This company, founded in 1927, manufactured shoe laces until World War II. [Through the 1960s] it remained dominant, supplying elastic braids for underwear and foundation garments throughout the United States.

Ross Matthews Corporation: Established in 1922 in Providence and currently located in Fall River. Founded by Max Strasmich.

Narragansett Braid Mills, Inc.: Established by the Silver brothers of Boston, operated at 191 Rand Street in Central Falls, producing elastic braids.

International Stretch Company: Established by Max Cohen and his sons, it is a conglomerate of several allied companies and produces elastic braids, tapes, webs, broad woven fabrics, and extruded rubber thread.

The braiding field includes many shoelace manufacturers. A prominent one is the Lincoln Lace & Braid Company of Providence, managed by the Gittleman family. Automatic packaging was a unique innovation in the shoelace industry. Nathan Berk, of Berk Lace & Braid Manufacturing Company, conducted his business for forty years in Providence and then Pawtucket before he sold it in 1962. He received credit for inventing the first automatic shoelace pairing machine in the industry. Another shoelace and drawcord manufacturer was the Biltmore Textile Company, of Providence, originally founded by Hyman G. Goldsmith.

Concord Webbing Company: A manufacturer of narrow fabrics, this company moved from New York to Pawtucket in the 1940s. Ably managed by Eugene Aaronson and his family, their chief products were venetian blind webbing. The company was discontinued in 1963.

American Insulated Wire Corp.: Founded in 1919 by Jacob and Barney Kenner and incorporated in 1921, the company was a giant in the wire and cable field, and had its origin in shoelace manufacturing. It moved from Providence to Pawtucket.

OTHER ENTERPRISES

Providence Fabric, Providence: An early narrow fabric company, producing shoelaces and cotton and silk braids.

Taunton Manufacturing Company: Incorporated in 1920, it wove tire fabrics in Providence.

Waldman Manufacturing Company, Providence: Established by Samuel Waldman, it was one of the larger braiding companies of the early 1920s, manufacturing shoelaces, braids, and tapes.

*The following lists are condensed for reasons of space. The original article also mentioned several concerns in nearby Massachusetts. Eds.

Arch Narrow Fabric Company, Cranston, was incorporated in 1920 with A. E. Levine and Alvin T. Sapinsley as its organizers. It manufactured braids, corset laces, darning cotton, and balling.

Colonial Braid Company, Pawtucket: Incorporated in 1916 by Sanford H. Cohen, its products included trimming, braid, and shoelaces, produced on 300 braiders.

Atlantic Tubing and Rubber Company: Cranston. Originally acquired by Philip P. Weinstein, the chief products are rubber and plastics.

Royal Electric Company: Founded by Joseph and Myer Riesman in 1921 in Chelsea, Massachusetts, with six employees, [in the late 1960s] the company employed over 1,000 workers in the manufacture of wire and cable and cords for the electric industries. In the late 1950s Royal became affiliated with International Telephone & Telegraph Corporation.

Hamilton Web Company, Inc., Hamilton, North Kingstown. Martin Nelson and Nathan Berlin acquired the business in July 1951 from the Greene family who controlled this company for four generations. Hamilton manufactures woven narrow fabrics.

Hope Webbing, Pawtucket, manufactures cotton and synthetic braids. This well established company was purchased by David and Frank Casty in the 1950s and merged into Chelsea Industries in 1964.

Elizabeth Webbing Company: Pawtucket, narrow fabric manufacturers. Purchased by Martin Lifland in March 1959.

PRE–WORLD WAR I, 1900–1919

Samuel Priest: Born in Lithuania, Priest first engaged in the waste and rag business in Providence as early as 1888. He founded the Imperial Printing and Finishing Company in Cranston in 1912. The business continued until 1937.

Austin T. Levy: Formed the Stillwater Worsted Mills in 1907 and purchased combing and yarn mills in Harrisville. All of his mills were incorporated in 1912 into Stillwater Worsted Mills, Inc., and at one time had twelve plants, reaching peak sales during the Korean War. They manufactured worsted cloth and wool tops as well as commissioned combed tops, specializing in the production of uniform and blended cloths. Levy's advocated improved working conditions and shortened hours of labor. His company also established the first profit-sharing plan in Rhode Island.

American Silk Spinning Company: Founded in 1909 by Edgar J. Lowenstein, taking over a mill in Providence. It spun silk and produced silk yarns, natural or dyed, in skeins, on cones, tubes, cops, and spools; and in warps for weaving, knitting, embroidering, sewing, and insulation. The mill employed 300 persons in 1911. The company was sold to the Top Company, Inc., in 1959.

S. Horvitz & Sons, Inc., Pawtucket: The firm is a manufacturer of upholstery paddings. Incorporated in Rhode Island in 1964, the business was successor to one originally started in 1910 by Samuel Horvitz.

Darlington Textile Company, Pawtucket: Producers of elastic cloths for corsets, girdles, slips, and shoes, the company was incorporated in 1912 (Joseph Siegle, president) and was liquidated in 1963.

Arthur I. Darman. Arthur Darman arrived in America in 1901 at age 11. He joined a theatrical company at an early age to become an actor. He then pursued the hotel and restaurant business successfully in a number of cities. He returned to

Woonsocket in 1914 to enter the woolen business with his father. He became a large dealer in wool wastes, wool taps, and similar products.

Young Bros. Mattress Company, Providence: Originally started by John Young in 1917 and incorporated in 1924, the company manufactured mattresses and upholstered furniture, couches and chairs, utilizing cotton stuffing.

I. Medoff Company, Woonsocket: Founded by Israel Medoff in the 1920s, the company is a leader in fashion fabrics for retail sales.

Nedra Mills, Pawtucket: Incorporated in 1919 by H. B. Feldman, Hyman Werner, and Jacob Werner, the company produced silk and cotton corset brocades on seventy-five looms. This was one of the earlier mills to operate outside the production of narrow fabrics.

PROSPERITY AND DEPRESSION, 1920–1939

John Marks Company, Central Falls: Founded by John Marks in the late 1920s as dealers and converters of cotton and synthetic yarns.

Cadillac Textiles, Pawtucket: Founded by David Schwartz, and run by the Schwartz brothers, Harry A. and Samuel, the company produces synthetic piece goods and tricot fabrics. The company moved to Pawtucket in 1928 and switched to synthetic fabrics in the early 1930s (having formerly woven silk fabrics).

Hassenfeld Brothers, Providence: Brothers Helal and Henry, with William Horowitz, established the firm in West Warwick as a finishing business. The company subsequently evolved into a toy and pencil manufacturing establishment and later developed into the giant Hasbro Industries.

Abraham A. Weiss: Founder of Vogue Textiles, Inc., Pawtucket, which manufactured fluorescent fabric safety materials.

Peerless Weaving Company, Pawtucket: Under the management of Abe C. Find and Harry L. Fine, the company wove rayon and synthetics, and was sold to Southern interests in the late 1940s.

Allie Zura: A prominent real estate operator who lived in Providence most of his life, Zura was among the pioneers in purchasing mill properties, which ultimately led to the revitalization of textile manufacturing in Rhode Island.

Lebanon Knitting Mill, Inc., Pawtucket: Founded in 1927 by Leo Grossman, the company produces tubular fabrics, primarily in worsted jersey cloth and double knits.

Atlantic Knitting Company, Providence: Founded by Joseph M. Finkelstein, the company concentrates on the knitting of woolen, worsted, and rayon fabrics.

Robison Rayon Company, Inc., Providence: A fine commission dyeing plant, well known as dyers of synthetic yarns, dyeing skeins and cakes as well as twisting filament yarns, distributed throughout the United States. Robison Co. was sold in 1954.

Standard Romper Company, Pawtucket and Central Falls: Manufacturers of children's wear, creepers, children's play garments, boys' polo shirts, and blouses made from knitted and woven fabrics, sold under the well-known trade names of "Stantogs" and "Health Tex."

Warren Handkerchief Company, Warren: Until 1965 produced satins on their own looms under the guidance of Albert J. Mann. [In the 1940s] they purchased handkerchief cloth and discontinued weaving.

David Dwares: Born in Russia and educated in Providence, his ventures included both textiles and real estate. He owned and operated the Slater Dye Works in Pawtucket. Damar Wool Combing Company, Inc., established in 1903, was under the control of the Dwares family from 1941 until 1959.

Sol Koffler: Founder and president of American Tourister, producers of luggage. While not directly involved in textiles, he purchased two former Berkshire Hathaway textile plants. The company was founded in Providence in 1932 and later moved to West Warwick and other locations.

Pansey Weaving Mills, Pawtucket: a major supplier of rayon and synthetic blended fabrics. Neil Pansey founded the company in 1937, which was run by three generations of the family.

Empire Woolen Mills, Woonsocket: Manufacturers of better grade men's and women's woolens, worsted, and uniform cloths.

WORLD WAR II AND AFTER

Martin Chase: Named by *Forbes Magazine* (January 1970) as "The Granddaddy of All Discounting," Chase was chairman of Ann & Hope stores. Chase began in the Ann & Hope Mills in Cumberland; the retail operations grew out of the original mill buildings. In the early 1950s, Ann & Hope was Rhode Island's largest volume department store. It pioneered in discounting and the use of shopping carts.

Providence Pile Fabric Corporation, Pawtucket: Founded by Louis J. I. Symonds in 1945, the company later moved to Fall River. The chief products were pile and flat fabrics manufactured from mohair, rayon, and blended yarns.

S. Granoff Manufacturing Company, Central Falls: Managed by Samuel Granoff and G. Sidney Granoff, the company engaged in the manufacture of knitted fabrics and in yarn sales. An affiliated company is the Ajax Manufacturing Company.

Sidney Blumenthal and Company: Founded in 1899, the business had plants in Valley Falls and Woonsocket as late as 1947. It manufactured mohair and fancy yarns and later moved to North Carolina.

Joseph H. Axelrod: Formed the Airdale Worsted Mills, Inc. in Woonsocket, which wove worsted fabrics on second-hand machinery. It added over five companies, including Crown Manufacturing in Pawtucket, a large complex for producing woolen worsted cloth. Crown was a uniquely progressive innovation. Its ivy covered walls and manicured landscaped lawns resembled a typical New England college. Axelrod also had controlling ownership with Fisher Abramson of the famed Wamsutta Manufacturing Company of New Bedford. This company was subsequently purchased by M. Lowenstein & Sons.

Mark Kahn: An outstanding figure in the region's textile growth, he helped revitalize a decaying industry. He controlled the Wanskuck Mills, Inc., in Providence, a producer of heavy damask and nun's habit cloth, which liquidated in the 1950s. He also had a foundation garment business and long-time interests in the New Hampshire textile industry.

Andrew Worsted Mills, Inc., Pascoag: Incorporated by Irving Hillelson in 1949, the company does commission weaving of broad woven woolen and worsted, cotton and blend fabrics, as well as dyeing and finishing.

Walter Marshall Spinning Corporation, Johnston: Spinner of worsted yarns.

William Heller, Inc., Woonsocket: Spins knitting yarns.

Allentown Mills, Inc., North Kingston: The company wholesaled broad woven cloths. Its operation commenced in 1951 and was discontinued in 1966.

Ace Dying & Finishing Company, West Warwick: Engaged in cutting, dyeing, and finishing of corduroys for jobbers and manufacturers.

Parflex Rubber Thread Corporation, Providence: Incorporated in 1952. Producers of latex rubber thread utilized in the textile industry.

A & C Woolen Mills, Inc., Providence: Commissioned weavers of woolen and worsted fabrics; incorporated in 1954.

Standish Mills, Inc., Esmond: Founded in 1955, it produced rayon, cotton, and elastic fabrics.

Woonsocket Sponging, Inc., Woonsocket: Incorporated in 1957, it is engaged in examining, shrinking, flameproofing, waterproofing, mildewproofing, and mothproofing cloth.

Pontiac Printing Works, Warwick: Established in the early nineteenth century, it was owned by Jack A. Goldfarb of New York City. It adopted the Fruit Of The Loom banner and in 1960 was sold. For many years this finishing plant was the largest roller printing firm in Rhode Island.

Hanora Looms, Inc., Oakland: The company manufactures woolen and worsted cloth for women's wear.

Recent Arrivals: Several new enterprises in the industry have been established. Among these is Tectra Industries of West Warwick [which] manufactures elastic webbing. Another is Highland Textile Printers Company, Inc., in Providence. This company processes and dyes cotton piece goods. Harry Ball of New York and his sons recently purchased the American Textile Company properties in Pawtucket. The Ball interests are leading producers of fabric quilting for outerwear.

The Jewelry Industry, Industrial Development, and Immigration in Providence, 1790–1993

RICHARD A. MECKEL

Jewish workers were relative newcomers to one of Rhode Island's principal industries, the manufacture of costume jewelry. Not until the twentieth century did sizable numbers of Jews come to that industry as laborers, managers, jobbers, and owners.

On February 12, 1919, when Rhode Island's World War I doughboys paraded triumphantly through a victory arch set up on Exchange Place in the heart of downtown Providence, they were returning to a city in which two thirds of the population was either immigrants or the children of immigrants, and to a state which, since 1870, had the highest percentage of foreign-born residents in the country. Rhode Island's doughboys were also returning to a city which, despite its location in the smallest state in the union, had for over half a century been one of the leading manufacturing centers in the nation. Indeed, having benefited from a wartime boom that had reversed a trend of industrial decline apparent in the first decade of the century, Providence could still boast that it was a world leader in the production of textile goods, especially woolens and worsteds, and that it was home to the world's largest machine tool factory (Brown & Sharpe), file factory (Nicholson File), screw factory (American Screw), and silverware factory (Gorham). It could also boast of being the home of a diverse collection of some fifteen hundred other manufacturers producing everything from rubber goods to salad oil.

That Providence, a major manufacturing city, was also an immigrant city was no accident. Limited in population and thus in its source of potential workers, Providence had long had to import workers as a prerequisite for industrial expansion. In the history of Providence, industrial growth and immigration have been inseparable partners.

This is especially true in the area of jewelry manufacturing, particularly the production of relatively inexpensive or costume jewelry. When World War I ended, Providence ranked as the nation's leading producer of costume jewelry, an honor it had held since the 1870s. Throughout the city, but concentrated especially in an area bounded by Pine, Chestnut, Dorrance, and Eddy Streets, close to three hundred manufacturers and jobbers, employing over 14,000 workers, combined to produce millions of dollars worth of costume jewelry findings (unfinished components). Among the manufacturers were a few big concerns. However, for the most part, the industry was made up of small concerns usually having no more than thirty or forty employees.

Because of the semiskilled nature of much costume jewelry work, the plethora of small production units, and the low level of capital required to start a factory or job shop, Providence's costume jewelry industry was one that lent itself to a high level of immigrant employment and entrepreneurial initiative — to both opportunity and exploitation. With the exception of a small number of skilled operatives and jewelry tool makers, wages of jewelry workers were the lowest in the manufacturing sector. Home work and piecework were common. And women, many of them immigrants or children of immigrants, constituted close to half of the labor force. Yet at the same time, workers

Excerpted from *Rhode Island Jewish Historical Notes*, Volume 13, Number 2 (November 2000): 244–258. This article appeared originally in Nadia D. Weisberg, ed., *Diamonds Are Forever, but Rhinestones Are for Everyone: An Oral History of the Costume Jewelry Industry of Rhode Island* (Providence: The Providence Jewelry Museum, 1998), 1–10.

were able to labor on their own at night, often with the help of their families, assembling parts jobbed out to them or easily purchased from findings shops. And the hope among Italian, Portuguese, Jewish, and other immigrants was always there that, from such work, savings might accumulate to establish a small concern and grow into something substantial.

In the eight decades since 1920, Providence's jewelry industry has undergone many changes. Although still containing some manufacturers and job shops, the jewelry district is no longer the hub of the industry. Many concerns have moved to exurbs, suburbs, or outlying industrial parks. Yet Providence can still justly claim to be the capital of the costume jewelry industry. Moreover, as was true in the early decades of the century, the majority of the industry's work force, as well as a significant proportion of its small producers and jobbers, continue to be immigrants or the children of immigrants.

THE DEVELOPMENT OF THE INDUSTRY IN PROVIDENCE, 1790–1850

Through the last decade of the eighteenth century, Providence's economy, like that of most American port cities, was essentially an agricultural and mercantile one, relying on the sea for trade with England, the Caribbean, and China. Manufacturing production was centered in the shops of small artisans.

Among these artisans was a small group of goldsmiths and silversmiths who hand-fashioned silver plates, teapots and trays, tankards and other fine housewares, and various types of eighteen-karat gold and sterling silver jewelry for wealthy area merchants.

Jewelry manufacturing continued to expand in Providence in the decades before the mid-nineteenth century, especially after 1844 when Thomas Lowe emigrated from England and introduced an improved and cheaper method for producing plated stock. The quality of rolled gold plate stock greatly increased the popularity of cheaper jewelry and helped create a boom in the trade that lasted until the panic of 1857. That boom was extremely good to the jewelry craftsmen-entrepreneurs. It took little capital to start a venture, only enough to purchase some stock. It was also good to jewelry workers. Skilled craftsmen that they were, they enjoyed among the highest wages of any workers in Providence.

As Providence was undergoing industrial development in the first half of the century, its population was changing dramatically in size and composition. Between 1790 and 1850, the number of people calling Providence their home increased from 7,614 to 41,513. During the early years of the nineteenth century, much of that growth was produced by natural increase and the in-migration of native born Americans from rural Rhode Island and other states. But immigration also played a part. English weavers, loomers, and spinners arrived to work in the state's and city's expanding textile industry. English and German jewelry craftsmen came for work in the expanding fine and costume jewelry industry as well as in the silver plate industry.

THE ERA OF EXPANSION AND HEAVY IMMIGRATION, 1850–1920

After suffering a severe but temporary setback during the panic of 1857, and a significant disruption during the Civil War, Providence's jewelry industry entered a period of tremendous expansion that by 1880 would make the city the country's leading jewelry producer. In 1875 Providence had 133 firms employing 2,667 workers. By 1900 there were over 200 firms, employing more than 7,000 workers and producing a product valued in excess of $13 million. By 1905 jewelry workers numbered almost 8,500, and the worth of the goods they produced had nearly doubled to $24 million. That growth continued for another decade and a half before leveling off.

As has been true throughout the history of the industry, the expansion was fueled by technological innovation and aggressive merchandising. Of particular importance was electroplating, which came into fairly widespread use in Providence after 1860. Essentially, electroplating involves coating a metal with another metal by immersing the object in a solution and applying low voltage electricity. This process is less expensive and more flexible than the older process. Electroplating can also produce various shades of gold; and individual pieces can be coated after they have been formed or assembled.

Providence's costume jewelry industry also benefited from the development of rolled gold seamless wire in the 1880s. This could be used to make chains with no exposed base metal. Combined with the growing popularity of inexpensive watches, that development enabled Providence manufacturers to fill large orders for plated gold watch chains. Finally, technological innovation in the machine tool industry, in which Providence was a national leader, gave the city's costume jewelry manufacturers access to an ever-increasing array of stamping and cutting machines that could be used to produce buckles, watch cases, and chains.

The period also witnessed aggressive merchandising and the opening of new markets, not only in the United States but also in South America, Europe, and even in Africa. Indeed, by 1900 costume jewelry and accessories produced in Providence could be found in most areas of the world.

During this period of expansion the center of costume jewelry production shifted from its traditional home on North Main Street to an area southwest of downtown. This is an area bordered today by Pine, Dorrance, Chestnut, and Eddy Streets. By the 1860s, firms were moving into existing buildings. Often several firms would occupy a single structure. Over the next half-century the area was architecturally transformed as several investors and some major manufacturers constructed buildings for the express purpose of housing jewelry manufacturers.

As Providence's jewelry industry was undergoing major expansion, the city itself was experiencing an industrial boom that made it one of the nation's leading manufacturing centers. At the center of the boom was the tremendous growth of the textile industry.

Consonant with the growth of the textile production in the second half of the nineteenth century had been the growth of other major industries. Chief among these were firms involved in metal work in the production of steam engines, machine tools, textile machinery, screws, and files.

Concurrent with its dramatic industrial expansion, Providence vastly increased its population. Between 1865 and 1925, the number of Providence residents increased almost fivefold, from 54,595 to 267,918. Only a small part of this growth was due to natural increase. Most came from in-migration and especially from immigration. Moreover, the source of that immigration changed significantly in the latter part of the period. In 1800, nine-tenths of the immigrant fathers of Providence school children came from the British Isles, primarily from Ireland. By 1900, only half did. The source of this new immigration was Southern and Eastern Europe, principally from Italy and to a lesser extent from Russia, Poland, Armenia, and the Azores.

Immigration provided the needed workers for that expansion; and industrial growth provided the motive for settling in Providence.

Opportunities for employment for unskilled male and female workers were also

plentiful in the jewelry industry after the turn of the century. Unlike the textile industry, however, this represented a major break with the past. For most of the nineteenth century, costume jewelry, like the higher grade jewelry, had been hand fashioned individually from base metal to finished product by skilled craftsmen; and they were distinguished from their brethren working in fine metal and precious stone jewelry only by the materials they worked with and the products they created rather than by skill. This began changing toward the end of the century with the development of machines to cut, shape, and cast the basic components of individual jewelry items. In short, mechanization and mass production came to the costume jewelry industry.

With mass production came a dramatic transformation of the work force. By the first decade of the twentieth century, the craftsmen capable of fashioning a piece of jewelry from beginning to end had largely disappeared from the costume jewelry work place, except for those few specialty concerns that fashioned "art" jewelry. In their place was a labor force stratified by function and skill. At the top were the precision toolmakers, die cutters, and mold makers who produced the machines and dies and molds that produced the jewelry components. Also at the top were senior platers who were responsible for regulating the chemical solutions and electrical energies to produce just the right shade of coloring. These machinists and platers were highly valued craftsmen and their wages reflected that fact.

At the next level were journeymen platers, polishers, and tool setters. And below them were the bench workers who increasingly made up the vast majority of the jewelry industry work force. Bench workers set stones, soldered findings, linked chains and rings, enameled pieces, and generally assembled the machine-cut or cast pieces into finished jewelry. Considered to be engaged in unskilled labor, bench workers were frequently women and sometimes children and were paid wages or piecework rates that placed their earnings among the lowest in the manufacturing sector. By 1905, women accounted for 35 percent of the jewelry manufacturing employees; by 1930, 54 percent; and by 1980 nearly 70 percent.

If mechanization divided up the work force, it also divided up the manufacturing process so that various components of that process could be "jobbed out." This led to the creation of small job shops specializing in one aspect of manufacture: plating, polishing, stamping, linking, or stone setting. It also led to the proliferation of home work; that is, the jobbing out at piecework rates of specific tasks (such as chain linking or stone setting) to individuals who, often with the help of their families, did the work in their homes. By 1918, home work in jewelry exceeded that in any other industry in Rhode Island.

The turn-of-the-century transformation of the manufacturing processes and work force in the costume jewelry industry was not replicated in the production of precious metal goods. Although Gorham and other silverware manufacturers mechanized, their work force remained largely male, native born or northern European, skilled, and well paid.

The disappearance of skilled craftsmen from the work forces, the declining wages, the increasing employment of women and sometimes children, and the mounting reliance on piecework and home work all earned for the industry criticism from social reformers and organized labor.

Not surprisingly, industry spokesmen and factory owners looked at the situation differently. Defending the piecework, homework, and jobbing out, Edgar M. Docherty, president of an industry trade group, explained in a 1922 interview with the *Providence Journal* that the practices were widespread because they allowed immigrant families to earn extra income and gave immigrant entrepreneurs the opportunity to become manufacturers themselves. Although self-interested, Docherty's explanation was not entirely incorrect.

To be sure, the criticized practices also immensely benefited jewelry concern owners, giving them a source of cheap labor that could be tapped during rush periods and ignored when things were slow. They also kept production costs low by depressing wages and by allowing for piecework rates that occasionally amounted to little more than a few cents an hour.

The small size of many of the jewelry concerns also attracted immigrant workers who tended to gravitate toward employment in places where others of the same nationality worked. Immigrants, historically, have tended to secure jobs through personal contacts. Between 1915 and 1935, for instance, over half of Federal Hill's Italian men who worked in jewelry factories had kin employed in the same place. Indeed, some small concerns, and especially those run by immigrant entrepreneurs, had their labor forces made up entirely of relatives and neighbors. Jewish families, though not as numerous as those of Italian and Portuguese background, were also attracted to the industry in increasing numbers during this period.

Jewelry factories also attracted female immigrants by shaping work hours and schedules to fit the needs of women with children. As is still true today, "mothers' shifts" paralleling school hours were common. The seasonal nature of employment was also attractive to women who saw their earnings as supplementary to their husbands' wages and rarely desired full-time, year-round employment. Yet, as in other "sweat shop" industries that job-out work, seasonally employ large numbers of women, and offer entrepreneurial opportunity to workers with little capital, immigrants paid a price for the benefits they derived from Providence's jewelry industry. Wages remained low; job security was always fleeting; union organization proved exceptionally difficult; and health and safety conditions in the small job shops run on razor-thin profit margin continued, in many cases, to be abominable.

CONTINUITY AMIDST DECLINING INDUSTRIAL PRODUCTION: 1920 TO THE PRESENT

In 1920 Providence was still an industrial giant, but it was one teetering on collapse. The incipient decline that had been interrupted by the war emerged during the twenties and became a headlong spiral during the Depression of the 1930s. With the end of the war the bottom fell out of the cotton textile industry. Other industries and businesses were also hard hit and jobs disappeared with frightening speed. By the time of Roosevelt's inauguration, 32 percent of Providence's workers were unemployed and some 230 businesses had failed.

The jewelry industry also suffered, but less so than most. And by 1939 it had recovered somewhat, registering only 6 percent fewer jobs than it had in 1919. Indeed, that would be the pattern for the rest of the century. As Providence's industrial base continued to shrink, the jewelry industry would occasionally falter but would retain its strength and size.

World War II brought a temporary respite for the industrial decline that had beset the state and its largest city since 1920. What was left of the textile industry disintegrated after the war. Other major industries also closed or departed.

Only the jewelry industry, specifically costume jewelry, remained a national manufacturing leader. In 1947, Rhode Island jewelry firms, most of which were located in Providence, were producing 40 percent of the nation's low-cost jewelry. Indeed, the decline of industrial manufacturing in Rhode Island in many ways benefited the jewelry industry. The steady loss of industrial jobs produced a growing pool of workers, many with metalworking skills, which could be tapped by jewelry firms. Hard times among Providence's and Rhode Island's working-class families also encouraged wives and daughters to seek work to supplement family incomes. Hence, the jewelry industry, which had always depended on seasonal employees, had a large supply of such employees available to it. Finally, the closing of mills and factories made available a large number of industrial work spaces that could be rented cheaply. Along with the sharp decline of other industrial employment opportunities, this encouraged many workers to start their own small manufacturing or job shops.

The postwar history of the jewelry industry was not, however, one of steady growth and prosperity. Although it increasingly dominated industrial manufacturing activity in the state, the industry had good periods and bad periods and underwent many changes. This was particularly true in Providence, which watched many firms fold or move to the exurbs, suburbs, or outlying industrial parks.

The postwar era also saw dramatic changes in Rhode Island's and Providence's immigrant population, the traditional source of so many jewelry industry workers. By 1950, three decades of war, depression, and restrictive immigration quotas had transformed the population from one heavily made up of new immigrants and their children to one in which the vast majority of the population had either been born here or had resided here for several decades.

This low level of immigration began to rise dramatically after 1965 when a new federal immigration law removed the national quota restrictions that had been in effect since the 1920s. Economic conditions in Asia and in Central America were propelling mounting numbers of Asian and Latino immigrants to Rhode Island and the rest of the country.

As with those who came before them, many of the new immigrants have found work in the jewelry industry, often laboring for the children or grandchildren of earlier waves of immigrants. In several ways, the industry they have entered is dramatically different from the one that employed Italians, Portuguese, Jewish, and other immigrants earlier in the century. Especially since the 1970s, many of the larger firms operate in modern plants where working conditions are relatively good and where employees receive benefit packages similar to those offered in other industries. But in several other ways the industry is similar. Seasonal employment and a high turnover rate still characterize it. So too does the hiring of women to do most of the semiskilled or unskilled bench-work. Estimates are that over 75 percent of the solderers and stamp press operators and over 90 percent of the carders, stringers, and linkers are women. As in the past, the industry offers these women such benefits as "mother's shifts" and employment when needed in exchange for low wages and little job security.

The industry is also still one that offers immigrant worker-entrepreneurs with little capital the opportunity to start their own shops with a few family members to help. And as immigrants continue to enter the city and the state, one suspects this will remain true for some time to come.

Beyond New York, a Second Look
The Occupations of Russian Jewish Immigrants in Providence, Rhode Island, and in Other Small Jewish Communities, 1900–1915

JOEL PERLMANN

I worked on the social history of Providence for the better part of fifteen years, and an important part of my effort focused on the city's East European Jewish immigrants and their children—specifically the occupations of the immigrants and the schooling and occupations of their children. This paper is therefore partly about the substance of American Jewish history, and about Rhode Island Jewish history in particular, and partly about evidence and historical methods for using certain kinds of evidence.

I was interested in the schooling and social mobility patterns of American ethnic groups. Just how differently had ethnic groups responded to American schooling? How much more schooling had some groups obtained compared to other groups? And just how much did the schooling they received help some ethnic groups to get ahead faster than other ethnic groups? Just how much, then, had schooling helped the children of the immigrants in the past? I was especially interested in the period of the great migrations at the end of the nineteenth century and the beginning of the twentieth.

In Providence I found excellent historical sources. The city boasted superb census records, school records that may well be unique in their comprehensiveness and detail, and, finally, city directories and marriage records (complete with wonderful indices). Moreover, Providence offered much more than merely the sources. Providence was a place of manageable size, a place that had a multifaceted economy.

In 1974 I began working on Providence social history, and I worked on it consistently thereafter. First, I and a small army of research assistants painstakingly collected samples of 12,000 school-age children from census records of 1880, 1900, 1915, and 1925; and we traced these 12,000 individuals to school records and then across time to their jobs as young adults. The work took the better part of three years. But in the end I had a unique source of evidence about social origins, schooling, and getting ahead in America at the turn of the century.

One of the great questions about Jews in America is why they have received such unusual amounts of education and why they have advanced so rapidly in socioeconomic terms. Some observers have stressed various cultural differences between Jews and others. One example is their tradition of learning. Also relevant may have been the long heritage of acting carefully as a minority group, behavior that conceivably may have led to resourcefulness. And a long history of involvement in trade in Europe (even if at humble levels of material well-being) may have encouraged initiative as opposed to fatalism. But other observers have stressed something other than the cultural attributes of Jews, namely the fact that so many Jews had basic job skills that turned out to be useful in this country and that helped them enter the skilled trades from which they could get a

Excerpted from *Rhode Island Jewish Historical Notes*, Volume 10, Number 3B (November 1989): 375–388.

The board of directors of Gemilath Chesed, later known as Hebrew Free Loan Association of Providence, 1903. Founded by and for immigrants, this was the first of many Hebrew Free Loans established throughout Rhode Island. In 2003 it celebrated its centenary.

leg up. Many, in particular, came with skills as tailors. Others came with skills in trade. Not that these Jewish immigrants were not impoverished—they were. But they had certain skills, the argument goes, that favored their more rapid advance in the marketplace.

But suppose we compare the children of immigrant Jews to the children of other families in the same social niches—compare the children of skilled workers who were Jews with the children of skilled workers who were not Jews, compare the children of petty traders who were Jews to the children of petty traders who were not Jews, and so on. In the end I concluded that while the differences in fathers' occupations between Jews and others were surely important, they cannot explain all of the difference between the children of East European Jews and the children of others in the same social niches in Providence, and I concluded, therefore, that the explanations of Jewish behavior that appeal to cultural attributes deserve serious attention. To assess arguments about Jewish upward mobility, I had to look carefully at the occupations of Jewish immigrants.

My questions had led me to take a close look at a group of school-age children around the turn of the century, and as part of that effort I took a close look at the occupations of their fathers. In the case of the East European Jews, I collected a sample of children of the Russian-born immigrants in Providence in 1915. I was consequently able to study the occupations of some 561 Russian-born fathers in that year.

The striking finding from that study was how heavily the Russian-born Jews were concentrated in the skilled trades and in commerce—and especially in commerce. In discussing commerce I do not mean to imply that the Jewish immigrants were well off; as often as not they were peddlers, and there is every indication that those who had their own small stores had also started as peddlers. But the concentration in commerce

Table 1. Occupations of Russian Jewish Immigrant Fathers and
Other Immigrant Fathers in Providence, 1915

	Russian Jews	Other immigrants
A. Percentage of self-employed		
Employer	11%	6%
"on own account"	60	14
all self-employed	71	20
B. Percentage in selected occupational categories		
Peddlers	22%	3%
Proprietors	23	8
Self-employed artisans	20	8
Semiskilled or unskilled employees	13	49

Source: A sample of fathers of school-age children drawn from the R.I. State Census of 1915 by J.
Perlmann. Included are 561 Russian Jews and 761 others.

meant that they were differently situated than other groups, possibly in ways that made a difference for later work. Just how differently situated these Russian Jewish fathers were than others in the city can be seen in Table 1. In 1915 fully 71 percent of the Russian Jewish fathers were self-employed, whereas only 20 percent of the other immigrant fathers were. Twenty-two percent of the fathers were peddlers, compared to 3 percent of other immigrant groups. Forty-three percent were proprietors or self-employed artisans, compared to 16 percent among other immigrants. At the other extreme, only 13 percent of the Russian Jewish immigrant fathers were semiskilled or unskilled wage workers—compared to 49 percent among other groups.

Moreover, the occupational profile of the Russian Jewish immigrants in Providence seemed remarkably different from that described in the common generalizations about East European Jewish immigrants in America. Those generalizations said that East European Jews started in the skilled trades, especially in the garment industry, and typically did not escape manual work during their lifetimes. It is not that I thought these generalizations wrong. Rather, the generalizations pertained to the giant Jewish communities that have been so well studied: chiefly New York, but also Chicago, Philadelphia, and Boston. And so in 1983 I published an article "Beyond New York" (in *American Jewish History*) that stressed how different the occupations of the Jews were in Providence from those in New York.[1]

In that article I compared East European Jewish occupations in New York and Providence. Then I presented some evidence that I had found in the published reports of the United States Census of 1900. That evidence suggested that in other middle-sized cities, the Jewish occupations were much more like those in Providence than like those in New York—much more likely to be rooted in trade than was the case in New York and much less likely to be rooted in the garment industry in particular. That data is summarized in Table 2. The table published in 1983 allowed me to compare four kinds of occupational groups across all the cities. Two of these occupations were in commerce: peddling and a broader category of retail trade including peddlers, merchants, and dealers. The other two occupations were in manufacturing: tailoring and a broader category of all manufacturing and mechanical pursuits.[2]

The difference between the occupational structure in the middle-sized cities and the occupational structure in New York, I reasoned, could have had important implications. From the starting position in commerce, in the smaller Jewish communities, upward

Table 2. "Beyond New York": Occupations of Russian-Born Immigrants, 1900

	Percentage of Russian male workers			
Location	Peddlers	All peddlers, merchants, dealers	Tailors	All manufac.
New York City only	5%	16%	28%	61%
5 big centers	7	19	25	53
31 other cities, pop. over 100,000	13	29	15	42
Providence only	24	42	7	39

Source: Published report of the 1900 US Census. 5 big centers include NYC, Chicago, Philadelphia, Boston, Baltimore. 31 other cities include Providence.

mobility might be more rapid, or at least it might take different paths, that is, be based on different kinds of jobs than elsewhere. Also, if the Jews of these communities were less likely to experience wage labor, and more likely to have remained self-employed, perhaps they were less likely to have been radicalized by the socialist movement that was so important in the lives of New York and Chicago Yiddish labor. So these occupational differences might have great importance.

Now of course most Jews were in New York—just over half—and about another two in five were in Chicago, Philadelphia, and Boston. Nevertheless, about three Jewish immigrants in ten were not to be found in those centers. They were in smaller Jewish communities, typically in middle-sized cities like Providence. And it is about these three in ten that I thought I had something valuable to say.

But recall: my really detailed evidence was only from Providence; from Providence I had my 1915 sample of many hundreds of fathers of school children. And from that sample I knew the sort of information summarized in Table 1. For the other cities I was limited to the much less detailed evidence published in the census reports of 1900.

The huge 1910 census public-use sample affords us two opportunities. First, we can look at the situation in a later year, in 1910 rather than in 1900, after a decade of massive new migrations. And, second, we can look at the East European Jews in *all* communities of the United States, since by looking at those of Yiddish origin we know we are dealing with Jews. The results of the new exploration are to be found in Table 3.

In 1910 the same occupational patterns that I noted earlier persisted. And the new data show that the same general argument that I made about the middle-sized places in 1900 can be extended with greater force to the small communities, those with populations under 100,000. There the reliance on commerce was especially great. Thirty-four percent of East European Jews are peddlers, merchants, and dealers, as against 12 percent in New York City. Only 27 percent are in manufacturing pursuits, as against 59 percent in New York.

On the other hand, I am also struck that the differences between the middle-sized communities and the five large communities of Jews were not so great—and in particular they were not as great as the difference between Providence and these five large centers. For perspective, recall that the middle-sized communities include all those in cities with populations of 100,000 except the five largest Jewish population centers (New York, Chicago, Philadelphia, Boston, and Baltimore). Providence had a population of some 175,000 in 1900 and 224,000 in 1910. The number of Russian-born in the city numbered 2,000 in 1900 and 6,000 in 1910. The Providence Jewish community was among the most extreme in the middle-sized group in its reliance on peddling and commerce. Thus in 1900 Providence had the third highest proportion of peddlers among the 36 cities; 24 percent, whereas the norm for the 31 middle-sized communities was 13 percent.

Table 3. Occupations of East European Jewish Immigrants, 1910

Location	Percentage of Russian male workers			
	Peddlers	All peddlers merchants, dealers	Apparel manufac.	All manufac.
A. Four categories of occupations				
New York City only	4%	12%	25%	49%
5 big centers	4	13	23	48
31 other cities, pop. over 100,000 in 1900	4	20	10	34
All other places	7	34	4	26
B. Self-employment				
	Employer	"On own" account	Total	Number in sample
New York City only	13%	20%	33%	936
5 big centers	13	21	34	1,252
31 other cities, pop. over 100,000 in 1900	14	26	40	197
All other places	21	40	61	213
C. Self-employment among men over 40 only				
5 big centers	18	33	51	293
31 other cities	25	21	46	57
All other places	29	49	78	55
Compare to: Fathers in Providence sample, 1915	11	60	71	561

Source: The public-use sample of the 1910 US Census (except last row). Apparel manufacturing includes all blue collar occupations in that industrial sector (thus more than tailors).

Also, consider the evidence on self-employment, that other remarkable feature of the Providence fathers in my 1915 sample. There was no comparative data from 1900. Fortunately, however, the 1910 census data now allow us to explore self-employment. Self-employment, like reliance on commerce, was more common in the middle-sized Jewish communities than in the five large ones (40 percent as against 34 percent). But the difference was fairly small. Once again, it is in the smallest communities that the fraction of self-employed was much greater than in New York. And, finally, nowhere was the fraction of self-employed as high as I had found in Providence among my sample of fathers in 1915.

However, there is a certain lack of comparability between my Providence samples and the national data; in Providence I had studied the fathers of adolescents. And the fathers of adolescents are older men than the group of all adult male workers (the average age of the fathers of the adolescents was 44). Could this lack of comparability explain the difference in the occupations of Providence men and others? To find the answer to this question, I compared men over 40 in the 1910 sample to my Providence fathers of 1915. In the 31 middle-sized cities, the difference from Providence is still clear: 46 percent, not 71 percent as in Providence, are self-employed. But in the smallest cities, under 100,000 in size, the fraction self-employed among the older men actually exceeded the fraction self-employed among the Providence fathers of 1915, with 78 percent of the small sample self-employed.

In sum, there were other communities like Providence, but they were typically in the third group, in the smaller cities, those with a population of under 100,000 in 1910. In those cities, among all gainfully employed East European Jewish men, 61 percent were self-employed, 34 percent were in commerce, and only 26 percent were in manufacturing.[3]

In my 1983 paper, "Beyond New York," I had speculated that the high proportion of Russian Jews in the workforce of some cities might have limited the opportunities to enter commerce—quite simply too many Jews may have wanted to engage in trade to permit them all to do so. Perhaps, too, in the larger cities the structure of retail trade made it harder for newcomers with very little capital to break in—perhaps, for example, larger stores were more common in larger cities or relations between wholesalers and retailers were tighter there. And just possibly, too, the Jews most interested in entering trade might have moved to the smaller cities where entry into trade was easier. And certainly, those Jewish immigrants with garment industry skills would have had a greater incentive, other things being equal, to come to garment industry centers. Finally, the extent of self-employment and peddling may have varied among the smaller Jewish communities as a result of the extent to which, on the one hand, ethnic hostility operated to limit Jewish opportunities to be hired by non-Jews and, on the other, by the extent to which earlier Jewish immigrations (principally from Germany) may have produced Jewish-owned enterprises that could hire the new Jewish immigrants.[4] These speculations remain only speculations; still, I continue to think they are about right. But I am now struck that even when one ventured beyond New York, Providence may have been fairly exceptional among the middle-sized Jewish communities, not in the greater reliance on commerce and self-employment than was typical in New York, but on the degree of that reliance.

NOTES

1. Joel Perlmann, "Beyond New York: The Occupations of Russian Jewish Immigrants in Providence, Rhode Island, and in Other Small Jewish Communities, 1900–1915" in *American Jewish History* (March 1983): 369–394.

2. The figures in Table 2 differ slightly from the comparable ones in my earlier paper, "Beyond New York," because in that paper I provided unweighted averages (each city in a size-category of cities counted the same as every other, regardless of the number of Jewish workers in the city). Here, by contrast, I used weighted averages (each city weighted according to the number of Jewish workers; or, to put it differently, all workers in one size-category of cities were viewed together just as though they had come from one city). The reason for the change is that the 1910 sample, large as it is, is not large enough to permit reliable estimates of the occupational profile of Jewish workers in many of the middle-sized cities.

3. Further work might determine the extent to which the patterns observed in the middle-sized cities were particularly influenced by one or two cities. For example, many of the garment workers in those cities were in Newark. Nevertheless, the 1900 data for individual cities, presented in Table A of "Beyond New York," show that the difference between Providence and these other middle-sized cities cannot be explained away by such a line of argument. Thus, for example, as noted in the text, the proportion of peddlers in 1900 was higher among Russian Jews in Providence than in all but three of the middle-sized cities.

4. I am grateful to Alice Goldstein for stressing these last two points in discussion with me.

Jews in Rhode Island Labor
An Introductory Investigation

PAUL M. BUHLE

I call this an introductory investigation because the study of Rhode Island labor is not even as advanced as the study of Rhode Island Jewry, and we must therefore attempt to put in place some elementary building blocks before we can begin to structure our analysis of this important but overlooked subject.

Jewish immigrants to the United States and their children, from the 1890s to the 1940s, created several of the most democratic unions in the United States, and those unions, especially but not only the Amalgamated Clothing Workers, had an impact upon all working Americans, lifting standards of living, standards of production, and quality of life.

I address Jewish labor history in Rhode Island not as a study of a finite number of workers in a finite series of institutions, but rather as a part of a larger Jewish tendency.

Rhode Island always lacked the critical number of Jewish industrial workers whose presence set the tone for progressive labor in greater New York and had a strong influence in Philadelphia, Chicago, Rochester, Boston, and even New Haven.

Therefore, lower and middle class Jews of Rhode Island, like those of many other places, intersected primarily as supporters of Jewish movements elsewhere—readers, members, financial contributors—and of labor and social movements not predominantly Jewish in character, both within and outside Rhode Island.

This does not mean that Rhode Island Jews were merely spectators of other movements. Smallish branches counted in Jewish movements, especially in times of need or disorientation. Readers counted; financial contributors counted a great deal. To give an example of national importance, the Poale Zionist Alter Boyman initiated in Providence the Third Seder, a major method of the Poale Zionists nationally to fund the colonization of Palestine. No city the size of Providence had so large and active a Poale Zionist movement generally. To give another kind of example: Rhode Island's Lawrence Spitz became the dynamo of textile and later steel workers, and of the major social reform movements in health, welfare, and housing desegregation movements of the 1950s. And the story does not end here.

To try to understand all this, I shall be working in two directions simultaneously: by deductive reasoning, from the general national and international movements to their local affiliates; and by inductive reasoning, from what I've been able to glean from interviews and from materials in the Rhode Island Historical Society and the Rhode Island Jewish Historical Association.

[In 1896, the *Providence Journal* published its] first descriptions of Jewish unionism and of union meetings at the old Liederkranz Hall on North Main Street. Not only did Jewish tailors organize a union; they entered, during the worst depression in the nation's history up to that point, into an audacious seven-week strike against the merchant tailors.

Excerpted from *Rhode Island Jewish Historical Notes*, Volume 10, Number 2 (November 1988): 146–156.

Only a few months or years in the country, the Journal seemed to imply, and Jews had already begun to act like the Irish, or worse, like the socialists, never very numerous in Rhode Island but always feared.[1]

About the same time, Providence Jews became active as socialists, supporting the desperate strikes of Olneyville textile workers against starvation wage-reductions in the early 1890s and helping in the attempt to form a new national industrial union of textile workers, headquartered in Providence, in 1896. These struggles also failed. But along with German-American brewery workers, the Karl Marx circle of Italian artisans, the Irish-American following of textile union leader James P. Reid, and a scattering of Yankee radicals, Jewish tailors and other Jews became the solid center of the Rhode Island Socialist Party. As socialists, they would play an important role in Rhode Island labor for two generations.[2]

The Journal took no apparent notice—none that I could find—of the organization of the Workmen's Circle around the turn of the century. The Workmen's Circle would be, for many Jews, the key mechanism by which they would gain an education in labor ideas and through which they would support the labor movement.

From the experience of the early Landsmanshaften, the organizations of immigrants from various areas, and from the German-American socialist Sterbe and Krankenvereine, death and sickness benefit societies, the Workmen's Circle drew its methods and goals during the 1890s. To workers, but through them also to the community at large, the Arbeiter Ring or Workmen's Circle offered insurance protection generations before Social Security existed. It was not much protection, but it was enough to keep a workman who was sick a short time from becoming destitute or to keep a widow from losing everything she had because of funeral expenses.

But even more than that. The Workmen's Circle from its earliest organizing was also a social and educational center, and sometimes an entertainment center too, for the whole Jewish community. It kept a library in Yiddish and English, it brought in Yiddish lecturers from New York or Boston when possible, it held weekly discussion meetings on world topics, and it generally encouraged self-education and enlightenment.

I do not yet have the necessary evidence to make a crucial case for Providence's importance in this regard. But we know that the Workmen's Circle failed in New York City in its initial period of the 1890s because of the terrible depression but also because it competed with so many other organizations and clubs. It succeeded and re-established itself, on a permanent basis, outside New York, in cities like Providence, where the competition was much less severe and the Workmen's Circle became the unquestioned center of Jewish working class life.[3]

But note that this is not to discount the role of other types of immigrant Jewish mutual benefit organizations in Providence working class life. The hevrahs (groups of men who came together to pray and study Torah in the old country) had a major role also, but not the same as the Workmen's Circle.

One particular contribution of the Workmen's Circle became very important in the next opportunity and crisis facing Rhode Island labor. In most of Rhode Island by 1905 or thereabouts, hardly any unionism had been securely established, except a narrow craft unionism in a few scattered trades, such as the building trades. The recession beginning in 1907 destroyed most of the unions that remained, as employers drove down wages and workers could not afford to pay dues. But beginning in 1909, and accelerating in 1911–1912, a new series of strikes by new immigrants, unskilled workers, shook the country, including Rhode Island.

The famous strike in Lawrence, Massachusetts, in 1912, set off great excitement in textile mills across our state shortly after. A parade of Providence socialists marched from Smith Hill to Federal Hill in support of the Lawrence strike leaders, who had been arrested on trumped-up charges. They were joined by a contingent from Olneyville, where an Irish-American Socialist had been elected in 1911 to the state legislature. From textiles, the center shifted to the garment industries. The International Ladies Garment Workers Union had just won a great strike for recognition in New York, and Boston tailors had struck in sympathy with local garment workers. In Providence, an organizing drive led by the Industrial Workers of the World sought a comprehensive contract with the department stores and finishing shops, employing more than a thousand. Mass meetings were held in Yiddish, English, and Italian.[4]

At this moment, Rhode Island Jews might have played an important national role in what was widely considered one of the most oppressive American sites of industrial labor. A breakthrough would have brought the kind of social improvement delayed until the 1930s and the Congress of Industrial Organizations. But police, employers, and conservative union leaders joined hands to ban demonstrations and forbade use of public halls. The local labor newspaper noted, "Never before in the history of the labor movement in this city has any organization of working men and women been more bitterly assailed."[5] The tailors were defeated.

There is a sequel to this defeat. During World War I, the labor shortage once again made great strikes possible, not only in textiles but also in the most oppressive and

The Providence Cornice Company, located at Charles and Smith Streets in Providence's North End, ca. 1900. Established in 1896, when Providence was a manufacturing powerhouse, the company produced copper and galvanized iron. Jewish laborers in this photograph include Abraham Nulman and Jacob Cohen (seated center); Louis Goldstein (standing, white coat); and Isaac Wolf and Joseph Jokovitch (location not identified).

dangerous of industrial trades, jewelry. Here, the mostly Jewish-Italian union, the International Jewelry Workers Union, came into a virtually open-shop environment and began to bring decent conditions into shops where $1.50 per day was an average wage, and child labor and unsanitary and extremely dangerous working conditions prevailed.

Here, perhaps for the first time, Jews operated in the Rhode Island labor movement as a minority of a workforce made up largely of new Italian immigrants, but represented a majority of the leadership—and also, it has to be said, a certain number of the employers who came to Providence to escape unionization in New York.

In a short time, 3,000 to 4,000 workers joined the union in Providence and the Attleboros; the most important jewelry workers' strike in New England history began at Ostby & Barton's. Again, history might have been made, all the more so because Providence would become the costume jewelry capital of America. But again, and for the last time in Rhode Island jewelry until the 1940s, jewelry workers had gone all out without improvement of conditions or pay. Employers successfully responded to the threat with firings, police attacks, and blacklisting of union members. In some cases, health standards would remain dangerously low until the passage of the Occupational Health and Safety Act of the 1970s. It was a Jewish defeat, without question, and a source of continuing shame for Rhode Islanders with a conscience.[6]

By the 1920s, conditions had improved somewhat for Jews in Rhode Island. Many were successful by this time in establishing small-scale businesses of their own; others got along in retail shops or managed in the tailoring trade. But America of the 1920s, including Rhode Island, was a time of fierce political reaction, of Ku Klux Klan parades at Roger Williams Park with echoes of anti-Semitism. In short, Jews had moved up, especially relative to other new immigrant groups, but American life had not become any more democratic, especially not in an ethnic or racial sense. Finally, all through this period of hopes and disappointments, unionism, war, and revolution, Jews remained in touch with their European families, whose condition and very existence grew more and more endangered.

For these reasons, Jewish communal life, emphasizing values of the labor movement even when not part of it in an industrial sense, flourished as never before in Rhode Island, from the 1920s to the 1940s. The Workmen's Circle, numbering a hundred or so active members and a periphery of perhaps 500 in all, stepped up its activities. It opened a Yiddish *shul* on the East Side in 1924 and soon another one in South Providence. The teacher, Beryl Segal (a recent immigrant from Russia, by way of the West) also led the Friday discussion group. It was a lively circle of people who, as his daughter Geraldine S. Foster says, should be described as working people in the most literal sense; they were Jews who worked with their hands whether they were one-man businesses, or carpenters, painters, or tailors. They represented Jewish progressive, communal activity at its highest point in Rhode Island history.

Segal had come to Providence because his wife's cousin, Alter Boyman, had already become a major figure of the Poale Zion, the labor Zionists, not only locally in Providence but nationally as well. A founder of labor Zionism and a mentor of David Ben Gurion, Pincus Caruso, who was ninety-seven when interviewed in Miami, said that Providence was a beehive of Poale Zionist activity. Under Boyman's dynamic leadership, the Poale Zion had a local membership of at least a hundred, with its own educational meetings and cultural affairs. The members and their children also participated in Workmen's Circle affairs.[7]

Alter's wife, Sara, and Chaya (Irene) Segal, meanwhile, soon led what would become the largest of any of the progressive Jewish organizations, the Pioneer Women (now called *Na'Amat*), with at least three hundred members. The depth of feeling for the communal spirit may be measured in how it spread through the entire family—father, mother, and child.[8]

It is worth emphasizing that the Poale Zion was a labor, socialist movement, despite the fact that its membership was considerably more middle class than that of the Workmen's Circle. This is not a contradiction in terms. Its enthusiasts, like Alter Boyman himself, moved up somewhat in business or the professions, but without losing the ideals of a different and better way of life, not only for Jews but for all people. (Poale Zion was militantly opposed to the Zionist "Revisionism" of the Likud Party's predecessors. For labor Zionists, Israel had to become a land of cooperative labor and of justice for all its citizens. As Pincus Caruso told me, they remained committed to those goals to the very end.)[9]

There was one dark spot in this development: the split between the left, the "Linkies" as they were called, and the Workmen's Circle. In many other cities, where a new influx of Jewish immigrants came into industrial work in the 1910s and 1920s, the Yiddish-speaking supporters of the Soviet Union were the younger and more vigorous activists who became the leaders of new communal institutions, such as Yiddish choirs and theaters and such unions as the furriers and others. They also led the popular movement against fascism, and later for a short period played a major role in supporting young Israel, strange as that now may seem.

In Rhode Island, where industrial conditions brought few new Jewish proletarians, this Jewish Left never had much strength. But its leaders played a major role in the unemployed movement, which used to fill what is now Kennedy Plaza with mass rallies in the early 1930s. Former Workmen's Circle members, along with newer recruits, were members of a lively International Workers Order (later Jewish People's Fraternal Order) branch in South Providence.[10] Years after the 1920s split of the Workmen's Circle branch ("down the middle," according to Beryl Segal) the two sides, as nationally, achieved a *modus vivendi* of sorts in anti-fascist causes and support of new industrial unions (including a few, such as the furriers, that had Jewish members locally). The strength was far less than it had been before the division.

The greater loss was to the power American culture held over the younger generation of Jews; to move up almost demanded assimilation in some form, at least the casting off of obvious Jewish accents. Public schools, radio, sports, the whole spectrum of youthful experiences tended to draw young Jews away from the communalism of the immigrants.

By the 1930s, losses could already be felt somewhat. On the one hand, as Judith Smith's book, *Family Connections*, points out, many older Jewish tailors lost their trade in fine clothes, so that the main area of Jewish participation in traditional unionism practically vanished. The Workmen's Circle and Poale Zion energetically supported Norman Thomas or followed other Rhode Islanders in supporting Franklin D. Roosevelt. Although the Providence Poale Zion maintained the vision of socialism into their members' old age of the 1940s–50s, the dream of great changes in the world passed increasingly to the singular vision of Palestine, not so much for themselves directly (very few Rhode islanders would make *aliyah*—immigration to Israel) as for a world community of Jews.[11]

The 1940s made these tendencies tragically absolute. The Holocaust made Israel a priority, even for many who had always opposed Zionism and continued to be unenthusiastic about Zionism as an ideology. World War II, for American Jews of younger generations, brought a new dimension of Americanization, social life in the army and the G.I. Bill afterward, with the prospect of suburbs and the baby boom just around the corner.

In some larger Jewish districts, like the Bronx, the Holocaust touched off a new urgency for Yiddish teaching; in Rhode Island, the distances students now had to travel and the cost of gasoline to get there proved too much—the Workmen's Circle *shuls* closed in 1946. On the other hand, the outburst of prosperity at the end of the 1940s plunged Americans, remembering the Depression, into a new world of consumerism and mass entertainments. The 1930s vision of a pluralistic America, with communities of different kinds and even different languages adding something decisive to democracy, was pretty much washed away. Every kind of ethnic life suffered culturally, and Jewish life, too. Yiddish lost its Eastern European center, and with Ben Gurion's decision for a monolingual Hebrew culture, its hopes for the foreseeable future in Israel, too.

But there were important gains along with these losses. Here we speak about Jews as individuals, rather than as representatives of Jewish groups in Rhode Island labor and social movements. These individuals grew out of, and represented, the finest traditions of the Jewish social movements in a wider arena.

The first I will discuss briefly is Larry Spitz, without a doubt the most dynamic labor leader of the industrial union movement in Rhode Island. From a South Providence background in the Depression, he found his way to New York where he observed the International Ladies Garment Workers Local 22, which had at the time the most extensive social and cultural program of any union in the United States. Relocating himself in Woonsocket, which he had quite accidentally toured in a union theater company for the labor play, *Waiting for Lefty,* he discovered the Independent Textile Union, a mostly French-Canadian organization that had led dramatic strikes in that city but had not yet stabilized itself.

In a short time, Spitz became the secretary general, the thinker, the speaker, and the leader of the first successful industrial union of textile workers in Rhode Island, and one of the most successful in any city in the nation. Through his leadership, the ITU developed a model program of comprehensive unionization, improvement of working conditions and wages, and also extensive cultural and educational programs, health care, and even cooperative housing. After service in World War II, Spitz returned to Providence, where he became sub-director of the steelworkers union.

Here again, but in a wider arena, he made the steelworkers a center for progressive unionism and social programs. Through his leadership, social-minded labor leaders joined with the Catholic diocese and Jewish leaders such as Irving Fain to push through programs such as open housing and to launch Rhode Island Group Health Association as a health plan for workers and the poor. Spitz also led the fight against corruption in unions and the corrupt use of business influence to distort the state's economic development. In these ways, Larry Spitz blazed the way for other Jewish leaders of Rhode Island trade unions from the 1950s to the 1960s, including Nat Kushner of the Retail Workers, Milton Bronstein of the American Federation of State, County, and Municipal Employees (AFSCME), Morton Miller of the Hotel and Restaurant workers, among others.[12]

From the 1930s to the 1960s, it almost seemed as if Jewish influence on Rhode Island labor was limited to leadership, but not because of the absence of Jewish employees. It was just that unionization had to catch up with the white-collar and professional worker, son or daughter of the tailor, the retail clerk and small businessman. The best single example is the high school teacher, historically undervalued and underpaid until unionization in the 1960s and 1970s began to add dignity and better pay, upgrading the profession. William Bernstein, president of the Coventry Teachers Union, stated that out of approximately 10,000 high school teachers in the state, at least 1,500 are Jews.

There is still another important sense, a sense still broader, of Jews and Rhode Island labor. Those Workmen's Circle and Poale Zion branches did not see the society they dreamed of creating in America actually come into being. But they saw, and supported, the rise of a New Deal coalition that brought the most democracy Rhode Island had seen in all its history. That coalition, supporting Governor T. F. Green, was an ethnic and working people's coalition foremost; it survived for almost two generations.[13]

Julius Michaelson, whose political career was foreshortened by the disintegration of that old alliance and by the emergence of a more conservative era in Rhode Island politics, may be seen as the last of that school, the last of the children of Jewish immigrants whose parents belonged to workingmen's benefit associations. But the story, as I have indicated, is not finished. We have another era before us, and the political questions of justice, peace, education, and all the others remain unanswered. What role will labor play in them, and what role will newer generations of Jews play in them within Rhode Island?

NOTES

1. *Providence Journal*, June 13, 1896.

2. The best discussion of this strike period is in Paul Buhle, "Italian-American Radicals and the Labor Movement, 1905–1930," *Radical History Review* 17 (spring 1977).

3. The standard source remains Sh. Sacks, *Di Geshikhte fun Arbeiter Ring* (New York: Arbeiter Ring, 1925), two volumes. There are, however, few direct mentions of Providence. Other citations of Providence Jewish labor (i.e., socialist) activity can be found scattered in Yiddish radical newspapers such as *Di Arbeiter Tseitung* and *Di Yiddish Kempfer*.

4. "Italian-American Radicals," op. cit. The ILGWU, in bitter hostility to the Industrial Workers of the World, joined employers and the *Providence Journal* in appealing to Jewish tailors to abandon the strike and return to work.

5. "The Garment Workers Strike," *Labor Advocate* (Providence), April 6, 1913.

6. See *The Jewelry Workers Monthly Bulletin* (New York), for 1917–1918, especially "Help to Win the Strike at Ostby and Barton's Shop, Providence, R.I.," May, 1917. *Report of the Commissioner of Labor . . . 1916–1919* (Providence, 1920), 179–83.

7. Beryl Segal Interview, 1977 (by Paul Buhle), Oral History of the American Left, Tamiment Library, New York University; duplicate in Rhode Island Jewish Historical Association library.

8. Chaya (Irene) Segal Interview, 1987 (by Paul Buhle), Oral History of the American Left, Tamiment Library; duplicate in Rhode Island Jewish Historical Association library.

9. See Paul Buhle, "Jews and American Communism: The Cultural Question," *Radical History Review* 23 (Spring 1980). His volume, *Marxism in the U.S.* (London: Verso, 1987), also has an extended reinterpretation of Jewish radical history in the U.S., based upon Yiddish sources and several hundred interviews with veterans of various causes.

10. David Kolodoff Interview (by Paul Buhle), Rhode Island Labor Oral History Project, Rhode Island Historical Society. Kolodoff, secretary of the Jewish People's Fraternal Order, has been most gracious and helpful.

11. Judith E. Smith, *Family Connections: A History of Italian and Jewish Immigrant Lives in Providence, Rhode Island, 1900–1940* (Albany: State University of New York Press, 1985), especially Chapter Two, "A Family Culture of Work." The *Pesach Blott* (later retitled in English, the *Providence Passover Journal*) is an extraordinary and evidently little-known source of Labor Zionist history, including some local

history. See, for instance, A. Boyman, "Letter to a Friend," in the 1938 number, describing the problems in maintaining Jewish fraternal activities. "He Created the Third Seder: A Tribute to Alter Boyman," *Histadrut Foto News*, March 1966, describes Boyman's (and Providence's) historic role in this tradition.

12. The Lawrence Spitz Papers, Rhode Island Historical Society, are the best source for this story. See also Buhle's *Working Lives: An Oral History of Rhode Island Labor* (Providence: Rhode Island Historical Society, 1987), especially Chapter Four, "Entering the Postindustrial Age, 1941–1960."

13. On the 1934 strike, see James Findlay, "The Great Textile Strike of 1934: Illuminating Rhode Island History in the Thirties," *Rhode Island History*, Vol. 42 (February 1983).

Jewish Farmers in Rhode Island

ELEANOR F. HORVITZ & GERALDINE S. FOSTER

INTRODUCTION

As we look at the history of the Jews in Rhode Island, the words *farm* and *farmer* seldom appear. The immigrants and their descendants generally chose occupations and professions other than agriculture even when they settled in suburban or rural areas. A closer study indicates that a small number of Jews—less than ten families that we know of—did try their hand at farming in Rhode Island. The earliest known to us was Abraham Shoshansky in 1889 in Foster. A family member said of him that each year he raised an excellent crop of rocks.[1]

In Czarist Russia and in other parts of Eastern Europe, most Jews lived in the *shtetlach* and, where permitted, in the towns and cities of the Pale of Settlement. During the early years of the nineteenth century the Czar initiated a movement to settle Jews on the land within the Pale and beyond. The process accelerated as the population expanded and the Russian economy deteriorated. Many Jews found themselves forced out of their traditional occupations. As a result, by the middle of that century, a goodly segment of the unemployed had turned to agriculture, particularly dairy or truck farming. They could thus earn a living on a small plot of land they either owned—or more likely—rented. Jewish farming settlements were found in parts of the Ukraine and White Russia, as well as in Poland, Galicia (Austria), and areas of Romania.[2]

Some of those opting for a life on the farm in Rhode Island, therefore, had already had farming experience in Europe which enabled them to succeed in their new homeland.

BARON MAURICE DE HIRSCH AND JEWISH AGRICULTURAL SOCIETY

Baron de Hirsch (1831–1896) was the scion of a family of Jewish court bankers in Germany. His wife, Clara Bischoffsheim (1833–1899), was the daughter of a senator in the German parliament and a partner in a prominent banking house. As a result of pioneering ventures in railroads and in industry, he amassed a great personal fortune.[3]

Through his travels to Turkey on behalf of his business interests, Baron de Hirsch became aware of the deplorable situations of oriental Jews, and in co-operation with the Alliance Israelite Universelle he established schools, many of them trade schools. By the 1880s, he turned his attention to the miserable social and economic conditions of the Jews of Eastern Europe. He established and funded two organizations designed to aid in the mass emigration of Jews from Eastern Europe and their resettlement in South America, the United States, and Canada: The Jewish Colonization

Excerpted from *Rhode Island Jewish Historical Notes*, Volume 10, Number 4 (November 1990): 442–478.

Association (ICA) for South American resettlement and the Baron de Hirsch Fund for North American resettlement.

A subsidiary of the Baron de Hirsch Fund, the Jewish Agricultural (and Industrial) Aid Society, was chartered in New York in 1900 to teach Eastern European Jewish immigrants how to farm "as free farmers on their own soil."[4] The society encouraged the formation of cooperatives, but its services were available to individuals as well. Among these services were aid in locating a farm, generally an abandoned one; Yiddish speaking agents and specialists who traveled throughout a region, for example, New England, New Jersey, and New York, to advise on crops and modern techniques; *The Jewish Farmer*, a Yiddish-English language monthly; and loans on generous terms for seed, machinery, livestock, or help in difficult times. Through the aegis of the Jewish Agricultural Society, a number of families resettled in Rhode Island.

THE GOLDMAN FARM

The origin of the present Greylawn Farms and Greylawn Foods and its distribution and warehouse centers can be traced to Samuel Goldman, who emigrated from Russia to Rhode Island. According to Sanford Goldman, his son,[5] he started a poultry business which he named the South End Live Poultry Market (1900) on Gay Street. His home and business at that time were in North Providence, but he later moved to Providence and lived on Charles Street. Samuel had six children: two sons, Frank and Sanford, and four daughters. Samuel died when Sanford was only 16.

In 1935, Frank Goldman bought a few acres of land on what was called the Greylawn plat in Warwick. On the land was a large chicken coop. Sanford joined him on the farm where they raised chickens and produced eggs. They also raised goats and sold goats' milk. Sanford raised a steer which they slaughtered for their own use. Vegetables were planted, and during the harvest season the children had a stand outside the farm where they sold some of the vegetables, but most of the produce was for their own use.

Sanford worked on the farm until he retired in 1985. He and his brother did not really consider themselves farmers but operators of an urban poultry business.

THE SKLUT FARM

In 1910 William and Pearl Sklut purchased a two-tenement house on 76 Sabra Street in Cranston.[6] Mr. Sklut converted that house to a one-family farm house with the first floor as the family's living quarters. The second floor was converted to a synagogue.

During the early teens of the twentieth century a number of Jewish families lived in the Cranston area. The closest synagogue was in the Willard Avenue district of South Providence, which in the pre-automobile era was a considerable distance away. Thus Mr. Sklut's area for worship filled a definite need. He had brought a Torah with him from Europe. He made a small *bima*. Tables and benches were placed around the room. An area in back of this large room was set aside for women. During the High Holidays the Jewish families gathered in this room. Although Mr. Sklut was well versed in Hebrew, a rabbi was hired to conduct the service.

Mr. Sklut's venture into farming was rather brief and a largely unsuccessful interlude in his business career as a tailor. According to his two daughters, he had no farming background. William Sklut left the family in Russia to seek his fortune in the United States. After he was established, he sent for his wife, children, and his wife's mother.

He had operated a small tailor shop in Olneyville. His brother-in-law, David Gerson, moved to Cranston where he purchased a farm, just one block from the Sklut home. In the interim William had an accident to one eye, resulting in the loss of sight. Persuaded by David Gerson, he gave up his tailoring business and invested in three cows to start his own dairy business. There was a barn on the property for the cows and a great deal of open space in the sparsely settled area for grazing.

On the Sklut property there was also a large open lot, but the family did not use this for farming. Instead they would picnic in the area, setting up a large table and chairs when the weather was clement. The oldest sister helped milk the cows. As the youngest children, Stella and Zelda's role was to watch over the cows in the nearby pastures where they grazed.

Stella did not recall how the milk was processed and marketed, but she remembered that is was her job to bring milk to a Hirschfield family who had a little grocery store in their home. Mrs. Sklut died in 1943, Mr. Sklut in 1957. Stella, who inherited the home, sold it in 1965. William Sklut had been a dairy farmer for only about five years, probably from 1915 to 1920.

THE FEINMAN FARMS

Joseph Feinman was different from the other Jewish farmers in this study, who were one-farm owners, in that he owned or rented a number of farms.[7] Unlike some Jews who became farmers with no experience in poultry or cattle raising, Joseph Feinman was the son of a cattle dealer in Russia. By the age of twelve Joseph had learned the trade of butcher.

Joseph was the only son of seven children, all born in Russia. Two older sisters emigrated to the United States and settled in the Newport area. He joined his sisters, living with one who was married to a baker. His first job was with a man who was called a provisioner (supplier of food). He traveled with him, helped with the slaughtering, and visited several different farms as they bought and sold cattle.

Joseph's first farm in the early 1920s was leased in the Wakefield area. During that period cows were milked by hand and horses pulled the tractors. He transported the milk himself to an East Greenwich dairy. He also leased a farm in Perryille. In the periods between farming, Joseph Feinman worked as a butcher in Newport and Providence.

The first farm he purchased was at Mackerel Cove in Jamestown. It was a 194-year-old farm of 103 acres. There were two houses on the farm, which had been in use since the American Revolution. Milk from the cows was transported by truck and then by ferry for sale to the dairies. Corn was raised for fodder, and sweet corn and green beans were raised for sale for human consumption. Eventually he sold the farm to a wealthy couple who restored the original farmhouse. The last farm Joseph Feinman owned was in Portsmouth, purchased in the late 1940s. This was basically a dairy farm, with milk stored in tanks to be picked up by Hood's Dairy. This farm was sold to developers for house lots in the 1960s.

Joseph's wife, Tillie, died in 1973, and Joseph Feinman in 1980.

Before Charles Fradin came to this country, he had already acquired a great deal of experience in agriculture. According to his daughter-in-law, Dorothy Fradin,[8] he had been a manager of a large farm belonging to a *poretz* in Russia. Charles and Bella Fradin first farmed in South Providence for a short time and then moved to the Hughesdale section of Cranston. There they established the Tobey Farm Dairy. Milk produced there was sold on a route through South Providence.

Their son, Hyman Fradin, went to a one-room schoolhouse where he was the only boy in his graduating class. Dorothy Fradin recalled his descriptions of how ice was cut from the pond on their property each winter and stored for refrigeration.

GARELICK FARMS

Soon after their arrival from Russia around 1900, the Garelick family had settled in Woonsocket. Israel Garelick started in the cattle business as a very young man with one cow. His daughter, Elinor Garelick Zelkind, stated: He would walk from one farm to another, going from Woonsocket to Bellingham, Massachusetts. He sold the first cow, bought another, and continued until he had enough money to buy a pickup truck. Then he could expand his business.

In 1931 Israel and Max Garelick purchased a farm in Franklin, Massachusetts, from the Ray family.[9] According to Elinor Garelick Zelkind, originally it was more like a gentleman's farm, an estate rather than a working farm. Her father and uncle had bought a "location," an excellent site for business interests—buying and selling cattle and producing milk. Max Garelick was the "inside man," supervising the daily operations of the dairy farm while Israel Garelick would travel, often as far as Vermont and New York, buying and selling cattle.

According to a history of Garelick Farms published in the company newsletter, at one point (probably before 1947) the Garelick brothers "maintained a herd of almost one thousand cows, grazing and milking them at five different farm locations." At first they sold the milk to others in the dairy business who had processing plants. When they could no longer find a large company to buy their milk, they decided to open their own plant. In 1947, the company was incorporated and headed by Israel Garelick.

The two Garelick brothers married two sisters from Boston. After the purchase of the farm "they lived together separately" in the mansion that was part of the original estate, each family occupying one floor. Mrs. Zelkind was one of five children (four girls and one boy); there were also four cousins. "In lieu of privacy we had the affection and warmth and security of growing up in an extended family. If I did not like what my mother was making for dinner, I would eat at my aunt's house upstairs. She made things considered indigenous to the country, like root beer and doughnuts."

From time to time, relatives came to work at the Garelick farm, and they lived in apartments in the wings of the huge main house. There were also apartments on another part of the property for farm workers and their families, and a boardinghouse for those who were single. A woman was hired to take care of their meals and the farm workers' cleaning and laundry as well.

The girls were not allowed to milk the cows or do agricultural chores. However, Mrs. Zelkind worked in the office. Her brother Daniel worked in the fields. Even while a student at Harvard he continued to bale hay, handle cows, and participate in the workings of the farm.

Israel Garelick enjoyed his work very much. He was involved in the buying and selling of cattle; he also knew a great deal about animal husbandry. Mrs. Zelkind remembers her father going off early in the morning to cattle auctions; she also recalls his assisting at the birth of calves and ministering to sick cows. Because of the nature of his work, he kept irregular hours, but at whatever hour he came home, Mrs. Zelkind said, her mother had dinner waiting for him.

COHN FARM

Hyman Cohn came to the United States about the time of World War I. He was a "commuting farmer," in the words of his daughter, Marcia Cohn Cohen.[10] He lived in Providence and traveled the eighteen miles to Lafayette in the town of North Kingstown, where he owned about sixty-five acres of land on which he kept up to one hundred head of cattle. Most were milk cows whose produce was sold to Hood's Dairy. A foreman and hired hands lived on the farm and took care of the animals as well as the planting and harvesting of the corn and hay. In addition, there was a special pasture in Saunderstown where dry cows were kept. Although Mr. Cohn did not visit the farm every day, he spoke with the foreman every morning (except *Shabbat*) to discuss what needed to be done and what had been done. He regularly traveled throughout Rhode Island and the northern New England states buying and selling cattle.

Marcia Cohen described her father's schedule. He rose at 4:00 A.M. and left home by 5:00 A.M. to begin his day's work. On those days when he planned to spend more time on the farm than on the road, he made a number of stops at other farms along the way to check their herds, perhaps to do some business, and would not arrive in Lafayette before about 1:00 P.M. But on Fridays he was home well before sundown in order to go to synagogue and properly usher in *Shabbat*.

All week long, Marcia Cohen recalled, her father wore overalls and a work shirt. On *Shabbat*, however, he dressed in a dark suit and white shirt. His neighbors in Providence called him the banker of Lancaster Street. On *Shabbat* morning, he was neither farmer nor banker but an Orthodox Jew walking to the synagogue to pray.

Mr. Cohn regularly brought cattle to the slaughterhouse in Brighton, Massachusetts. On Tuesday nights, Marcia Cohen recounted, he would come home after dark and park his truck in the driveway on Dana Street, behind the family house on Lancaster Street. What most of the neighbors did not know was that there were usually three to four cows in the back of the parked truck. Mr. Cohn would leave for Brighton very early in the morning while it was still dark. Since cows "moo" and become active only when there is light, the secret remained safe, and those who knew did not object.

The Cohn family did not live on the family farm in Lafayette, but they almost became summer residents. A house was built at a distance from the barns.

Mr. Cohn had a prize bull, a huge animal, who was his pet, trained to respond to his commands. Mrs. Cohn, however, was afraid of him. The bull, who had free run of the farm, would stand outside the house and watch the family eat breakfast, making Mrs.

Cohn rather uneasy. Then, one morning she came into the kitchen and went over to the sink. There, poking its head into the open window was the bull, all 2,500 pounds of him, his nose ring gleaming in the sunlight. Mrs. Cohn immediately packed their bags and never lived on the farm again.

FARM VISITORS

Before television, before organized recreation, and before the individual activities of a mobile society, families spent their Sundays and holidays together. A favorite pastime was a visit to the country and to a farm. Dr. Irving Beck recalled,[11] "going into the country for fresh air and the raw eggs."

The Beck family, among others, held picnics on a spacious stretch of land, Lubofsky's Farm, at 187 Pleasant Street in Cranston. Actually it was not a farm at all but a large piece of land with a grove on Spectacle Pond, ideal for picnics. Not only individual families but also groups of families and organizations held their outings on this land. It was a chance for *landsleit* to play and to discuss pertinent issues.

Another group of visitors to the farms rented rooms from the families. Some did their own cooking; others came as boarders and were served their meals.

Lillian Horvitz Levitt[12] spent several summers as a child with her mother and brother on a farm in Seekonk, Massachusetts, owned by the Klein family, who rented rooms in their home. Her mother cooked in the common kitchen. For a city girl this was her first exposure to chickens and cows and eating fresh vegetables such as corn and peas right from the gardens. Mr. Horvitz stayed in the city to work, but on weekends Mr. Klein, who commuted from his window-washing business in South Providence, brought Mr. Horvitz to spend the weekend on the farm. The accommodations, Lillian Levitt recalled, were rather primitive and had outhouse facilities.

At the same time that the Horvitz family was vacationing at Klein's Farm in Seekonk, Pearl Finkelstein Braude, together with her mother, father, sister, and brother, were also "roomers" at the farm.[13] Their accommodations were different from those occupied by the Horvitz family; the Finklesteins rented cabins on the farm property. Thus, some Jewish-owned farms provided recreation and vacation facilities to urban, hard-working immigrant families.

THE FARMER'S WIFE

For the early Jewish farmers, farming was more than a livelihood. It was a way of life in which all the members of the family participated. The men worked in the fields and with the livestock; perhaps there was also a milk, egg, or vegetable delivery route as an outlet for the produce. Children, too, had their chores. On the shoulders of the wife fell the responsibilities for tending the household and caring for the children plus assisting with a variety of tasks about the farm. Often her help and, in some cases, her expertise, made the difference between economic survival or failure.

In the Sklut family, Mrs. Sklut's mother, Dora Benamovitz, had farming experience.[14] According to her granddaughters, Zelda Hittner and Stella Sklut, *Bubbe*, while very young, had worked in the fields in Russia, and she, of all the family, enjoyed gardening. On one of the lots adjacent to their home, she raised vegetables for the family. Her granddaughters remembered with pleasure her tasty cucumbers. It was *Bubbe*, according to grandson Harry Sklut, who supervised the milking of cows, and it was she who ran the household. "She was," he added, "the whole *macher* in the family." It was said with affection and admiration.

Preparing three meals each day for a family and often additional workers consumed a great deal of time and energy for farm women. There were also problems of food storage and preservation. At harvest, time had to be found for canning fruits and vegetables or preparing them in some other fashion for use during the winter seasons. Cooking was not an easy task, since it involved using a coal or wood-burning stove. Yet from the interviews, it is apparent that, despite all the difficulties, delicious meals came out of those kitchens.

By the 1930s, a change had taken place. The newer farms were considered by their owners as places where one earned one's livelihood, not necessarily where the family lived. The farm no longer engaged all the members of the family or depended on women sharing in the physical labor. For example, the Garelick family lived on a farm but was not a farm family. Neither Mrs. Garelick nor her daughters participated in the work of the farm. Although very much occupied with her home and raising five children, Mrs. Garelick could afford the time to pursue her own interests. As an adult she decided to take piano lessons,[15] and she learned to play well. She was a gracious hostess whose home was always open to friends and relatives or for community functions. Mrs. Zelkind told of Sundays when their table was always set for company, because their farm was a pleasant drive from the city. Her mother and aunt did all the cooking for the guests, who could number as many as twenty-five. Mrs. Garelick also took an active role in a number of Jewish organizations.

EDUCATION

Going to school, getting an education, played a major role in the lives of the second generation of the farming families. The Garelick cousins were probably the only Jewish children in their school. According to Elinor Zelkind, the other students respected them because they did well. However, because of the distance they lived from school, they could not walk home with classmates or play with neighborhood children. Instead, they enjoyed their own company and always found something to do by using their imaginations.[16]

The school day was a long one for the cousins. To get to school, they had to be ready early in the morning. Since no school bus was available to them, arrangements were made for an inter-city bus to stop across the road from the farm. Each morning one youngster would keep a lookout and shout, "The bus!" when it approached. At the word, the others came flying out of the house with books and lunches. Because they could not readily come home for the noon meal as all the other students did, they remained in the school building all day and then had to catch a bus again to bring them home. It was all part of the adventure.

IN RETROSPECT

Looking back on their experience of growing up on a farm, almost all those interviewed would have agreed with Harry Halpern when he stated that he was "very grateful for his farm upbringing. . . . It was a nice life" that taught him to be responsible, to work hard, and to see a job through. He continued, "You know a thing has to be done and you do it. You are tied to living things and have to take care of living things."[17]

Elinor Zelkind expressed a regret that her children, who grew up in Woonsocket, did not have the pleasure of living on the farm as she did, of enjoying the pace of life there, of being attuned to the natural world. There was no need for planned activities; there was always something to do—tobogganing in the fields in winter or walking along the top of the farm's stone walls or picking berries. Her children did not do these kinds of things once they had moved to town.[18]

CODA

William Sklut was a dairy farmer for perhaps five years. However, the Skluts remained in the converted two-family house in Cranston after Mr. Sklut opened his tailor shop in Olneyville Square.

Sanford Goldman retired in 1985. The Goldman farm land has been developed into house lots.

The Feinman farm in Portsmouth was sold to real estate developers in the 1960s, according to his daughter Marcia Cohen, when ill health forced him to retire. Although he wished to sell the land as a working farm, no one was interested in the property for that purpose. It was subsequently developed into home sites.

The Garelick farm is now the headquarters for the large and varied business enterprise known as Garelick Farms, Inc.

NOTES
1. Interview with Sarah (Mrs. Joseph) Webber, July 19, 1976.
2. *Encyclopedia Judaica* (Jerusalem: Keter Publishing House. Corrected Edition, Vol. 2, pp. 406–411).
3. Ibid., Vol. 8, p. 506.
4. Ibid., Vol. 10, p. 35.
5. Telephone interview with Sanford Goldman, July 15, 1990.
6. Interview with Zelda Hittner and Stella Sklut, May 10, 1990.
7. Telephone interview with David Feinman, July 2, 1990.
8. Telephone interview with Dorothy Fradin, May 16, 1990.
9. Interview with Elinor Garelick Zelkind, May 31, 1990.
10. Interview with Marcia Cohn Cohen, June 25, 1990.
11. Interview with Dr. Irving A. Beck, March 26, 1990.
12. Interview with Lillian Horvitz Levitt, June 2, 1990.
13. Written reminiscences by Pearl Finklestein Braude, 1990.
14. Hittner and Sklut interview.
15. Zelkind interview.
16. Zelkind interview.
17. Interview with Harry Halpern, August 22, 1990.
18. Zelkind interview.

"The Capman Boys and the Fashionettes," ca. 1920. Thelma Winnerman (bottom left), a Providence native, adopted the stage name "Billie Winn" for this traveling variety act.

Joseph Teller in 1923, the year he opened his market on Lonsdale Avenue in Central Falls.

Hope High School Baseball Team June 1921

Hope High School baseball team, Providence, 1921. Its Jewish members include Fred Abrams (in uniform, back row, far left); Robert Hochberg (in uniform next to him); and Jacob Temkin (seated, far left, suit and tie).

Young Men's Hebrew Association basketball team, Newport, 1923–24. Top row, left to right: J. Mirman, J. Feldman, Benjamin Horowitz, M. Rosen, Morris Dannin, Robert Dannin. Bottom row, left to right: M. Dannin, (?) Rudick, Maurice Katzmann, Sam Lippitt, (?) Rudick. Touro Synagogue.

The Miriam Hospital, Parade Street, Providence, date unknown. "The Miriam" opened in this former apartment building in 1925. While caring for patients of all denominations, the hospital served kosher food, welcomed Yiddish speakers, and provided opportunities for Jewish physicians and nurses.

The Jewish Home for the Aged, 191 Orms Street, North End, Providence. Established by the Ladies Hebrew Association, "The Home" opened in 1912 and remained on Orms Street until it moved to Hillside Avenue on the East Side in 1932.

Residents and staff in the front room of The Jewish Home for the Aged, 1925.

A home economics class at the Jewish Community Center, Providence, late 1920s. Organized in 1925, the JCC occupied the former Hebrew Education Institute on Benefit Street. The JCC taught domestic, vocational, and language skills to immigrants and their children.

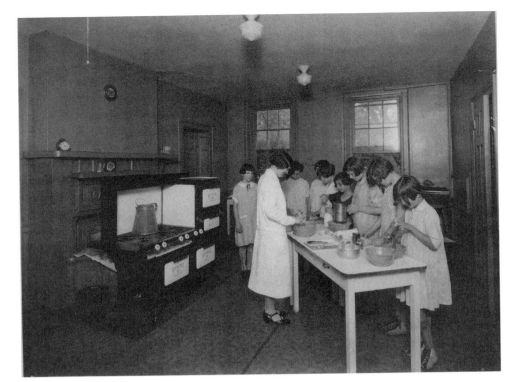

Chaim Weizmann, president of the World Zionist Organization, greeted on the steps of the Rhode Island State House, Providence, probably 1921. Among Rhode Island's Zionist leaders are Dr. Ilie Berger (smiling, with glasses, behind Weizmann's left shoulder) and Alter Boyman (front row, far left).

Officers, captains, and workers of the United Palestine Appeal Committee, Providence, June, 1927.

The third annual donors' luncheon of Senior Hadassah of Pawtucket and Central Falls was held at the Narragansett Hotel, Providence, March 21, 1939. With its kosher kitchen and large ballroom, the Narragansett Hotel, under the supervision of Max Zinn, hosted hundreds of Jewish functions from the 1920s through the 1950s.

Halsband's, 99 Main Street, East Greenwich, 1920. Established in 1912 by John Halsband, this store, like many operated by Jews in small towns across Rhode Island, sold stationery, candies, and cigars.

Benny's, 87 Fountain Street, Providence, 1931. The "everything for your auto store" was founded in 1925 by Benjamin Bromberg and was one of several tire businesses owned and operated by Jews. The Bromberg family still operates dozens of Benny's stores through Rhode Island and nearby Massachusetts.

Adler's Army-Navy Store, 173 Wickenden Street, Providence, 1932. Founded in 1919 by Fred Adler,
the business is now run by the family's third generation as a hardware and home decorating store.

Morris Stepak, a Providence
policeman, date unknown. Stepak
joined the motorcycle division in
1933 and retired as a lieutenant in
1960.

Arrest photographs of a Jewish
larceny suspect, Providence,
February 1932. Under suspicion
for jewelry theft, he was 22 years
old, 5'4", and 154 pounds with
"slender build, brown eyes, and
brown hair." Disposition of the
case is unknown.

Providence College football team, 1930. Left to right: Irving Katznelson '34, Charles McCormick, William McCarthy, Charles Burge, Emmett Shea, and Mark McGovern (captain). Founded by Dominicans in 1917, "PC" accepted Jewish men when many other universities were closed to them and when the State College was too great a distance from Providence for commuters. Providence College Archives.

The American team at the World Jewish Games in Ramat Gan, Palestine, 1935. Swimmer Doris Kelman of Providence is at the far right.

Camp JORI, near Point Judith in Narragansett. Opened in 1937 by the Jewish Orphanage of Rhode Island, the camp served its own children until the orphanage closed in 1942. JORI, which relocated to Wakefield in 2003, is still the only Jewish overnight camp in Rhode Island.

AUGUST-14-1936

Olneyville Hebrew Club, August 14, 1936. Left to right: Leo Miller, Sam Shindler, George Labush, Eddie Wexler, and Sam Kagan.

Ladies Hebrew Free Loan Association, Providence, October 16, 1934. Rhode Island's only Hebrew Free Loan organization governed by and serving women was most active during the Great Depression.

Sisterhood reception of Congregation Ahavath Shalom ("The Howell Street Shul"), Providence, ca. 1940. The congregation was founded in 1896 in the North End. Usually excluded from positions of authority on synagogue boards, women led their own social service and charitable auxiliaries.

Providence Hebrew Day School, founded in 1947, in its original location on Waterman Street. It moved to its present location on Elmgrove Avenue on Providence's East Side, in 1962.

Willard Avenue in South Providence, ca. 1945. A bakery, delicatessen, and kosher meat market reflect the Jewish character of this neighborhood. Removal to outlying towns and suburbs would soon accelerate.

Three generations of the Morris Feinberg family celebrate Shevouth on June 9, 1943 at Morris's home on Creighton Street on Providence's East Side. A samovar, probably brought from Eastern Europe, can be seen on the cupboard.

Members of the Providence chapter of the Workmen's Circle prepare holiday packages for servicemen and women during World War II. Rebecca Kelman Fine, far left. Richard J. Israel Family.

Kosher Dinner To Service Men (All War Casualties) From Naval Hospital Newport, R.I. Given at the Prov. Hebrew Sheltering Society Mar. 11, 1945. Sponsored By Mr. L. Fain

A kosher dinner for sailors, all war casualties from the Newport Naval Hospital, was held at Providence's Hebrew Sheltering Society on March 11, 1945.

Learning and Leisure

Since the colonial era, Jews have participated in the intellectual life of Rhode Island. Shalom Goldman demonstrates, moreover, that the study of Hebrew remained important even during the period when Jews were no longer living here. Jewish culture has not been limited to literary affairs, however. Recreation and music have been integral to physical, emotional, and spiritual well-being.

Several articles in *The Notes* have focused on Jews at Brown University. While Goldman emphasizes the importance of Hebrew in early American learning, he shows its continuing influence at Brown through the early twentieth century.

Karen Lamoree examines Brown when women students were relegated to the Women's College, a forerunner of Pembroke College, which disappeared with coeducation. Lamoree concludes that during the 1920s and 1930s, when many universities limited Jewish enrollment, Brown was somewhat more tolerant, at least toward Jewish women who commuted from home.

Geraldine Foster and Eleanor Horvitz, Brown alumnae, take readers to the beach. This was the first of three vivid articles on Jewish vacation communities along Narragansett Bay. It captures idyllic moments enjoyed by families, especially children, in an era before a monstrous hurricane and World War II.

Finally, George Goodwin spotlights the Newport Folk Festival, one of the most daring and popular cultural events of the postwar era. He shows that although the producer and many performers, songwriters, agents, and record executives were Jews, none were Rhode Islanders. Yet, Jewish and universal themes of peace, freedom, justice, and equality transfixed audiences at the rousing outdoor concerts.

Rho chapter of Alpha Epsilon Pi
Fraternity, Rhode Island State
College (now University of Rhode
Island), Kingston, April 27, 1930.
Although fraternities were
established at the College in 1908,
this Jewish fraternity was not
chartered until 1928.

Christians, Jews, and the Hebrew Language in Rhode Island

SHALOM GOLDMAN

The study of Hebrew in Colonial America and in the early republic was, for the most part, a Protestant endeavor. The few Jews resident in the thirteen colonies (estimates range from 1,000 to 1,500) used Hebrew for liturgical and other religious reasons, but theirs was a Hebrew quite different from the language studied in the early American colleges and in the homes of ministers, professors, and legislators. Colonial American Jews, be they of Sephardic or Ashkenazic extraction, used and studied a rabbinic Hebrew that had a long history of continuous development. Their Protestant counterparts were students of what a modern scholar has dubbed "Divinity School Hebrew, the original language of the text sacred to Protestants, a text created by a 'primitive people,' Jews, who were of little contemporary relevance except for millennial groups." The pedigree of Divinity School Hebrew was then approximately two centuries old. Its origins lie in sixteenth-century German humanism, and in the related Reformation idea of *sola scriptura*, the notion that the text of the Bible was the only source of revealed truth.[1]

It is important to make this distinction between Christian Hebraism and Jewish use of Hebrew. It should serve as a corrective to the prevailing notion that European and American Christian study of Hebrew language and Hebrew texts implied a sympathetic interest in Jews, be they individual Jews or members of an established Jewish community. To the contrary, some Christian Hebraists, in their zeal to demonstrate the "Christian truth" through the study of Hebrew, were most vocal and active in their anti-Judaism. In some cases this took the form of missionary activity; in other cases Hebrew learning was a tool used to expose the alleged iniquities of the Jews. Though valuable, these sharply drawn distinctions between rabbinic Hebrew and divinity school Hebrew, and between Hebraism and philo-Judaism, break down when we examine the case of Hebrew in Rhode Island. Famed for its religious tolerance and distinguished by the presence of a flourishing Jewish community of Newport, Rhode Island offers the student of American Hebraism a model with which to examine the relationship between Christian Hebraism and Jewish cultural and religious life in eighteenth-century America. As I hope to demonstrate, it is a model in which the sharply drawn distinctions mentioned above tend to blur or break down.

In 1626, Roger Williams completed his degree at Pembroke College, Cambridge University. As a student he excelled in the study of languages, an aptitude he demonstrated during his earlier studies at Sutton's Hospital (Charter House), London. At Cambridge in the early seventeenth century, the aspiration of the college tutors was that each of their students would achieve the perfection of the "tri-lingual man," the scholar who could read the Greek, the Latin, and the Hebrew. At Pembroke, "Latin was the language of instruction although students were encouraged to converse in Greek and in Hebrew." Williams mastered the classical languages and proceeded to modern languages. In his

Originally published in *Rhode Island Jewish Historical Notes*, Volume 11, Number 3 (November 1993): 344–353.

careers as teacher, writer, polemicist, and legislator, Williams often called upon his knowledge of the classical and modern languages to illustrate a point. In his later years he was considered "well versed in five languages besides his own: French, Dutch, Latin, Greek and Hebrew."

Williams spent an additional two years at Cambridge preparing for the ministry and in 1631 embarked on his voyage to America. In the colonies, despite the hardships that he endured, he continued his language and textual studies. His facility with languages enabled him to quickly gain facility in some of the American Indian languages. "My desire is that I may intent at what I long after, the Native's Soul, a constant, zealous desire to dive into the native language so burned in me that God pleased give me a painful, patient spirit to lodge with them in their filthy smoke holes even while I live at Plymouth and Salem, to gain their tongue."

There is a striking similarity in Williams's approach to Indian languages and the Christian Hebraist approach to Hebrew as the Jewish language. Williams sees the Indian language as a window into "the Indian soul" intended as a tool for preaching the gospel; Christian Hebraists often saw knowledge of Hebrew as a tool to be utilized in arguments with the Jews and in convincing the Jews of the Christian truth.

On a 1643 trip to England, made for the purpose of seeking an English charter for Rhode Island, Williams wrote *A Key into the Language of America*: "It established Mr. Williams as a scholar, linguist, Indian authority, and foremost English missionary. The members of Parliament were so favorably impressed that this pamphlet had great influence in their granting of three charters in 1644." In *A Key to the Language of America*, Williams implies that there is validity to what is now dubbed the "Jewish-Indian Theory," a notion that the Natives of the Americas were descended from the lost tribes of Israel and that, therefore, the languages of the Native Americans had affinities with Hebrew, Aramaic, and other Near Eastern languages.

Williams, in a letter to Thomas Thorogood, author of *Jews in America or Probabilities That the Americans are of That Race* (London, 1650), observed cultural affinities between the Indians of his day and the biblical Jews. Among these observations: "The Indians separate menstruating women in a little wigwam as the Jews separate themselves under such circumstance," and that the Indians believe in a God above who made heaven and earth.

It seems that on a trip to England, Williams availed himself of the opportunity to study his beloved learned languages. From the winter of 1652 to the summer of 1654, he was resident in England. This was the most turbulent period in English political and ecclesiastical history, and Williams took the opportunity to express himself forcefully on the issues of the day. He was an advocate of voluntarism as against the power of the established church, and he advocated the adoption in England of those very principles on which Rhode Island was founded: "Absolute voluntarism in religion or no state church of any kind."

Especially stimulating for Williams were his frequent meetings with the poet John Milton, whom Cromwell had appointed "Secretary for the Foreign Tongues" to the Council of State which replaced the monarch. No doubt some matters of state were discussed at the Williams-Milton meetings, but most of their time together was devoted to what we would now call a "language exchange." Milton, then in the first years of his blindness, gave Williams the opportunity to practice speaking in Hebrew, Greek, Latin, and French, and in exchange, Williams taught Milton some Dutch. On this same trip to England, Williams wrote forcefully to advocate the readmission of the Jews to England

and he put his ideas on Jewish rights into practice when he later admitted Jews as full citizens of Rhode Island.[2]

Though the leap made by modern authors from Hebraism to philo-Semitism is often too easily made, in Williams's case it would seem that the leap is justified. His abiding interest in the biblical languages and his advocacy of the admission of the Jews to England set the stage for the admission of Jews to Rhode Island. Williams thus set the tone for Rhode Island's cultural and religious future; the ideological function of Hebrew in Williams's thought was later manifested in Rhode Island cultural life.

Cultural institutions which developed in eighteenth-century Rhode Island, among them Newport's Redwood Library and Brown University, demonstrated an unusual connection between Hebraism and the Jewish community. The Jews of Rhode Island played a role in the formation and growth of these institutions. This is in marked contrast to Massachusetts, whose cultural institutions were purely Protestant, al-

The headstone of Martha Moravia is found in Newport's Jewish cemetery. The daughter of Moses Seixas, she died on July 12, 1787 (26 Tamuz 5547). The inscription was incised in Hebrew, transliterated Hebrew, and English by the prominent Newport carver, John Stevens III.

though Jewish and Hebrew terminology is often used to describe them. Cotton Mather's description of Cambridge, Massachusetts, as *Kiryat Sefer* (city of a book, Hebrew) and of Harvard College and other schools as the *Batei Midrash* (houses of study, Hebrew) of the Commonwealth are playful linguistic borrowings from the Hebrew. No Jewish connection or affiliation is implied. To the contrary, in Mather's thought Jewish learning was now supplanted by Christian study of the sacred languages and texts. We have to distinguish between Hebraism as appropriations, which we see very clearly in the work of Cotton Mather, and Christian Hebraism as empathic identification with Jewish life and texts, which manifested itself in Williams's work and subsequent Rhode Island history.[3]

This is not to say that Williams, in his liberalism, did not hope for the ultimate conversion of the Jews, but rather, he saw this, and the fulfillment of other eschatological predictions, as something in the distant future. As Arthur Hertzberg has noted, Williams has argued that the only way to achieve the ultimate triumph of Christianity was to create a civil society in which Christianity would be taught but not forced.[4] Our earlier observation that Christian Hebraism and philo-Judaism are not to be confused still stands, but it is an observation that needs to be further refined. Williams, though hoping for the ultimate conversion of the Jews, argued for their readmission into England and only a few years later enabled the Jews to settle in Rhode Island. Their conversion would come at the end of time, and not through human agency. Williams's thoughts on Jewish rights in a Christian society are summed up in response to the readmission controversy in England:

> I humbly conceive it to be the *Duty of the Civil Magistrate* to break down that superstitious *wall of separation* (as to Civil things) between us Gentiles and the Jews, and freely (without this asking) to make way for their free and peaceable Habitation amongst us.
>
> As other *nations*, so this especially, and the *Kings* thereof have had just cause to fear, that the *unchristian oppressions, incivilities* and *inhumanities* of this *Nation* against the *Jews*, have cried to *Heaven* against this *Nation* and the *Kings* and *Princes* of it.
>
> What horrible *oppressions* and horrible *slaughters* have the *Jews* suffered from the *Kings* and peoples of this Nation, in the Reigns of *Henry* 2, *K. John, Richard* 1 and *Edward* 1. Concerning which not only we, but the *Jews* themselves keep Chronicles.[5]

In the eighteenth century we find a similar tension in the life and work of Ezra Stiles, pastor of the First Congregational Church of Newport. Resident in Newport for twenty-three years (1755–1778), Stiles evinced a lifelong interest in Hebrew and the Jews. In Stiles's case, this was not an occasional, though significant, interest as it was with Williams. It was not an interest dictated by political issues or questions of civil rights, but rather, it was a grand lifelong obsession. As G. A. Kohut pointed out at the beginning of the [twentieth] century (in his *Ezra Stiles and the Jews*) both Stiles's diary and correspondence were replete with references to matters Jewish and Hebraic. Arthur Chiel, in his important work on Stiles at Yale, has analyzed Stiles's ambivalence towards the Jews: "Ezra Stiles kept an open mind throughout his lifetime, allowing knowledge and ideas to flow freely through it. And although there was undoubtedly an ambivalence in his attitude to the Jews he had not allowed the scales of judgment to tip over into the fixed antipathetic stance on his part."[6] Stiles's continuing study of Hebraic sources, which extended throughout his lifetime, his intimate association with Newport Jews and their visiting rabbis, his very profound feelings for Rabbi Carigal, all of these had their cumulatively positive effect upon him. For Stiles the conversionist issue was always there. Ultimately, as he saw it, the Jews would see the Christian truth. But his hostility to the Jews did not triumph over his interest in them.

The attitudes of Roger Williams and Ezra Stiles contributed towards the formation of a "Rhode Island Hebraism," a configuration of (1) interest in Jewish texts and Jewish language (2) ambivalence towards the Jews (3) toleration of and interest in Jewish community. This created the climate for an interesting cultural ferment: a ferment we can see operating in the relationship between Stiles, the Jews of Newport, and the visiting rabbis of Europe and Palestine. This then sets the stage for the inclusion of Jewish elements in the formation and early history of two Rhode Island cultural institutions: the Redwood Library of Newport and Rhode Island College (later Brown University).

When the Redwood Library opened in 1750, prominent members of the Newport community contributed books from their personal libraries or contributed toward the purchase of books to be shipped to London. It is significant that, at the time of the opening of the library, members of the Newport Jewish community donated a copy of Leusden's edition of the *Biblia Hebraica* (a very sumptuous printing of the Hebrew Bible) and a copy of David Nieto's *Matteh Dan.* This was not a random choice. Nieto, *Haham* (1654–1728) of the Spanish and Portuguese Synagogue in London, wrote *Matteh Dan* in response to attacks by Christians on the rabbinic tradition, and the treatise is a defense of rabbinic tradition against these attacks. The donation of the book can be viewed as an act of resistance to conversionist pressure, and it demonstrated a willingness to stake a claim for the Jewish community's integrity and individuality. A quarter century later, some of the elders of the Jewish community, among them Jacob Rodriquez Rivera, Aaron Lopez, and Isaac Stark, together with Ezra Stiles, donated a copy of Montano's Bible in Hebrew, Aramaic, Greek and Latin in eight volumes. According to Robert Behra, curator of special collections at the Redwood Library, "Ezra Stiles was made an honorary member of the Library in 1755 and in 1756 he was elected librarian, a post he held until 1764. And he was again elected librarian between 1768 and 1777."[7]

At Rhode Island College, founded in 1764, we see an early flowering of Hebrew studies. Some of the founders of the College were educated at the College of New Jersey (Princeton) where Hebrew was taught to the freshman class. In contrast to Hebrew studies at the other American colleges (Hebrew was taught at the nine American colleges founded before the American Revolution), the history of Hebrew at Rhode Island College is linked to the Jewish community.

In this early period there were no Jewish students at Brown, just as there were no Jewish students at any of the American colleges. The Jewish community of Newport dispersed after the Revolution; before the Revolution they sent no students to the College. There were offers from the Jewish community to pay for a professor of Hebrew. Some have suggested that the offer was to pay for a Jewish professor of Hebrew, although I don't see this directly reflected in the correspondence. There is a letter to the Trustees, within a few years of the founding of the College, from a South Carolina Jewish merchant, Moses Lindo. Lindo inquired whether Jews would be admitted to the new Baptist college. The Trustees assured him that they would accept Jewish students. It is clear from the College records that the trustees expected donations to pour in as a result of this liberalism. Mr. Lindo, for his part, seemed satisfied to donate his original £20 and did not explore this matter further. But here too, in these early years of Brown, we have an unusual interaction between members of the Newport Jewish community, the founders of Rhode Island College, and Jewish merchants elsewhere in the Colonies. Though nominally a Baptist school, the college was open to all students, and it was not doctrinal in its teaching. And this in line with Rhode Island's reputation for liberalism in matters of religion must have attracted interest from a merchant such as Lindo.

Brown's first class studied Hebrew; their teacher was David Howell (1747–1824). Instruction was from the text of the Hebrew Bible. The College Library had a manuscript volume entitled *A New and Short Method to Learn the Hebrew Tongue without the Assistance of a Master* by one Adam Joseph Rheiner, and the college's first catalogue also lists a Hebrew dictionary.[8] As the method used in learned languages was recitation, that is, the students would prepare the text on their own and read it to the professor in class, the grammar and the dictionary were the only teaching aids at their disposal.

Professor Howell, who taught the "learned languages," was also a mathematician and a linguist. One must remember that in the early American colleges, there were very few professors, and each professor was obligated to teach a number of subjects. Howell, who later became Rhode Island's most eminent jurist and a member of the Continental Congress, imbued his students with a love of the biblical texts in its original languages. In the diary of one of these students, Solomon Drowne, we can see Howell's influence at work. Drowne, who kept a diary throughout his college career, tended to use Latin when he was making notes about his women friends in Newport. Matters of the heart, it seems, had to be recorded in a classical, private language. Drowne was smitten with one Emilia, a young woman of Providence, and for a number of years his diary is full of references to her, all written in Latin. But when Solomon Drowne reflects on matters religious or spiritual it is not Latin that he turns to, but Hebrew. In March 1773 Drowne wrote, "Arouse my soul, look around you, consider how and what thou art. But what can I do in this grace divine? Assist me. I trust I am sincere when I say as in Psalm 130, verse 5, 'I wait for the lord, my soul does wait, and in his word do I hope.' [The biblical quotation is in Hebrew with no English translation provided.] I return my most sincere thanks on my kind preserver for thy protection of me this last year . . . Make I beseech thee my gratitude adequate to the favors I have received."[9]

A few lines later Drowne writes, "I humbly entreat thee, my Creator, thy may arrive with light knowledge my Redeemer, Jesus the Son of thy love." So it is clear that for Drowne Hebrew is reserved for the theological-spiritual sphere; Latin is for the conjugal-erotic—and it is equally clear that the reference here is Christian, with no reference to matters Jewish.

Professor Howell and James Manning, founder of the College, were, for long periods, the only two faculty members at the new college. Howell continued as professor until 1779 when, owing to the Revolutionary War, all College exercises were temporarily suspended.

While Solomon Drowne's use of Hebrew is noteworthy, it is not unheard of in Colonial American circles. We know of other seventeenth- and eighteenth-century American Protestant students of the learned languages who peppered their diaries with words and phrases in Hebrew, Greek, and Latin. What is remarkable is that later in his diary Drowne recorded his impressions of the Jewish community of Newport and he did so in a humorous and at the same time respectful manner.

It seems that Solomon Drowne and his Rhode Island College classmates would slip out of their residences and try to find some diversion (and more interesting food) in town. If they were caught, the penalties were quite stiff, especially if they were caught drinking liquor. On October 6, 1773, they went out on the town, intending to use a visit to the synagogue as both a diversion and an excuse for not returning to their boarding house for dinner. To their surprise the Jews were not eating that day (they did not realize they had picked Yom Kippur as a day to visit.) But the opportunity to actually linger at the synagogue, or at least to tell their professor that they had, provided them with a fine excuse when they appeared at their house in the middle of the night, and professed to a complete lack of appetite.

At Rhode Island College, as at other colonial American colleges, commencement orations were delivered both in English and in the "learned languages." At the Commencements of 1776 and again in 1778, one of the orations was delivered in Hebrew. (Some college documents of the Revolutionary period have been lost, but college records confirm the existence of Hebrew orations on at least these two occasions.) Similarly, at Dartmouth, we find Hebrew orations delivered over a period of almost forty years—from the founding of the college until the death of Professor Smith in 1809. At Harvard this tradition was intact until 1817. As with the study of Hebrew generally, the tradition had no relation to matters Jewish. The orations were the usual exhortations to good behavior and were Christian in character. The one interesting exception, an 1800 rabbinic Hebrew oration at Columbia, proves the rule.[10]

After a hiatus of about thirty years, Hebrew was again offered at Brown in the early 1830s. In this period, the teacher of Hebrew was Horatio Hackett (1808–1875), who was later to be the pre-eminent teacher of the New Testament in the United States. Hackett left Brown in 1839. He moved to Newton Theological Seminary, where he taught for thirty years. He was a pioneer in forging a relationship between Hebraic studies and Holy Land exploration. In 1852, he traveled to the Levant. The resulting volume, *Illustrations of Scripture: Suggested by a Tour Through the Holy Land*, was a serious contribution to the growing American literature on the topic.

But the story of Hebrew in Rhode Island and its relationship to the Jewish community did not end with the decline of the Newport community. John Hay, who was educated at Brown and seems to have studied Hebrew there, became the Secretary of State at the beginning of the twentieth century. Hay took a lively interest in the welfare of European Jews, most particularly in the situation of the Jews of Romania. This community had long been an object of concern for American Jews. The first U.S. Counsel to Romania—from 1871 to 1875—was Benjamin Peixotto of the colonial American Sephardic family. He was concerned with the situation of the Jews of that country, as were many of his co-religionists in the United States. As a result, the Order of B'nai Brith in America contributed to the building of the first U.S. Consulate in Bucharest. When Hay became Secretary of State he expressed his concern for the Jews of Romania in a letter to a midwestern rabbi. This letter is written in Hebrew and indicates that Hay was trained in Hebrew at Brown.[11] A pattern emerges here in which the intellectual legacy of eighteenth-century America, in the form of Hebrew instruction at Brown, influenced American diplomatic affairs in the early twentieth century.

In 1896 Brown granted an honorary degree to Oscar Straus. Brother of Isidor and Nathan Straus of department store fame, Oscar became a scholar and United States diplomat. He was an advocate for Jewish rights, and, as U.S. diplomatic representative in Constantinople, he supported the Jews of Palestine in their struggle against Ottoman restrictions of Jewish emigration and land purchase. Straus wrote a biography of Roger Williams, an act of homage in which he seemed to indicate that he owed his advancement in the American educational and diplomatic worlds to the liberalism exemplified in Williams's attitude toward the Jews. He named his son, who also became a public figure, Roger Williams Straus. Thus in an almost novelistic fashion the circle is now completed. In the 1650s Roger Williams advocated the readmission of the Jews to England and enabled the Jews to settle in Newport, Rhode Island. In the late 1890s Oscar Straus, recipient of a Brown honorary degree and biographer of Roger Williams, used his influence to help persecuted Jews in Europe. And in 1902 John Hay, American Secretary of State, expressed, in Hebrew, his concern for the persecuted Jews of Romania. Both Hay and Straus were the products of a unique tradition of Rhode Island Hebraism, a tradition which still lives and thrives at Rhode Island's cultural institutions.

NOTES

1. For the cultural background of American Hebraism see the introduction to Shalom Goldman, ed., *Hebrew and the Bible in America* (Hanover and London: University Press of New England, 1993). The description of Divinity School Hebrew is from Arnold Band in Alan Mintz, ed., *Hebrew in America* (Detroit: Wayne State University Press, 1993).

2. On Roger Williams and matters Hebraic see R. B. Morris, "The Jewish Interests of Roger Williams," in *The American Hebrew*, Dec. 9, 1921.

3. On Mather and the Jews see Louis Feldman, "The Influence of Josephus on Cotton Mather's *Biblia Americana*: A Study in Ambiguity," in Goldman, *Hebrew and the Bible in America*, pp. 122–155.

4. A. Hertzberg, "The New England Puritans and the Jews," in Goldman, *Hebrew and the Bible in America*, pp. 105–121.

5. O. Straus, *Roger Williams, the Pioneer of Religious Liberty*, 1894.

6. Arthur A. Chiel, "Ezra Stiles and the Jews: A Study in Ambivalence," in Goldman, *Hebrew and the Bible in America*, pp. 156–167.

7. Correspondence with R. Behra of the Redwood Library, 1992.

8. Correspondence with M. Mitchell, Archivist, Brown University, 1992.

9. *The Diary of Solomon Drowne, 1770–1774* (Brown University Library).

10. On these orations see Dr. Goldman's recent paper, "Two American Hebrew Orations" in *Hebrew Annual Review*, 1991.

11. Jay's Hebrew letter is reproduced in Moshe Davis, ed., *With Eyes Toward Zion: Scholars Colloquium on America–Holy Land Studies* (New York: Arno Press, 1977).

"Why Not a Jewish Girl?"

The Jewish Experience at Pembroke College in Brown University

The February 21, 1896, issue of *The Organ*, published by Congregation Sons of Israel and David, reported in its women's column that Brown University's newly established Women's College was raising money for its endowment and urged the women of the congregation to contribute to the cause of educating the women of Rhode Island. The first Jewish woman to graduate from Brown was probably Clara Gomberg, class of 1897, who listed her address as 214 Benefit Street, Providence. The number of Jewish women increased slowly but steadily over the years. By 1942, however, the dean of the college, by then known as Pembroke College in Brown University, noted an admissions policy "... We accept all [Jewish women] who come to us from Providence, and enough others to make a proper proportion in each dormitory. We reject each year now 100 to 150 Jewish applicants, nearly all of whom are fully prepared." Clearly, between 1891 and 1942 attitudes and policies became less hospitable to the admission of Jewish women.[1]

These changes reflect not only the issue of anti-Semitism, but issues of class, race, ethnicity and gender, common to many institutions of higher education. The admission of women to Brown was engendered by nearly twenty years of community agitation by educator Sarah E. Doyle, the Rhode Island Women's Club, the *Providence Journal*, and parents of prospective students. Brown was established in 1764 by Baptists and although the president was required to be a Baptist minister until 1926, its charter stated that "into this liberal and catholic institution shall never be admitted any religious tests." The people of Rhode Island viewed the school, which had educated so many of their sons, with proprietary interest. The admission of women was promoted successfully, therefore, by appeals to state pride and progressive sensibilities of justice.

Brown began admitting women in 1891 under its coordinate system with a mandate to provide a collegiate education for the women of Rhode Island, particularly those who were unable to afford to attend school away from home. Southeastern New England women responded immediately to this long-awaited opportunity, and the enrollment went from seven in the first year to approximately two hundred by 1900. The coordinate system was designed to provide women with the advantages of both a university faculty and curriculum and those of a small women's college. The women were admitted and graduated under the same requirements, but lower-level classes were usually segregated by gender. The women's classes took place in storefront buildings on Benefit Street until Pembroke Hall was built in 1897 by the women of the Rhode Island Society for the Collegiate Education of Women.[2]

This early period, under President E. Benjamin Andrews, a passionate and charismatic advocate of women's education, was one in which all students academically prepared to begin collegiate study were admitted. Under the coordinate system the college maintained a separate admissions office. The only information required of

Excerpted from *Rhode Island Jewish Historical Notes*, Volume 10, Number 2 (November 1998): 122–140.

The Banjo and Guitar Club of the Women's College in Brown University, 1896. Clara Gomberg, back row right, was the first Jewish graduate of the college in 1897. The college's name was later changed to Pembroke and eventually merged with Brown.

applicants was name, address, parents' name, and high school grades. While many of the applicants were known to Andrews or the college's dean, Louis Snow, interviews were not required.[3]

The vast majority of students came from the lower-middle and middle socio-economic classes and were local residents, living with family or friends. No dormitory accommodations were available until 1900, so non-commuting students lived in approved boarding houses. Many women were special students who arranged their classes around work schedules and were past the standard age for college enrollment. The only college-wide organization for women was the Christian Association, then an auxiliary of the national, evangelical Young Women's Christian Association.

The women were aware of the need to prove their capability to doubters. The general atmosphere encouraged the women to band together and to excel, to the extent that the women invariably outperformed the men scholastically. Women were equated with that group of people who, in the college man's eye, did not approach college from the "proper" perspective. Typically, the college man, interested in sports and fraternity life above all else, viewed scholastic achievers as belonging to either immigrant groups, the lower classes, or the religious. The men[4] vilified women as "greasy grinds," although acceptance of individual women was the norm. Jewish women, therefore, if they conformed to the stereotype of the Jewish student—studious, serious of purpose, not wealthy, urban—would have conformed to the norm for almost all of the women at Brown University in the 1890s.

To some extent the atmosphere of studiousness, casual social life, and haphazard discipline would change when Andrews's successor, William H. P. Faunce, hired Dr. Anne Emery because he felt it improper for a man to be dean of a women's college. Emery was not only a classical scholar and creator of a separate "life together" for the women at the University of Wisconsin, but also was most definitely a gracious "lady."

Faunce hired her, in part, to help him enforce middle-class mores and codes of behavior. Ladylike behavior was prescribed and taught, particularly by Emery in her role as housemother of the new dormitory on Benefit Street and by the Student Government Association established under her aegis. The women were encouraged to form their own separate clubs, and sororities boomed. Unsurprisingly, the flourishing of exclusiveness resulted in bigotry. By 1903 the Catholic women, most of whom were Irish, had formed a separate sorority, Beta Delta Phi—undoubtedly a result of discrimination and not a desire for their own club. The membership of Jewish women in sororities, however, varied, with some in Alpha Beta (the most prestigious) or Zeta Zeta Zeta, while others were not members of any Greek letter society.[5]

Emery and Faunce were successful in their design of the separate "life together" for the women at a time when coeducation was coming under attack, particularly by private universities. Emery resigned in 1905 and was replaced by Lida Shaw King. Under King, the first known overt discrimination occurred against Blacks.

In June 1917 the Executive Committee of the college reported that:

It was the opinion of the committee that the admission of young women of the colored race to classes was not objectionable; that for the present their admission to college dormitories was undesirable, also that colored young women from a distance should not be encouraged to enter the college.[6]

This policy statement was a compromise between desires to limit Black enrollment and the college's mandate to educate Rhode Island women. King, nonetheless, continued to allow a steady increase in Jewish enrollment during her tenure, and in 1922 the Christian Association reported that there were twenty Jewish women at Brown,[7] making an average of five per class or approximately 5 percent of the total. In contrast only 2.9 percent of Brown men were Jewish.[8]

Faunce replaced King in 1922 with Dr. Margaret Shove Morriss. Morriss is an enigmatic figure, and her personal feelings on race, class, and ethnicity are unclear. Although she befriended individual Jewish women, the architecture for the Jewish quota system was created during her tenure. Morriss was dean of the college from 1922 to 1950. Under her guidance Pembroke went from a regional school to one of national reputation. As the college became increasingly popular among applicants, it could be more selective. Under Morriss's tenure it became more difficult for women to obtain admission to Pembroke than it was for men to be admitted to Brown. Morriss accomplished Pembroke's transformation during a period when the existence of women's higher education was under attack.

The 1920s were a period in which issues of race, ethnicity, class, and gender intensified and became ever more interrelated. The presence of women on campus again became an issue of class. Jews became associated with the immigrant urban poor at many colleges, paralleling societal trends, and quotas reflective of academic nativism were enacted at Harvard and Yale, for example.[9] In this context of class, racial, and sexual prejudice, it became increasingly important for women at Pembroke to adhere to white, middle-class, Protestant codes of behavior. The equation of Jews with immigrant behavior resulted in discrimination at other institutions of higher learning,[10] and it is possible that it also affected Pembroke.

Although admissions standards were tightened during the early to mid-1920s, Pembroke continued to admit the academically qualified without making distinctions for class, race, and religion with the exception of Black resident students. While most other colleges seem to have enacted Jewish quotas in the 1920s,[11] evidence of concentrated efforts to homogenize the racial and ethnic background of the student body do not appear in Pembroke application forms until the mid-1930s. Eva A. Mooar, a Radcliffe graduate, was hired as a dean of admissions in 1927, and it was under her administration that the admissions process changed,[12] although we do not know at whose instigation. The application form, the first screening device of all admissions offices, was not amended until 1936.[13] In that year the form began to ask prospects for the first time to self-report their race, and, significantly for Blacks and Jews, proposed living arrangements.

An interview summary sheet in each student's file included sections for an interviewer's evaluation of the applicant's "personal appearance, family background, mental equipment, traits, financial, activities, interests, goal." The acquisition of this subjective descriptive information occurred prior to student self-reporting or preparatory school correspondence in the admission process. Through the 1930s and early 1940s Mooar and/or her assistants commented most often on the characteristics of women who might be Jewish. Examples of Mooar's attempts at characterizing students include[14]

Student '33: "Can't tell whether Jewish or not."
Student '36: "Father has wavy hair, few front teeth and a marked accent. Says they speak German at home. Germans or Jews? Are blonde, so probably the former."
Student '37: "Pretty girl with a southern accent."
Student '44: "Not especially Jewish features."
Student '44: "Tall, dark, rather attractive recognizable Jewish features."
Student '48: "Looks Italian."
Student '48: "Splendid all-around type, Exactly what we want."
Student '49: "Nice, 'money' people."

It is in 1942 that the first discussion of the Jewish quota appears in the records of Pembroke's Advisory Committee. Dean Morriss was a national leader in championing the war effort and the causes for which the United States was fighting, which makes her quota policies all the more ironic.

Also revealing is a 1943 report from Eva Mooar which groups Jewish women with financial aid applicants and public school students, i.e., with a "lower" class of students.[15]

Throughout the 1920s and 1930s the Executive Committee heard complaints about dormitory room shortage, and in 1940 the deanery reported that applications for admissions had doubled since 1930.[16] It seems clear from these reports that Jewish women were applying to colleges in numbers admissions offices considered higher than in previous years. Goldstein and Goldscheider's 1967 study of Providence Jews revealed that Jewish women over the age of twenty-five were more than three times as likely to have attended college as non-Jewish Providence women. They also reported little significant difference between the median years of schooling for Jewish women from 25–44 and 45–64 years of age, except for those who were third-generation Americans (which were not part of the Pembroke cohort, in general).[17] We can assume, therefore, that the women entering Brown in the period under discussion, largely the 45–64 age group in 1967, were more likely to attend college than their non-Jewish contemporaries and were also more likely to enter college than those 65 and over. Unlike other schools, Pembroke seems to have treated its Jewish students equally once an applicant passed through the admissions gauntlet.

The experience of Jewish women after matriculation as reported in oral history interviews was a positive one. Most do not mention any awareness of quotas or remember any subtle or overt discrimination. A typical comment was that of Celia Ernstof Adler '25, "I was the only Jewish girl in my class but I never felt anything anti-Semitic."[18] Much of the cohort were Russian immigrants, or as time went on, the children of Russian immigrants, while others were of Polish or German extraction. This distribution was typical of Providence's Jewish population, of which three-quarters of its naturalized citizens in 1906 were of Russian or Polish nationality.[19]

For Zelda Fisher Gourse '36,[20] the highlight of her four years was her election to the position of Student Government Association president. She was the first Jewish woman to attain that position, and her background was a factor in the election. The 1934–1935 election, Zelda recalls, was different from previous elections. "It had been a closed circuit, but that year . . . it was open to the whole student body and you could campaign. I remember a Jewish girl in my class who came from Boise, Idaho, who went to my best friend and said I'd never make it. My best friend, who's not Jewish, didn't think I'd make it either." While the votes were counted, Zelda said, "I got into my car and drove to the Seekonk River and said to myself, 'Dear God, Why not a Jewish girl?' The girl running against me was not Jewish . . . that night my mother said I had a phone call, I'd been elected!"

Zelda also played a leading role in her sophomore class masque and was senior speaker on Ivy Day, the ritual culminating four years at Pembroke. In an ironic twist, the first Jewish president of student government was also a member of the Christian Association board. Zelda characterized the Christian Association, however, as "not necessarily Christian, [but rather] it was a religious organization to further understanding." Although a list of places of worship in the student handbook in the 1930s did not include synagogues, as early as 1933 the Freshmen Council advised its successors to change the traditional date of the freshman reception as it fell on a Jewish holiday.[21] It seems clear that the acceptance of which Morriss spoke did indeed exist on the women's campus. This level of tolerance and freedom from racism on the part of students was not true for the men, if one only glances through some of their publications.[22]

The period of discrimination against the admission of resident Jewish women followed early efforts to ban Black women from the dormitories and occurred during a time in the 1930s when the world was becoming aware of German actions against Jews. Clearly the Pembroke administration failed to see any connection between their policies and anti-Semitism. No reasons were ever given for these policies, but factors included anti-Semitism, issues of class, and the creation of a "proper" residential atmosphere which precluded Black women entirely and limited Jewish residency. These problems do not seem to have intruded, however, on the Jewish women's experiences after admission.

One of Morriss's accomplishments was changing Pembroke from a commuter school to a residential college. Because admission for resident Jews was more selective than for resident non-Jews, it was the marginal student who suffered. This selectivity was particularly problematic prior to the 1947 erection of the large dormitory, Andrews Hall. Morriss had been stymied in her efforts to create a residential college by the lack of modern dormitory facilities, and many students were housed in haphazard fashion. The influx of students during World War II under Morriss's accelerated curriculum exacerbated the housing problem, particularly since the Pembroke dormitories were used for navy personnel. After 1947, however, adequate housing became available.

Concurrently with the erection of new dormitory facilities came a national trend against discrimination, particularly discrimination toward Jews in higher education. In Mooar's 1940–1949 Admissions "Policy" file are two items that demonstrate that she was aware of this trend and its possible consequences. One letter was from an alumna with a different perspective.

The alumna, class of 1900, reported in 1944 to Mooar that an acquaintance had told her that a Pembroke student left the college because there were too many Jews there. The alumna went on, "I'm wondering if this statement is correct." Mooar's reply carefully straddled the fence:

> The number of Jewish girls at Pembroke College is not large. Generally we are very proud of our Jewish students for they are unusually fine girls, and their contribution to the life of the College is good. Occasionally, of course, we have a student who is disappointing, but that is true of the Christian girls also.[23]

Mooar complimented the Jewish women while maintaining limitations on their numbers. Discrimination would become less acceptable as World War II went on.

The Pembroke deanery was also made aware of possible financial repercussions from the quota system. These considerations, combined, perhaps, with available housing, probably engendered a more sensitive approach to Jewish admissions. The admission of and assignment of dormitory space to Blacks would await the 1950s–60s for amelioration.

The history of Jewish admissions to Pembroke College in Brown University, then, can be broken down into at least three distinct periods. The early period, 1891–1927, was characterized by open admissions to the academically qualified. The students were highly motivated, and the women's community was one in which scholastic achievement and seriousness of purpose were considered the goal and the norm, respectively. The Women's College was largely a commuter school of urban lower-middle and middle-class students. Attempts were made to inculcate ladylike behavior in the students, especially in the backlash against the supposed connection between coeducation and lower-class colleges. Black women were forbidden from residing in the dormitories, although local women continued to be admitted.

Dean Morriss's entrance in 1922 marks the beginning of Pembroke's emergence as a college attracting a national student body. This coincided with increasing national emphasis on non-scholastic endeavors and behaviors, increasing admissions of women from upper classes, an influx of Jews into colleges and universities, and a trend toward prejudice. Into this context came reports of quotas at other Ivy League institutions, and it should not be surprising, therefore, to see Pembroke following the lead of its Ivy League peers as it attempted to become ever more competitive on a national basis. It should be noted, however, that the quotas were only for residential students. Pembroke still operated under a mandate to educate the women of Rhode Island. Commuting Jewish women were accepted on the same basis as their non-Jewish peers. The best residential Jewish students were also judged on the same basis as the other applicants. It was the marginal residential Jewish woman who was less likely to be accepted than a marginal non-Jewish woman. After matriculation, Jewish women seem to have been fully accepted by the students and faculty, according to our oral histories. Jewish women were aware of other members of their cohort, but underestimated their number and may have felt isolated.

The era following World War II seems to show some evidence of a growing economic and social sensitivity to the potential problems of quotas. Further research will no doubt show that the quota system was dropped shortly thereafter. Morriss retired in 1950 and Mooar followed shortly thereafter.

NOTES

1. *The Organ*, Congregation Sons of Israel and David, v. 1. (5), February 21, 1896, p. 1. Pembroke College Dean Margaret Shove Morriss in the Pembroke College Advisory Committee minutes, August 5, 1942, p. 1.

2. For information on the history of Pembroke College see, for example: Linda M. Eisenmann, *Women at Brown, 1891–1930, "Academically Identical, But Socially Quite Distinct,"* Harvard University, Graduate School of Education, Doctoral Dissertation, 1987, and Grace E. Hawk, *Pembroke College in Brown University 1891–1966* (Providence: Brown University, 1966).

3. Pembroke College—Admissions Record Book

4. For information on relations between the sexes at Brown and Pembroke see, for example: Karen M. Lamoree, "An Historic Relationship: Pembroke Women and Brown Men," address given March 8, 1987, Brown University, and Mary Ann Miller, "'The Pembroke Problem'": Defining Women's Place in Brown University, 1891–1928," Brown University Honors Thesis, 1985, American Civilization Department.

5. Louise Bauer and William T. Hastings, eds., *Historical Catalogue of Brown University, 1764–1934* (Providence: Brown University, 1934); *Liber Brunensis*, 1893–1908; and *Brun Mael*, 1909–1914.

6. Pembroke College—Executive Committee—Meeting Minutes, June 15, 1917.

7. Lucille Rogers, general secretary, Christian Association, Women's College in Brown University, December 7, 1922, to Rabbi Samuel M. Gup of Providence in Topic file Pembroke College—Students, Jewish. The figure given in 1922 should not be used as an indication for subsequent years because an unscientific survey of the class composition seems to indicate growth. Increases in this period would have been tied to the Rhode Island Jewish population, as the college remained largely local through the end of the 1920s.

8. Marcia Graham Synott, *The Half-Opened Door: Discrimination and Admissions at Harvard, Yale, and Princeton, 1900–1970* (Westport, Conn.: Greenwood Press, 1979), p. 16. An example of the connection between minority groups is Brown Dean Otis Randall's proposal to discuss limitation of Jewish and Black men at the 1920 meeting of the Association of Academic Officers of New England. In Synott, p. 16.

9. See, for example: Dan A. Oren, *Joining the Club: Jews and Yale, 1900–1970* (New Haven, Conn.: Yale University, 1985), pp. 38ff., and Synott, especially pp. xvii and 17.

10. Barnard's Dean Virginia Gildersleeve, for example, wrote, "Many of our Jewish students have been charming and creative human beings . . . on the other hand . . . the intense ambition of the Jews for education has brought to college girls from a lower social level than that of most of the non-Jewish students." In Lynn D. Gordon, "Annie Nathan Meyer and Barnard College: Mission and Identity in Women's Higher Education, 1889–1950," *History of Education Quarterly*, vol. 26 (4), Winter 1986, p. 516.

11. Synott, p. 17.

12. The information following in the text was retrieved from the Pembroke deanery's individual student files. Concerns for privacy do not allow us to identify the individual file from which a quotation is drawn.

13. Radcliffe seems to have instituted a limitations program around 1936 also. The percentage of Jewish freshwomen there increased from 17.7% in 1934–35, to a high of 24.8% in 1936–37, to a new low of 16.5% in 1937–38. In Barbara Miller Solomon, *In the Company of Educated Women* (New Haven, Conn.: Yale University, 1985), p. 144. It seems probable that the number of Jewish women would have continued to increase if a limitations program was not at work.

14. No identification of identity is possible for reasons of privacy, but the quotations come from the Pembroke deanery's individual student files.

15. Morriss in the Pembroke College Advisory Committee meeting minutes, April 6, 1943, p. 1.

16. Pembroke College—Executive Committee meeting minutes, October 29, 1940.

17. Sidney Goldstein and Calvin Goldschneider, *Jewish Americans: Three Generations in a Jewish Community* (Englewood Cliffs, N.J.: Prentice-Hall, Inc., 1968), pp. 65-71.

18. Celia Ernstof Adler, Interview by Judith Weiss Cohen, September 24, 1988.

19. Information on the students' backgrounds comes from oral history interviews and the Pembroke deanery's individual student files. Information on Providence's Jewish community is available from, for example, Goldstein and Goldschneider, p. 26, and Geraldine S. Foster, *The Jews in Rhode Island: A Brief History* (Rhode Island Ethnic Heritage Commission and Rhode Island Publications Society, 1985).

20. Zelda Fisher Gourse, Interview by Sasha Oster, May 13, 1988.

21. Pembroke College—Student Handbooks, 1933, 1935 and Pembroke College—Freshman Council Notebook, 1933.

22. See, for example, the *Brown Jug*.

23. Margaret N. Goodwin, August 15, 1944, to Pembroke College Registrar. Eva A. Mooar, associate dean and director of admission at Pembroke College to Margaret N. Goodwin, August 21, 1944, in Pembroke College—Admissions Office—Policies, 1940-1949 file. Note that Mooar does not mention scholastic achievements, but rather the Jewish students' "contribution to the life of the college." This is an example of the confusion over the purposes of women's education and the increasing importance of being an "all-around girl," rather than an intellectual or "grind."

Summers Along Upper Narragansett Bay, 1910–1938

GERALDINE S. FOSTER & ELEANOR F. HORVITZ

For Eastern European Jews who came to Rhode Island between 1880 and 1914, the idea of a summer vacation home or, for that matter, a vacation, was something quite new, beyond their personal experience. Wealthy people in the old country went to a *dacha* (villa), a resort by the sea, or to the countryside, where they could enjoy the pleasures of life away from the summer heat of the city. However, for the impoverished, oppressed residents of the *shtetl*, or crowded urban quarters, activities of this sort were not possible. Here in their new home in America, Eastern European Jews learned what earlier Jewish immigrants had already experienced. A vacation home by the sea in Rhode Island was feasible even for those of modest means. Such a home might be a summer rental of the most primitive sort, but a vacation lay within reach, often just a trolley ride away.

The upper reaches of Narragansett Bay, to the east and west of Providence, sheltered many seaside communities where families could spend hot months in the healthy environment of the shore. Although these communities lacked the cachet and the broad sandy beaches of Narragansett or Newport, they had their own attractions. If the beaches were narrow and stony, if seaweed accumulated at the shore and jellyfish often washed ashore, still the water was clear and not too deep even at high tide. Children could swim and play with a minimum of supervision. All those interviewed for this survey used the same word, *safe*, in describing not only the swimming areas but the entire locale as well.

Those who first summered at these seaside communities along the upper Bay are not fully known. Available information suggests that in the years following World War I Jews came to these shore areas in increasing numbers. Their presence must have been small.

BEGINNINGS

One summer around 1910, Ethel Reffkin Gertsacov accepted the invitation of Bess Finberg to visit with her children for a few weeks at Old Buttonwoods.[1] On the last day of her stay, she decided to take a walk along the shore while awaiting the van to take her family and their goods back to their city home. Since the tide was low, she could cross Baker's Creek, which she did for the first time. From its farther bank, she saw Nausauket; it fascinated her. There beside the water she found two houses, one a large farmhouse. So taken was she with the place that she knocked on the door to ask the owner if he rented rooms. The reply, according to Ethel's daughter, Irma Gertsacov Slavit, was "Well, we never have, and we don't have a stove." Unfazed, she responded, "Then I'll buy a [kerosene] stove." They concluded their arrangements, and, when the van arrived in Buttonwoods to bring her and her children home, Mrs. Gertsacov sent word to her

Excerpted from *Rhode Island Jewish Historical Notes*, Volume 11, Number 1 (November 1991): 14–39.

A day trip by the Jewish Orphanage of Rhode Island to Scarboro Beach in Narragansett, August 1940. Maurice Stollerman, the superintendent, is in top row, second from right.

husband on the unexpected change in plans and then rerouted the movers to Nausau-ket, where the family spent the remainder of the summer and many summers to come. This summer colony soon attracted members of the Gertsacovs' extended family as well as other Jewish families.

On a summer day in 1916, sixteen-year-old Samuel Salk filled a container with an assortment of items from his father's dry goods store at 249 Plain Street, near Willard Avenue in Providence, and boarded a trolley for Oakland Beach. He walked the length of the beach selling his wares. By the end of the day he had sold his entire stock. As a result of his son's successful venture, Hyman Salk rented a store the following year and opened a business there. That was the beginning of the Salk enterprises in Oakland Beach and Conimicut.[2]

Jews began to buy and build summer homes in Barrington, in the East Bay, around 1922. The Fales estate was purchased by Herman Rosner, Dr. Ilie Berger, Abraham Weiner, and Philip Weinstein. According to Evelyn Berger Hendel, the Easton estate was purchased by Herman Rosner.[3] According to Eleanor Turoff Radin, Mr. Rosner was instrumental in the development of both properties.[4] Jack Temkin characterized the Barrington summer colony as "a microcosm of the state." "There was the Providence plat, the Pawtucket plat, the Central Falls plat, and the Woonsocket plat," because Jews from those communities tended to purchase property (or in rare instances rented) near their city neighbors.[5]

LIVING QUARTERS

The summer homes ran the gamut from primitive to magnificent; from very simple cabins on cinder blocks to spacious, shingled houses with full cellars and large porches.

The amenities also ranged from the basic (water pumps, outhouses, ice boxes, and kerosene stoves) to all the comforts of a modern 1920s–style home with indoor plumbing, radio, and phonograph. Refrigerators and gas stoves began to appear in the late 1930s; telephones were in short supply.

Vivian Orodenker Kolodny described her dwelling on Conimicut Point as a small, four-room house with an unfinished interior. One could see the frame of the structure as well as the timbers of the roof through the spaces in the ceiling. Curtains hung over the doorways to bedrooms for a modicum of privacy. An icebox provided refrigeration, while a gas stove served for cooking, with an attached heating unit for keeping the chill out of the rooms when needed.

The Brodsky family did not want a fancy place, according to Anna Brodsky Musen. "The many relatives who came to spend their vacation with us did not mind. The main thing was to enjoy the sun and the beach."[6] The simple life did present its own problems, however. Freda Ernstof Rosenberg described the cottage her parents rented in Longmeadow for seven summers, beginning in 1916. When they first moved in, there was an outhouse to be reckoned with and a kerosene stove. She recalled that the pump had to be primed every evening to have water the next morning.

B. Ruby Winnerman's mother rented a cottage in Riverside along the East Bay. Although the rental of fifty dollars entitled the family to a whole year of occupancy, they spent only the months of school vacation there. The house had no indoor plumbing and no shower. The family improvised a shower by hanging a can with a hole punched in it, then threading the garden hose through the hole. There were no telephones in private homes in their area of Riverside, but there was a phone in a nearby drugstore. On the rare occasions when one might have an urgent call, the druggist or clerk would take the message and give it to whomever was walking by at the time, who in turn would relay it to the proper person.[7]

According to Doris Fain Hirsch, daughter of B. Alfred and Tillie Blacher Fain, the Blacher home at Bay View Avenue and Prospect Street in Oakland Beach was spacious enough to house four families in great comfort.[8] Pearl Burbill Lavine remembered the sleeping quarters on the third floor for maids.[9] "Having twelve people sit down to dinner was nothing," Doris Hirsch stated. The house, purchased in 1921, had porches on three sides. A lawn reached to the bay and a private beach. It was suitable for year-round use, because it had a full cellar and heating system, but was occupied only in the summer. A large barn behind the house served as a garage and was later remodeled to include a shower room and dressing area. Although the house had indoor plumbing, a working pump remained in the yard. Doris Hirsch remembered her grandmother Lena Blacher carefully washing fruit and vegetables under the pump as she prepared meals.

Some Oakland Beach vacationers stayed at the Pleasant View Hotel, where individuals or families could rent rooms for short periods of time or on a seasonal basis.

Jack Temkin recalled that cottages in Barrington were for the most part occupied by their owners, who were middle-class or well-to-do. Interiors were finished, most often with plasterboard, and small front porches were for sitting and socializing. Although the cottages had indoor plumbing and hot water provided by a vulcan heater, most had outside showers for use after a visit to the beach. The reason was pragmatic, said Eleanor Radin.[10] Allowing the water to run freely from an outside shower eased the burden on the individual cesspools to which each house was connected.

Dr. Nathaniel Robinson wrote about the purchase in 1925 or 1926 of a house and adjacent land facing Barrington Beach. His family lived there for five summers. Their house was one of the few in Barrington where rooms were rented out to other summer vacationers. Across the road, the Robinsons also operated a small refreshment stand where they sold soda, hot dogs, ice cream, and candy.[11] Rita Millen stated that the Robinsons also sold milk, bread, and some canned goods, eliminating the need for a trip to the center of town when one ran out of such necessities. In bad weather the stand did not open, but food items were still sold at the "round house," as the Robinson residence was called.

RHYTHMS OF THE SEASON

Memorial Day weekend figured prominently in planning for the season by the sea, especially for property owners. About that time most families went to inspect their homes for possible ravages of winter, to mow the lawns, and to clean away the accumulations of dust and cobwebs. Rita Millen recalled how her family spent the three days at the various tasks. Pillows and mattresses required airing, while windows needed washing. The awnings went up, and the furniture covers came off. Walls and floors were cleaned and mopped. In between came explorations of the beach and visits with others who had come with their parents to "open their houses."

Anna Musen remembered moving day as a "pain in the neck," a *shlep* (drag). Each year her mother would say, "I hate this," but continued the practice for many years. Claire Ernstof's mother also wondered why they were always "shlepping" things down when the house was completely furnished and all they needed were linens and clothes.

Summers on the shores of upper Narragansett Bay were idyllic, according to those interviewed. Freed from school, schedules, and restrictions imposed by city life, young people spent happy days at the beach or exploring the neighborhood. In the words of Anna Musen, they were wonderful times. "I always had playmates. There was always something to do." A field was always available for a ballgame or a porch could be found where youngsters could play card games or just sit and talk. They learned the pleasures of creating their own plays and games; they enjoyed the luxury of minimal adult supervision. Throughout the interviews came the refrain, "Things were different then. Parents did not have to worry about all the dangers."[12]

SUMMER FUN

"We had the freedom to roam in those days," stated Jack Temkin. Freedom to roam meant—for Eleanor Radin and her friends—being able to walk to Maple Avenue in the center of Barrington to buy penny candy or for Rita Millen and her cousins and friends to explore the coastal and inland areas of the town. It also allowed Vivian Kolodny and her friends to ride their bikes to Rocky Point from Riverview without undue parental concern for their well-being. Or Ralph Einstein, with his brother Ted on the handlebars, could ride to Rocky Point from Shawomet or could canvass households, selling *The Saturday Evening Post*.[13]

In Conimicut, children as young as eight and nine years old were able to go to the beach or play in a vacant field or pick wild blueberries, taking care to be home by the time the 6:00 P.M. siren sounded from the firehouse.

Freedom to roam also included—within limits—the bay as well as the land. Each of the Temkin boys kept a boat on the beach in front of their home: Jack a motorboat, Noah a rowboat, and Martin a sailboat, from which they explored the sea around them.

The summer that David and Abraham Horvitz were seven and nine years old, they and their thirteen-year-old uncle decided to build a boat. After studying other craft, they used canvas to cover barrel staves bound with hoops, which they then sealed with tar. After a great deal of work they felt confident enough for the launch. As they guided the boat into shallow water, they were elated that it stayed afloat. A few moments later it sank. It was amazing how a deserted shore suddenly became crowded with spectators watching this catastrophe. Undaunted, the three mariners retrieved their boat and remedied the problem with additional coats of tar. The now seaworthy craft afforded them a summer of pleasure. However, sometime during the winter the boat, which had been stored in the garage of "The Maples," their cottage, was stolen. The Horvitz boys suspected that it was the work of neighborhood boys who caused them trouble because they were Jewish. Sure enough, in the yard of one of the troublemakers they found their boat and retrieved it for another summer of enjoyment. The following year the same thing happened, but this time it was gone.[14]

At Conimicut, Celia Horvitz Zuckerberg enjoyed the company of her young cousin who lived with the family each summer. They had a circle of friends who sunned themselves, swam, played croquet and other outdoor games. To cope with boredom on rainy days, the two cousins started a newspaper called "The Pumpkin Seed," a name inspired by the quantity of pumpkin seeds they consumed that summer. On its pages appeared articles about the fictitious happenings and the latest news of a mythical kingdom they created. They conferred titles on their friends and included them in the news of the realm.[15]

Across the road from the Jewish-owned summer homes on lower Bay Road stood a large, fully furnished but unoccupied house, a magnet for adventurous children. On rainy days Rita Millen, her sister, Selma Halpern, and friends would pack lunches and candy bars, sneak into the house, and spend the time telling ghost stories. The dark, shuttered mansion provided a wonderful backdrop.

On Sundays Doris Fain Hirsch and her family enjoyed a special treat—homemade ice cream. She recalled cranking the handle of the ice cream maker. It was one of their traditions like salmon, peas, and mashed potatoes on the Fourth of July. However, as tasty as the homemade treat was, there was a special pleasure of "forbidden fruit" in buying an ice cream cone. Her grandmother, who was very scrupulous in her observance of *kashrut*, did not consider ice cream kosher and frowned upon its consumption by her family.

Doris Hirsch used to practice her piano lessons daily at the upright piano at the yacht club in Oakland Beach. Although her family were not members, her mother was able to arrange for the practice session, following which Doris would get a treat. Another feature of Doris Hirsch's day was the walk to the post office for the mail, since there was no home delivery. She was always dressed for the occasion, with a starched skirt and Mary Jane shoes.

There was trolley service from Providence to Conimicut Point, but its route was not always convenient for those living along the shores. According to Claire Ernstof, "Everyone hitchhiked because the trolley was some distance away."

The Ernstofs had a Victrola in their living room, a natural magnet for young people at the beach. On Saturdays, when her mother went to work in the family business, Claire, her brother, and their friends had dance parties that were enjoyed by all.

A popular summer activity in Nausauket was quahogging, according to Irma Slavit. The mollusks were also prevalent and popular in Conimicut. Anna Musen told of hunting for them, but her mother did not allow them to be brought into the house because they were not kosher. Instead they were given to an Italian neighbor down the street.

COMPANY

Having company was a fact of life for most of the families by the shore. Jack Temkin felt that his folks thrived on all the company. They had "lots of visitors"—family outings every weekend. Many cousins, from as far as New York, came on vacation.

Beatrice Wattman Miller, a summer resident in Barrington, used to say that if you saw someone walking with a suitcase, they were going to the "Heller Hotel." The Hellers had loads of cousins, including six from Central Falls. Every two weeks two would come down. Cousins from out of state would also visit. Rita Heller Millen and Selma Heller Halpern recall that their house had eight rooms, a porch, and one bathroom. Everyone had to double up, and there were still people sleeping downstairs. All the girls went into the bathroom at one time. The same with the boys. You slept wherever you found a place. Selma slept on two chairs. On Friday afternoons, when Mrs. Heller washed the kitchen floor, children were not allowed in the house. When they came up from the beach for lunch, she handed sandwiches and milk through the open door at the back of the house. The kids ate in the backyard.

"In Conimicut Point we had company who came for the day," Vivian Kolodny recalled. "The house was so small there was no room for overnight company." However, each year her parents would have a party for the members of the Farband (the Jewish Workers Alliance). All the members came out for the day. "It was a great occasion to me," she recalled. "Nothing formal was organized. People brought their own lunches, and they just came to enjoy an outing together. The Farband members impressed me greatly. They were important people in the community, like Alter Boyman."

TRADESMEN

Food shopping was made easier by tradesmen who came into the neighborhoods to sell their wares. Bakers, milkmen, fruit and vegetable vendors, the egg man, and fishmongers regularly made the rounds of the beach areas. At first, kosher meat and other kosher products had to be brought back from Providence or other towns. An order placed early in the day was picked up in the afternoon by a father or a neighbor. B. Ruby Winnerman stated that her mother shopped after work for the products she needed and brought food with her on the trolley. Being strictly observant, she bought only in stores selling kosher food.

It did not take long for the Jewish bakers and grocers to begin regular routes in the shore communities, as more and more customers began spending their summers away from the city. It was a while before kosher butchers began deliveries, however. Eleanor Radin spoke of her uncle David Malin, a grocer, who owned a summer cottage in Barrington. He made it a practice to drive to customers' homes, where he opened the back door of his truck to sell dairy items and canned goods from the miniature store inside.

A most important person in the days before refrigeration was the iceman, who called at any home where his card was displayed in a window. The card also indicated the size of the block requested. "On hot days," Eleanor Radin remembered, "we children would run after the truck and be grateful for any chip of ice he would give us."

During the work week, beach communities were populated mainly by women and children. Men drove off to work early in the morning, leaving their families behind. It was not always an easy commute. Gertrude Fruit Pansey recalled that it took her father an hour to reach his business in Pawtucket from their cottage in Shawomet.[16]

Evenings and weekends were the time for the men to relax. For Vivian Kolodny's father it meant going for a swim—whether the tide was high or low—as soon as he arrived home, and then tending to his vegetable garden. Anna Musen's father also raised vegetables, and he kept chickens as well in order to have fresh eggs.

A father's homecoming was eagerly awaited, particularly by children, who often waited a short distance from home to spot his car. Sometimes kids stood on the running board and hung precariously onto the strut between the open windows for the short distance home.

Alex Rumpler's homecoming to Barrington each evening was happily awaited by his wife and two sons and by the family's pet duck, which Leonard Rumpler had brought home at the close of the school year. "It was," said Mr. Rumpler, "an unusual creature. When I would be coming up Bluff Road, that duck would be at the edge of the road waiting for me. Then he would follow me home." At the end of the summer season, the duck was given to a neighboring farmer, because he could not keep him in Pawtucket.[17]

Another facet following work was the *minyan*. One was held at the Ernstof home in Conimicut, another at the home of Philip Abrams in Barrington. Mr. Abrams had a Torah in his home. Jack Temkin recalled how his grandfather, George Pullman, read the weekly portion on Shabbat mornings.

After dinner it was not difficult to find a poker or a pinochle game. These took place on front porches. In the morning children would crawl under the porches to find coins which had fallen through the slats. "We made out all right," said many interviewees. For the non-card players, there were discussions of current events or political philosophies. Though often heated, they were always friendly.

A few women "went to business" every day. For those who remained at home, a goodly portion of each morning was given over to household chores before going to the beach. Edith Gordon said that swimmers in Shawomet waited until high tide. "Mrs. Harry Norman [Mae] would inform the neighborhood that the tide was in by calling out, 'Everyone come to the beach.'"[18]

Whenever they went to the shore, mothers, particularly those of younger children, came equipped with blanket, beach chair, towels, extra child-sized bathing suits, and, of course, food. Ralph Einstein described the fruit and sandwiches as always being sandy. Women congregated on the shore to chat and to socialize, but mainly to keep watch.

The sense of togetherness extended to all occasions. Neighbors came together for beach parties and cookouts, events involving children and adults. Couples met for informal visits and evenings out. Every Saturday night during the summer, the Rumplers and a group of friends with beach homes in Barrington went to the Warren Inn for dinner and dancing. Others remembered Saturday night bridge clubs that met in various homes.

Yet the needs of the Jewish community in Rhode Island and overseas were never out of mind. Jack Temkin recalled that his father, Charles, and his grandfather, George Pullman, used to go out collecting money each summer in Barrington for the Jewish National Fund. Other collectors were Samuel Michaelson and Abraham Heller.

The women, though, carried on the bulk of fundraising activities. Anna Musen spoke of her mother's close friend, Esther Adler, who each year held a bridge party to benefit Pioneer Women (now *Na'Amat*) for aid to Palestine. Esther and Anna Musen's mother, along with Jessie Gordon and Celia (Mrs. Max) Brown, started early in the summer preparing for the event. They sold tickets and they baked. Esther had at least twenty tables for cards spread out on her lawn. All pitched in to welcome and serve the players. That party constituted *the* social event of the year. There were additional events, however. Leah Michaelson held a fundraising tea at her home in Barrington each year for Providence Hadassah. A bridge party held in Barrington during the summer of 1927 earned $46.50 for the Pawtucket–Central Falls Hadassah.[19] Mrs. Samuel Ernstof annually chaired a major fundraising affair in Conimicut for the benefit of the Jewish Home for the Aged.

CARNIVALS AND FIRECRACKERS

Sunny days were spent out of doors, but what did one do on a rainy day? Or for a change of pace? In several communities the public library provided an alternative to rounds of checkers, lotto, and cards. Going to the movies offered another source of entertainment. Movies were shown several times a week at the Shawomet Chapel; Barrington people went to the theater in Warren. Pearl Lavine recalled the hall in Oakland Beach, where silent films, complete with piano accompaniment, could be enjoyed. The audience sat on wooden benches and stamped their feet when the feature began. Oakland Beach could also boast of a wooden boardwalk next to the yacht club. A bowling alley and a dance hall above the lanes were popular with the "younger set." Another feature was the amusement park, with its "dobby horses," "the whip," and a Ferris wheel.[20]

There were two amusement parks on opposite sides of Narragansett Bay: Crescent Park on the east shore and Rocky Point on the west shore. Giant midways and roller coasters lured residents from nearby summer places. Itinerant carnivals, sometimes sponsored by churches or other organizations, traveled to various shore areas of Warwick.

Fourth of July was a special time at the beach communities. Cookouts, barbecues, and entertaining visitors were the order of the day. Crescent Park and Rocky Point sponsored extravagant fireworks displays. Rockets and flares shot out over the bay, evoking delighted applause from spectators near and far.

Yet it was not uncommon for individuals to shoot off fireworks for the enjoyment of families and neighbors. In Conimicut the fire department made a huge bonfire of railroad ties and scrap wood. This pile of discards rose twelve to fifteen feet. As a child, Robert Kotlen thought the bonfire was at least four stories high. Everyone watched in fascination as the flames crackled and consumed the pile, sending sparks high into the air.

CODA

The devastating hurricane of September 21, 1938 caused extensive damage to Oakland Beach, Conimicut Point, and Shawomet Beach.

Eleanor Turoff Radin remembered experiencing the hurricane when she was a child on Fales Avenue in Barrington. "I was here alone with my mother, Ruth. There were no houses around except for one house up the hill, a small bungalow across the street. At that time all this land was quite barren. My father was in the city with my brother, Lloyd. My mother was holding me in an old wicker rocking chair trying to comfort me. The electricity was off, the telephone service was not working. I can remember seeing the garage go up in the air and disappear. It was a terrifying time."

Though the hurricane of 1938 caused little damage in the Barrington Beach enclave, time and demographics brought change. Of the once thriving summer colony, perhaps only three or four cottages remain as they were.

The busiest years of the Jewish summer colonies along upper Narragansett Bay were during the 1920s and '30s. Irma Gertsacov Slavit noted the demise of Nausauket as a resort when families started sending their children to camp. During the housing shortage after World War II, people who couldn't find affordable houses in the cities bought summer cottages, which they winterized for year-round living. Another factor contributing to the decreased popularity of upper Narragansett Bay communities after World War II was the increased popularity of lower bay communities. Narragansett and Newport became attainable and more fashionable. Thus ended a lively chapter in the history of the Jews in Rhode Island.

NOTES

1. Interview with Irma Gertsacov Slavit, June 12, 1991.
2. Interview with Harold Salk, August 22, 1991.
3. Interview with Evelyn Berger Hendel, June 12, 1991.
4. Interview with Eleanor Turoff Radin, August 2, 1991.
5. Interview with Jack Temkin, June 11, 1991.
6. Interview with Anna Brodsky Musen, August 5, 1991.
7. Interview with B. Ruby Winnerman, July 3, 1991.
8. Interview with Doris Fain Hirsch, August 13, 1991.
9. Interview with Pearl Burbill Lavine, August 23, 1991.
10. Interview with Dora Fain Paster, July 18, 1991.
11. Letter from Dr. Nathan Robinson, Naples, Florida, July 12, 1991.
12. Musen interview.
13. Interview with Ralph Einstein, September 23, 1991.
14. Interview with Dr. Abraham Horvitz, August 15, 1991.
15. Interview with Celia Horvitz Zuckerberg, August 5, 1991.
16. Interview with Gertrude Fruit Pansey, October 2, 1991.
17. Interview with Celia and Alex Rumpler, June 24, 1991.
18. Interview with Edith Sonkin Gordon, September 16, 1991.
19. *Rhode Island Jewish Historical Notes*, Vol. 10, No. 4 (November 1990), p. 505.
20. Lavine interview.

The Newport Folk Festival
A Jewish Perspective

GEORGE M. GOODWIN

A jewel of the North Atlantic, Newport has for centuries symbolized maritime trade, naval power, religious tolerance, and pleasure—especially for the rich and debonair. To such observers as Edith Wharton and John Huston, even its decadence has been alluring. In recent decades, the miniature city on Aquidneck Island has enjoyed wide renown through music. In keeping with its own heterodox traditions, Newport has welcomed sounds from across the seas and around the nation; it has harbored extraordinary creativity. Given their involvement in countless artistic endeavors, it is not surprising to discover that Jews have played a part in that creativity. Yet the story of Jewish involvement in Newport's musical fame is not primarily about Newport's Jewish citizens. Instead, it resides with Jews from elsewhere, who lent their skills, talents, and daring to help create the ambience in which Newport's music flourished.

While Newport's jazz, opera, and chamber festivals deserve studies of their own, this essay focuses on the folk festivals, particularly their early period, from 1959 through 1969. Thanks to a flurry of scholarly studies and reminiscences by key participants, it is possible to look back with some ease and insight; the heady experience of ballads, banjos, bluegrass, and Baez has not been forgotten.[1]

During the early 1950s, Newport was a delightful but sleepy place. In 1953, a few adventurous aristocrats, led by George Warren, a New Yorker, sought to provide greater musical sustenance. Their Newport Music Festival engaged the New York Philharmonic for two outdoor concerts, but due to inclement weather the effort was a resounding flop.

The next step was the introduction of jazz. Some controversy remains over who deserves credit for the idea of a Newport jazz festival. According to Burt Goldblatt, a photographer who attended all the concerts and published a documentary study, credit goes to John Maxon, the director of the Museum of Art at Rhode Island School of Design.[2] Though not himself a jazz fan, he predicted that a summer festival in Newport would be a wild success. Strangely, Maxon never made the effort to attend the concerts, and he left Providence in 1959 to become curator of modern paintings at the Art Institute of Chicago.

Without question, Louis Lorillard and his wife, Elaine, were instrumental in the creation of the jazz festivals. A Newport native, Lorillard was a descendant of Pierre Lorillard, the tobacco tycoon. He was descended from Livingston Beekman, a governor of Rhode Island, and Robert Livingston, a signer of the Declaration of Independence.[3] While serving in Italy during World War II, he met Elaine Guthrie, a jazz aficionado and pianist who eventually claimed credit for the concept of a small summer festival in Newport.

Agreeing to bankroll the first concerts, the Lorillards contributed $20,000. Among sixty-five prominent families who were invited to lend support, only George Warren ac-

Originally published in *Rhode Island Jewish Historical Notes*, Volume 12, Number 4 (November 1998): 484–495.

cepted. When the Jazz Foundation of Newport, Rhode Island, was chartered in April, 1954, Louis Lorillard agreed to serve as its president. Sensing that a professional concert organizer was needed, Elaine turned to George Wein, a Jewish jazz promoter and band-leader working in Boston. As later events demonstrated, this was a fateful decision.[4]

Born in Boston in 1925, Wein, the son of a plastic surgeon, grew up in Newton. By fifteen years of age, he already led his own jazz band. After military service during World War II, he pursued pre-med studies at Boston University and graduated in 1950. He immediately launched a career as both a jazz musician and as a jazz promoter. His Storyville Club opened in Kenmore Square and soon moved to the Copley Square Hotel. The Hotel also became the site of his Mahogany Hall, which showcased his own Dixieland band as well as numerous stars.

When hired by the Lorillards for $1,000, Wein was asked to produce two evenings of outdoor entertainment in July, 1954, at the Newport Casino. Seeking the best talent, he enlisted Ella Fitzgerald, Billie Holiday, Gerry Mulligan, Stan Kenton, and The Modern Jazz Quartet. When thirteen thousand fans attended, an annual concert series seemed only natural, and Newport quickly became home to the outstanding American jazz festival of the late 1950s despite the facts that the town was accessible only by the Jamestown ferry and Mount Hope bridge, had few hotels, motels, or campgrounds, and was reluctant to accommodate Blacks or interracial couples. In 1959, Wein's own marriage to a Black earned his father's disapproval.

Brilliant and egotistical, Wein became one of the century's most successful impresarios. His illustrious Jewish colleagues would include Sol Hurock, David Merrick, Joseph Papp, and Harvey Lichtenstein. Based on the success of Newport, Wein launched jazz festivals in Atlanta, Boston, Buffalo, Chicago, Cincinnati, Detroit, and Pittsburgh. With the addition of festivals in Toronto, Nice, and Tokyo, his Festival Productions, headquartered in New York City, exerted an international influence.

The significance of the early Newport jazz festivals has been gauged, in remarkable personal terms, by Michael Fink, a Providence native.[5] Growing up near North Main Street's Rhode Island Auditorium, he always felt the excitement of live entertainment. While still a student at Classical High (but looking considerably younger), Fink frequented the Celebrity Club, where he heard Sarah Vaughan and Ella Fitzgerald, and he also became acquainted with New York's cellar jazz clubs. While living in Paris for two years, he met other jazz musicians. Consequently, when Fink returned to Rhode Island in 1957 to teach literature at Rhode Island School of Design, he felt that "the world had come to him" during the summer concerts. While seated on the lawn at the festival beneath a starry sky and a glaring moon, he was enraptured. Simultaneously, Fink felt excited, he reports, to be a spectator at the performance of first-rate jazz, a supporter of civil rights, and a witness to Newport's colonial Jewish heritage of discovery and innovation.

Another Jewish native of Rhode Island, James Tobak, grew up in Newport, and thought that his hometown was musically cosmopolitan even if it had only one traffic light. He attended his first jazz concert in 1958, at twelve years of age.[6] Years later, when the folk festivals were in their prime, Tobak hosted many fraternity buddies who came to town. Sleeping on Middletown's Second Beach was the "cool" thing to do. But Tobak's older sister, Helen, scored even more points when she dated Bob Dylan's cousin, who was at Officer Candidate School in Newport.

Despite their extraordinary quality and popularity, the jazz festivals were not yet profitable. By 1959, Wein began searching for a new way to bolster revenues. He and his supporters, who had received a new charter as the American Jazz Festival, thought of attracting a somewhat larger audience through another genre, folk music. Toward the end of the Eisenhower administration, audiences were being captivated by lively and authentic American music. Since early in the century, in fact, folk music had been sought out, recorded, studied, performed, and interpreted—as if it might disappear forever. A small circle of devotees included literature professors, anthropologists, folklorists, enthnomusicologists, archivists, and amateur enthusiasts.

Many specialists believed that folk music still existed in various rural or isolated settings, where self-taught singers, instrumentalists, and dancers perpetuated traditional sounds not only for their personal gratification but for larger, communal needs. Accordingly, talented individuals were willing to forsake professional careers in order to protect their cultural identity and purity: there were important differences separating folk and commercial art. Even without Newport's folk festival, therefore, there would have been a folk music craze. During the late 1950s and early 1960s, it enjoyed widespread appeal, as demonstrated by the long-playing records (monaural at the time, not stereo) that were charted by *Billboard* magazine as the "Top 20 Pop Albums."[7]

The Kingston Trio, for example, enjoyed enormous sales, as did Harry Belafonte, especially his recordings of two concerts at Carnegie Hall. Joan Baez prevailed in 1962 and 1963 as a highly popular entertainer, though she was soon eclipsed by Peter, Paul and Mary, who enjoyed top sales through 1965. Jewish tastes fit this popular trend: in 1963, one of the most beloved albums was Allan Sherman's "My Son, The Folk Singer," a zany parody.

The Newport Folk Festival, under Wein's direction, appealed to this widespread interest. Robert Cantwell, author of *When We Were Good: The Folk Revival*, views the success of the Newport folk concerts in symbolic terms.[8] The concerts, he claims, were not only exceptional events or experiences—"happenings" to use the parlance of that era—but also a trenchant critique of middle-class values in a capitalist society. For Cantwell, Newport also represented a dark and bitter morality play that juxtaposed old age and youth, wealth and modesty, corruption and idealism, past and future.

But perhaps the Newport Festival was even more remarkable because there was no living folk tradition in Rhode Island. The concerts could not feature any indigenous school or talent; indeed, few professional musicians even vacationed there. So as a shrewd businessman, George Wein had to find ways to exploit the national craving for folk music in a remote location. During his first summer, in 1959, he was eager to welcome stars such as the Kingston Trio. And he had the foresight to recognize the stars of an earlier era. Like the Newport jazz festival, the folk festival could soon be seen not as a completely innovative endeavor but as a link in a long chain of revivals.

Huddie Ledbetter ("Leadbelly"), the singer, songwriter, and master of the twelve-string guitar, who served long terms in Texas and Louisiana prisons, would have been a major attraction in Newport, but he had died a decade earlier. Similarly, Woody Guthrie, the legendary guitarist and singer from Okemah, Oklahoma, who had written and popularized hundreds of ballads such as "This Train Is Bound for Glory" and "This Land Is Your Land," would also have been ideal, but he was stricken with a debilitating disease and unable to perform.[9]

Instead, Wein turned to one of Guthrie's most accomplished acolytes, Pete Seeger (born 1919), the son of a musicologist, who had taught and inspired his own legions of admirers and imitators over a two-decade career. With banjo in hand and chin uplifted, Seeger, like Guthrie, used music as a powerful weapon to oppose war, tyranny, hatred, exploitation, and misery.[10] Seeger had become an outcast for his support of trade unions and other left-wing causes, and in 1952, when he defied a Congressional subpoena, he was blacklisted. By the time he came to Newport, his career was not yet fully rehabilitated.

Wein also had the foresight to recruit another key figure in the folk movement revival, this one a Jew like himself. Born in Vienna in 1924, Theodore Bikel fled with his family to Palestine in 1939. Trained as an actor in Tel Aviv and London, he came to New York in 1955 to pursue roles on stage, in film, and on television. Though some of his colleagues could sing ballads in Spanish or Gaelic, Bikel was the most worldly. He mastered numerous tongues, including Hebrew, Yiddish, Ladino, French, German, Greek, Italian, Russian, and Zulu.

Like aspiring actors such as Belafonte and the Clancy Brothers, Bikel found stature as a singer, and in 1960 he published an anthology, *Folksongs and Footnotes: An International Songbook*. Bikel defined a folk song not in terms of who might sing it but what it could do, its emotional power: "It admonishes, lulls to sleep, calls to battle, rings with hope for the prisoner, with threat for the jailer, with joy for lovers, and with bitterness for him who might have but didn't. It heralds birth, boyhood, wedlock. It soothes, the weary, the sick, and the aged, and it mourns the dead."[11] At its richest and fullest, folk music is a celebration of life, an affirmation of human dignity, and a plea for social justice. In its quest to repair a ruptured world, Bikel believes, folk music conveys many values essential to Judaism.

Bikel occupies a special place in one family's memory. On Friday, November 22, 1963, Eugene and Arline Weinberg moved into their new home on Olney Street in Providence.[12] They planned to attend a Bikel concert that evening at Veterans' Auditorium. The artist transformed it into a memorial to the assassinated president.

Bikel's memoirs open a window on the role played by Jews within the folk music panorama. Though few singers were observant, many practiced music as both an artistic and spiritual calling. Peter Yarrow of Peter, Paul and Mary was born a Jew. One of The Limeliters was Lou Gottlieb, who had earned a doctorate in musicology. Some of the original members of The Tarriers included Alan Arkin and Marshall Brickman; a third member, Eric Weissberg, had previously sung with The Greenbriar Boys. Jewish members of The New Lost City Ramblers were John Cohen and Tracy Schwarz.

The outstanding independent talent agent of the period was Harold Leventhal, who managed The Weavers, Pete Seeger, and a young troubadour from Minnesota named Dylan. In an earlier era, Millard Lampell was the Jewish member of The Almanac Singers. Pete Seeger's Jewish colleague in The Weavers was Fred Hellerman. Even Woody Guthrie found a Jewish partner. His second wife, Marjorie Mazia, was the daughter of a Yiddish poet, Aliza Greenblatt.

Equally important, a national folk music revival would never have occurred without the existence of a record industry in which Jews played prominent roles. In 1950, Jack Holtzman founded Elektra Records in New York City. Vanguard Records was founded by two brothers, Maynard and Seymour Solomon, in New York in the early 1950s (highlights of the Newport folk festival are currently available on twenty CDs issued by Vanguard). And Goddard Lieberson was president of Columbia Records.

But the record company executive most involved in American and international folk music was Moses Asch. Asch (1905–1986), who created and owned for most of its years the Folkways label, is a particularly fascinating and perplexing figure within a Jewish context. He had a meager Jewish education, was nonobservant, but gave his son an Orthodox Bar Mitzvah. Moses was the second son of Sholem Asch, probably the world's most popular Yiddish novelist and playwright before World War II. Born in Poland, reared in France and New York, educated in New Jersey and Germany, and a resident of New York City, Moses helped nurture an extraordinary number and variety of famous and anonymous artists. Still available, there are more than two thousand Folkways recordings.

Asch was clever enough to understand that Yiddish stories and cantorial music would eventually serve as a bridge to larger markets. He was assisted by a dedicated and perceptive staff, which included such Jewish universalists as Marian Distler and Irwin Silber. Because its heyday was the 1950s, Folkways—more than any other recording or distributing company—paved the way for Newport. Asch signed a few of the artists whom the festivals introduced, but as Peter Goldsmith clearly demonstrates, he was not fundamentally interested in commercial success. His interest lay in assembling the century's most comprehensive and authoritative folk music archive.[13]

In numerous ways the early folk festival set high standards and bold precedents. Though the first, in 1959, lasted only two days, it was amazingly popular. More than 10,000 adults and children attended the major evening concerts in Freebody Park as well as a series of daytime panel discussions and workshops held at other locales. Because most programs were held outside, however, the elements often caused havoc.

Each festival featured scores of performers—veterans and neophytes, the brilliant and mediocre, magnetic and shy—drawn from throughout America. The professionals received only fifty dollars and an honorarium for transportation and lodging. While the most expensive seat (on a folding chair) was five dollars, many events were free. There was little intention of making a profit, but small surpluses were shared with grassroots organizations. Pulsating with energy, roaring with excitement, and overflowing with good will, the folk festivals were a natural preamble to the nation's Bicentennial celebrations in 1976.

Long before the term became a political slogan, the festivals were joyfully "multicultural." Without minority artists, the festivals would not have thrived. There were Native American and Hispanic performers, and women artists abounded, but given the pioneering contributions made by "Leadbelly," Josh White, Sonny Terry, and others, the music of Black America was pivotal. Such groups as The Freedom Singers, which originated with civil rights protests in the South, came to Newport to rally support and recruit activists. If the Newport festival had an anthem, it was "We Shall Overcome," a ballad learned by Pete Seeger in 1947 and popularized by him a decade later. Almost all of the evening concerts, which ran well past midnight, closed with performers and audiences singing the hymn's simple but profoundly moving chorus.

As a result of riots at the 1960 jazz festival, the 1961 and 1962 festivals were canceled. Fifty spectators had been injured in a drunken melee at Freebody Park.[14] When the festivals resumed in 1963, staggering crowds created vexing complications. Four-day attendance at the folk concerts was 46,000, surpassing the jazz concerts by 10,000. Newport had not yet devised a plan to feed, house, move, and control such an invasion. Many residents were alarmed to find fans sleeping in their yards. "Chickie" Friedman, who lived on Kay Street, was always upset to hear crying babies.[15] She would invite them and their mothers inside her home. David Lansky, who had opened the Music Box on Thames Street in 1958, put in long hours as a concessionaire at the concerts.[16] He was often irritated by the fans' inconsiderate behavior. One morning, before he could even open his booth, a customer reached inside for an album. When he went to reproach her, he noticed the biggest blue eyes he had ever seen. Judy Collins had not yet received a copy of her latest recording.

In 1964, editorial writers for the *Providence Journal* urged state officials to construct a suitable performance facility. They claimed that Newport "has what it takes to be the summer music center of the East—perhaps of the world."[17] By 1965, without government subsidy, the main venue was moved to "Festival Field," an open site on Connell Highway north of downtown. This space accommodated up to 19,000 spectators. Jeff Brown, then a post-confirmation student at Temple Beth-El in Providence, remembers attending a Peter, Paul and Mary concert that year.[18] When they sang Fanny Lou Hamer's "This Little Light of Mine," he recalls, the night was set aglow by thousands of matches and cigarette lighters.

For many fans and historians, the folk festival's most significant phase was 1963 through 1965. Attendance did not begin to dip until 1967, and there was a momentary lull before wrenching national upheavals. Pete Seeger and Theodore Bikel would continue their steady leadership, and new participants would include Richie Havens, Janis Ian, Joni Mitchell, and Buffy Sainte-Marie. But these three years were especially notable because of the participation of two musicians, both electrifying performers—especially when brought together.

Joan Baez, a minister's granddaughter, was born on Staten Island and attended Boston University.[19] She appeared on the November 23, 1962 cover of *Time* magazine, and her version of "We Shall Overcome," which she recorded in Birmingham in 1963, became the standard.

Robert Allen Zimmerman, better known as Bob Dylan, was born a Jew in Minnesota's harsh Iron Range.[20] An admirer of the Welsh poet, he took the name Dylan after moving to Minneapolis. Like Baez, Dylan was self-taught. He became a folksinger by immersing himself in recordings. By 1961 he found his way to New York City, both to meet his ailing idol, Woody Guthrie (also a harmonica player), and to seek his destiny. Within a year, Dylan gained a contract with Columbia and released his first album. By the spring of 1963, he acquired a manager, Harold Leventhal, and made his debut at Town Hall in New York. By July, he performed at a civil rights rally in Greenwood, Mississippi.

Only a few weeks later, Dylan made his first appearance at Newport, where he also cut three songs: "Blowin' in the Wind," "We Shall Overcome," and "With God on Our Side." Referring to Dylan and others, Ted Holmberg of the *Providence Journal* wrote: "It was one of those rare evenings when everything is so close to right that it is almost frightening, when the program builds to a certain climax inexorably and when even the elements combine to make loveliness a tangible thing: so tangible one feels as though one can reach out and touch it.[21] More than any musical artist of his generation, Dylan decried the fragmenting social order. His extraordinary and provocative lyrics were echoed by many other singers.

When Dylan returned to Newport in 1964, Ted Holmberg described him as "a genius."[22] The following summer, Holmberg called him "a hero" and "a demigod."[23] The journalist did not seem to care that the musician had moved in another direction. Embracing electric guitar with an entire band, Dylan was no longer "a folkie" but "a rocker." Pete Seeger was so incensed that he attempted to cut off his power supply, but Dylan's era at Newport was already over.

As rock music became deafening and apocalyptic, folk music grew mellower and more sentimental. Woody Guthrie died in 1967, so the 1968 festival included a tribute to him. His half-Jewish son Arlo was introduced to Newport audiences but though a personable entertainer, later known for doing rambling ballads, he did not inherit the Guthrie mantle. Ever a marketing genius, George Wein offered three post-festival concerts that year, the peak year for attendance at the folk festival, when more than 73,000 made a pilgrimage to Newport. By the following year, however, attendance plummeted to 51,000. Seeger and Bikel performed, as did Baez, but there was little trailblazing talent.

This was the same summer that the Newport bridge (later renamed in honor of Claiborne Pell) opened; even the improved access did not help the festival. David Fenton, a Jewish member of the Newport city council until 1968, encouraged the festivals, which he thought most Newporters only grudgingly tolerated, but in vain.[24] Newport's robust encounter with folk music had reached a sudden standstill. Wein had been requesting better facilities since 1963; without them, he warned, a move elsewhere might be necessary.

But Fenton, among others, could not visualize another venue in town. Newport officials had grown weary of unruly and disruptive behavior, especially the drinking and marijuana smoking among fans at the jazz concerts, which continued to be well attended (in 1969, 80,000 spectators attended the jazz festival). According to Fenton, many Newporters resented the musicians' leftist sympathies, and they detested rowdy or raucous young people. In 1969, a rampage occurred at a jazz concert, which forced Wein to hire more police and erect additional barricades. In 1971, there was a worse disturbance, and city fathers closed the jazz festival two days ahead of schedule. "Festival Field," only leased for concerts, had become highly attractive to developers; it eventually became a shopping center.

Wein was not discouraged. In 1972 he moved the Newport jazz festival to New York City, where he expanded it to forty-five concerts at five locations, taking place over nine days. Attendance climbed to 100,000. The master impresario attracted extensive corporate sponsorship, including Playboy and Schlitz. When Brown & Williamson, the tobacco company, became the festival's largest sponsor, the Newport moniker was replaced by "Kool." To date, more than twenty "Kool" jazz festivals have been held around the country. In 1981, Wein brought "Kool" back home to Newport. It seemed an ironic gesture, for the "Newport" brand belonged to Lorillard tobacco.

In 1986, Louis Lorillard, only 67 years but long divorced from Elaine, was laid to rest in Portsmouth. His former wife still resides in Newport, but she is troubled by the small coverage given to the festivals by the new Museum of Newport History. By the close of the Newport festivals, Pete Seeger had found a new cause, devoting his music to conservation and the clean-up of the Hudson River. Before his death in 1986, Moses Asch negotiated the purchase of the Folkways archive by the Smithsonian Institution. Though he never found stardom as an actor, Theodore Bikel became highly regarded as a humanitarian. He was a national leader of the American Jewish Congress, and from 1975 to 1982 he served as president of the Academy of Television Arts and Sciences. He continued to sing, and his most enthusiastic audiences were often found in synagogues; in the last several years he has performed twice at Temple Beth-El in Providence.

In 1997, Dylan received government honors at the Kennedy Center. It is difficult to argue with the assessment, however, that his most seminal work was created decades ago, during the period when he performed at Newport. Among her contemporaries, Joan Baez has been most loyal to Newport. She has appeared in summer concerts at Fort Adams State Park on a regular basis since 1988, when the ice cream moguls, Ben Cohen and Jerry Greenfield, revived the folk festival. Except for these Fort Adams concerts and Saturday afternoon programming on Boston's WGBH radio, there are no reminders in

Newport of a movement that has faded away from the local scene. Has Newport erected any kind of memorial, or is a sculpture or a marker even appropriate?

Songs of freedom, equality, justice, and hope will forever be sung around campfires and in Sunday schools. They are part of our American and our Jewish inheritance. In time, folk music will surely experience still another revival. When that occurs, the adventure on Aquidneck Island will seem not so quaint or distant but quite vivid and timely—a marvelous prologue and a powerful prototype.

NOTES

1. See Terry E. Miller, *Folk Music in America: A Reference Guide* (New York: Garland, 1986); this bibliography lists nearly 2,000 items. See also Neil V. Rosenberg, ed., *Transforming Tradition: Folk Music Revivals Examined* (Urbana: University of Illinois Press, 1993).

2. Burt Goldblatt, *Newport Jazz Festival: The Illustrated History* (New York: Dial Press, 1977), p. xi.

3. D. Morgan McVicar, "Louis Lorillard: Founder of Folk Festival," *Providence Journal*, November 7, 1986, p. C, 2.

4. See Charles Mortiz, ed., *Current Biography Yearbook 1985* (New York: H. H. Wilson, 1985); and Barry Kernfeld, *The New Grove Dictionary of Jazz*, Vol. 2 (New York: Macmillan, 1988), pp. 193–194.

5. Interview in Providence on October 25, 1998.

6. Interview in Providence on October 31, 1998.

7. Bruce C. Elrod, *Your Hit Parade and American Top Ten Hits*, 4th ed. (Ann Arbor: Popular Culture, 1994). For biographical sketches of prominent folk artists, see Julia M. Rubiner, ed., *Contemporary Musicians: Profiles of the People in Music*, 22 Vols. (Detroit: Gale Research, 1993); and Colin Lark, ed., *The Guinness Encyclopedia of Popular Music*, 6 Vols. (New York: Stockton, 1995). See also references such as Albert Christ-Janer, and others, *American Hymns Old and New* (New York: Columbia University Press, 1980); B. Lee Cooper: *A Resource Guide to Themes in Contemporary American Song Lyrics, 1950–1985* (New York: Greenwood, 1986); and Robert Lissauer, *Lissauer's Encyclopedia of Popular Music in America: 1888 to the Present* (New York: Paragon House, 1991).

8. Robert Cantwell, *When We Were Good: The Folk Revival* (Cambridge: Harvard University Press, 1996), pp. 293–310.

9. See David Marsh and Harold Leventhal, eds., *Woody Guthrie's Pastures of Plenty: A Self-Portrait* (New York: Harper Collins, 1990).

10. See Robbie Lieberman, *"My Song Is My Weapon": People's Songs, American Communism, and The Politics of Culture, 1930–1950* (Urbana: University of Illinois Press, 1989); and R. Serge Denisoff, *Great Day Coming: Folk Music and the American Left* (Urbana: University of Illinois Press, 1971).

11. Theodore Bikel, *Theo: The Autobiography of Theodore Bikel* (New York: Harper Collins, 1994), p. 168.

12. Interview in Providence on October 25, 1998.

13. Peter D. Goldsmith, *Making People's Music: Moe Asch and Folkways Records* (Washington: Smithsonian Institution Press, 1998).

14. See Nicolas Slonimsky, *Music Since 1900*, 5th ed. (New York: Schirmer, 1994), p. 687.

15. Telephone interview in Middletown on October 25, 1998.

16. Telephone interview in Newport on October 25, 1998.

17. "Newport's Festivals Need Statewide Help," *Providence Journal*, July 28, 1964, p. 14.

18. Interview in Providence on October 23, 1998.

19. Joan Baez, *And a Voice to Sing with: A Memoir* (New York: Summit, 1987).

20. See, for example: Robert Shelton, *No Direction Home: The Life and Music of Bob Dylan* (New York: Morrow, 1986); Bob Spitz, *Dylan: A Biography* (New York: McGraw-Hill, 1989); and Anthony DeCurtis and James Henke, eds., *The Rolling Stone Illustrated History of Rock & Roll* (New York: Random House, 1992).

21. Ted Holmberg, "A Few Rare Hours of Beauty, Triumph," *Providence Journal*, July 29, 1963, p. 1.

22. Ted Holmberg, "A Magnificent Windup," *Providence Journal*, July 27, 1964, p. 1.

23. Ted Holmberg, "A Triumph to the Final Note," *Providence Journal*, July 26, 1965, p. 1.

24. Telephone interview in Portland, Maine, on October 30, 1998.

The Postwar Era and Recent Decades

Three generations of ambulances given by Rhode Islanders to Israel through the American Red Mogen Dovid, from 1947 to 2002.

Top photograph: 1947, gift of Providence's General Jewish Committee. Ida Silverman, second from right, achieved international prominence as a Zionist leader.

Middle photograph: 1974 gift of the Alperin/Hirsch Family in honor of the 35th anniversary of their parents, Max and Ruth Alperin.

Bottom photograph: 2002 gift of the Jewish Federation of Rhode Island.

The Miriam Hospital, Summit Avenue, on Providence's East Side, date unknown. Having purchased the Jewish Orphanage of Rhode Island in 1944, "The Miriam" rebuilt the facility in 1952. Later a teaching hospital of Brown University, it has expanded in every decade.

The sanctuary of Temple Beth-El in 1954, when the congregation's new building was dedicated on Orchard Avenue on Providence's East Side. Designed by Percival Goodman, this is one of the earliest and finest examples of modern synagogue architecture in New England. The sanctuary was later named in honor of Rosalie and Norman Fain. Photograph by Alexander Georges. Temple Beth-El.

The synagogue of Sons of Jacob, 10 Douglas Avenue, Providence. Founded in 1896, the congregation dedicated this building in 1906. Still in use, it is the only surviving synagogue building in Providence's North End.

The choir of Sons of Jacob, 1947. This is an extremely rare view of a synagogue interior built before World War I. Front row, left to right: Eugene Cornfield (choirmaster), Sheldon Broder, Haskell Leach, William Rabinowitz (cantor from Boston), Bernard Zuckerman, Irving Schmuger. Second row, left to right: Leon Cornfield, Isadore Wuraftic, Morris Gordon, Herbert Nussbaum, Samuel Berditch.

A rehearsal of the Jewish
Community Center orchestra,
Benefit Street, Providence, 1948.
Harry Ellis Dickson, longtime
concertmaster of the Boston Pops,
conducts.

A Purim party sponsored by the Hebrew Culture Council of the Bureau of Jewish Education,
Providence, 1955. The Bureau was organized two years earlier. Right to left: Barbara Labush,
Sheila Berger Kaplan, Marsha Perry, Marion Gilbert, Elaine Segal, Sondra Smith, unidentified,
Sandra Mendelsohn, Betty Brown, Rena Cohen, rest unidentified. Photograph by Fred Kelman.

A banquet for Israel Bonds held at the Sheraton-Biltmore Hotel, Providence, June 13, 1955. Left to right: Frank Licht (later governor of Rhode Island), Senator John Pastore, Irving Fain (a civil rights leader), Abba Eban (Israel's ambassador to the United States), Henry Hassenfeld, unidentified, Governor Dennis Roberts. Photograph by Fred Kelman.

Selma Pilavin was the first of the three national chairs of the Women's Division of the United Jewish Appeal from Rhode Island. David Ben-Gurion, President of Israel, greets her during a visit in 1953. Temple Beth-El.

Professor Michael Fink in his office at Rhode Island School of Design, 1989. A faculty member since 1957, he has taught courses on Jewish and Holocaust literature and has brought many prominent Jewish writers to the "RISD" campus. Providence Journal Company.

Temple Emanu-El, Sessions Street, Providence, ca. 1960. Dedicated in 1927, this was the first synagogue built on the East Side. The property had belonged to Brown University, whose football stadium is visible in the upper left. The temple's domed sanctuary, evoking Roman and Byzantine architecture, was typical of American synagogues erected during the 1920s. Photograph courtesy of Temple Emanu-El.

Congregation Beth David, 102 Kingston Road, Narragansett, date unknown. Built in 1961, this synagogue resembles the cottages used by summer vacationers.

Members of Temple Emanu-El's Troop 20 lead services at Yawgoog Scout Reservation, Rockville, ca. 1960. In this era nearly every synagogue in Rhode Island sponsored Scout troops or Cub packs. Jewish boys, guided by rabbis, teachers, and parents, were encouraged to earn "Ner Tamid" merit badges. Narragansett Council, Boy Scouts of America.

Barbara Orson as "Georgette" in Trinity Repertory Company's 1972 production of Molière's School for Wives. Not only a founder in 1964, Orson acted, sang, and danced on the "Trinity Rep" stage for thirty-five years. (Pictured here with William Damkoehler.) William L. Smith, Trinity Repertory Company.

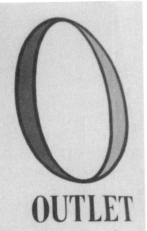

Groundbreaking ceremony at the Garden City branch of The Outlet Company, Cranston, ca. 1962. Among the dignitaries were Kenneth Logowitz, company president (behind and to the left of the man with the shovel), and his board of directors (from left to right). These were Bruce Sundlun (later governor of Rhode Island), Joseph "Dody" Sinclair (a grandson of the founders), John Chafee (later governor and senator from Rhode Island), and John Notte, Jr. (the then-current governor). The Outlet Co. [Ground Breaking Ceremony at the Garden City Branch of the Outlet Company.] Cranston, RI. c. 1962. Silver Gelatin Print. PHOTOGRAPH. Outlet Company Collection 1985 (?). Photo/Eph 30400. RHi X3 7607. Courtesy of the Rhode Island Historical Society.

Managers and senior sales staff of American Tourister luggage company, 1962. Sol Koffler, president and treasurer (seated, second from right), developed patented concepts for affordable luggage since founding American Tourister in 1932. By the 1970s, with five factories in Rhode Island, American Tourister had become one of the world's largest manufacturers of luggage. Though he never graduated from high school, Koffler donated buildings to Brown University, Bryant College, Providence College, and Rhode Island School of Design as well as to Jewish institutions. The Koffler/Bornstein Families.

Temple Emanu-El's Men's Club preparing a Sunday brunch, 1974.

The sanctuary of Temple B'nai Israel, Woonsocket. After worshipping for nearly sixty years in a former church, the congregation built its first synagogue in 1962 under the leadership of Arthur Darman and the Medoff brothers (Israel and Samuel). The magnificent sanctuary windows, designed by Israeli artist Avigdor Arikha, are perhaps the finest in an American synagogue of the postwar era. Photograph by Paul Caponigro. Constance G. Kantar.

Interiors, Touro Synagogue, Newport.

Top photograph: The celebration of the 200th anniversary of Touro's building, 1963. Senator Claiborne Pell of Rhode Island reading; Senator Jacob Javits of New York, front row, far right. Touro Synagogue.

Bottom photograph: Cantor Ely Katz (at left on the bimah) served the congregation from 1944 to 1986; Rabbi Theodore Lewis, from 1949 to 1985. These clergymen officiate at an interfaith celebration of the George Washington letter, ca. 1965. Touro Synagogue.

Rhode Island Board of Rabbis, 1963. Bottom row, left to right: Abraham Chill, Eli Bohnen, Saul Leeman (president), Pesach Krauss, William Braude, and Nathan Rosen. Top row, left to right: Joel Zaiman, Robert Layman, Pesach Sobel, Jerome Gurland, Donald Heskins, Charles Rubel, and Hershel Solnica. Photograph by Fred Kelman.

Executives of Rhode Island's Jewish communal agencies meet in the Jewish Federation's board room, Providence, ca. 1971. Left to right: Joseph Galkin (Jewish Federation); unidentified; Jerry Sapolsky (Miriam Hospital); Dr. Eliot Schwartz (Bureau of Jewish Education); unidentified; Sigmund Hellmann (Jewish Community Center); Paul Segal (Jewish Family Services).

A rally for Soviet Jewry held on Hope Street, Providence, early 1970s.

Dedication of the Alperin Family Building, Jordan Valley Regional College, Zemah junction, Emek Hayarden, Israel, 1974. Following additional gifts by the Alperin/Hirsch family, the institution's name was changed to the Alperin Regional College of the Jordan Valley. Left to right, Robert Riesman, then president of the Jewish Federation of Rhode Island, and Ruth Alperin. Max Alperin (glasses) stands between college staff members.

Frank Licht in Jerusalem, August 1971. Previously a Superior Court judge and president of the Jewish Federation, Licht was elected Rhode Island's first Jewish governor in 1969 and was re-elected in 1971. In 1987, shortly before his death, the Providence County Courthouse was named in his honor.

Richard Israel campaigning, 1971. Israel was elected Rhode Island's first Jewish attorney general in 1971 and was re-elected in 1973. He subsequently served as a Superior Court judge. Richard J. Israel Family.

Lila Sapinsley (center) campaigning for the state senate in 1973. The first Jewish woman legislator in the state's history, she became senate minority leader in 1975. Lila Sapinsley.

David Cicilline, Providence's first Jewish mayor, was inaugurated in 2003. He previously served as a state senator. Providence Journal Company.

Rabbi Yehoshua Laufer (back, center) and his wife, Rebbetzin Michla Laufer (next to him) with their children and her parents on the occasion of their son's Upsherenish (ceremonial cutting of a three-year-old boy's hair), 1989. Rabbi Laufer directs Chabad House on Hope Street in Providence. His son, Rabbi Yossi Laufer, directs Chabad of the West Bay, Warwick. Another son, Rabbi Menachem Laufer, directs Chabad of College Hill, Providence. Jonathan Sharlin.

Deborah and Daniel Weisman in front of Nathan Bishop Middle School on the East Side of Providence. In 1989 the Weismans sued the Providence School Committee for sponsoring a rabbi's prayer at a Bishop graduation. In 1992, in an important decision on church-state relations, the U.S. Supreme Court ruled in favor of the Weisman family. Providence Journal Company.

Darrell Ross, Class of 1965, chaired Moses Brown School's board of overseers from 1996 through 2003. Ross House, shown under construction and dedicated in 2003, honors his leadership of and generosity to this Quaker institution, founded in 1784. Ross exemplifies the Jewish tradition of support for educational and cultural institutions begun in colonial Newport. (Pictured here with Joanne Hoffman, head of the school, 2002.) Photograph by David O'Connor. Moses Brown School.

Alan G. Hassenfeld with Mr. Potato Head® and © 2003 Hasbro, Inc. A former chief executive officer, Hassenfeld continues to serve as chairman of Hasbro, Inc. Founded in 1923 by the Hassenfeld brothers (Henry and Helal), Hasbro began selling textile remnants and manufacturing pencil boxes. Mr. Potato Head®, created in 1952, helped the company become one of the world's largest manufacturers of toys and games. In 1994 Hasbro Children's Hospital was dedicated at Rhode Island Hospital. MR. POTATO HEAD® & ©2003 Hasbro, Inc. Used with permission.

"I Remember"

History is written from many sources: official and unofficial records, stories told, and objects saved. Over its fifty years, the editors of *Rhode Island Jewish Historical Notes* have published a wide variety of evidence from which the Rhode Island Jewish community describes and remembers itself.

These four memoirs potray not only world events but deep emotions. Though Seebert Goldowsky wrote dozens of article for *The Notes*, probably none is more heartfelt than this tribute to his father, Rhode Island's first Jewish detective.

By contrast, Saul Barber hardly knew his father. His recollection of a childhood spent in the Jewish Orphanage of Rhode Island is a rare published account. Yet, such an experience was not uncommon among Jewish youth during the Great Depression.

Rabbi Eli Bohnen recalls his service as an American chaplain in Europe during and after World War II. He knew that he was both a party and a witness to epochal events.

The last word in this anthology belongs to William Braude, the Rhode Island rabbi with the longest tenure of congregational leadership. In addition to his joys and frustrations, he shares highlights of his brilliant career as a teacher and a learner.

These stories will speak to and for many others. This is why memoirs and autobiographies remain so widely read and cherished.

Our Children
Passover Sedar
April 7, 1936.

The Gray
Studio
Prov R.I.

A Passover Seder for "Our Children,"
staff, and guests of the Jewish
Orphanage of Rhode Island,
Providence, April 7, 1936.

Bernard Manuel Goldowsky, 1864–1936

SEEBERT J. GOLDOWSKY

Those of my father's contemporaries who remember him thirty-five years after his death are more than likely to associate his name prominently with Jewish communal affairs. While his contributions to these activities were important, they alone would not justify more than a brief sketch. A few will remember him as the operator of a private detective agency that served the jewelry industry in Rhode Island and southeastern Massachusetts. Those who knew him well will concede that he was a colorful character. He was in fact the first Jewish detective in Rhode Island and a man of considerable attainments in his chosen profession. There are more valid reasons for this undertaking.

My father was born on January 3, 1864, in the village (*shtetl*) of Alexot, near the city of Kovno (Kovnogoberne) in Russian Lithuania, the son and oldest child of Samuel and Elenor (Chia Libbe) Goldowsky. He was named Beryl Mendel. My grandfather had been the proprietor of a small tavern and bakery, which, my father recalled, was patronized by the Russian soldiers in the area. From them he picked up a few Russian words and phrases. That Samuel Goldowsky had for some time planned to emigrate from Russia is evident, although he seems to have been reasonably comfortable, and his precise motivation is not clear. A communication from America, however, was the specific inducement which led him to take that fateful step. He had received a letter from a lawyer in Washington, D.C., stating than an uncle in America had died and that there was an estate to be settled. Leaving his family behind, he embarked for New York, arriving there after a stormy and harrowing voyage of seven weeks. This event occurred probably sometime in the late 1860s, certainly not later than 1871.

In the confusion of landing, and perhaps as a result of the hardships encountered during the lengthy voyage, the letter was lost. He traveled to Washington, but no one there was able to help him locate the proper person. After knocking on many doors, encountering only frustration and disappointment, he returned to New York City, where he determined to settle.

Before my grandfather left for America (at which time my father could not have been more than seven years old), he arranged for his eldest son's education. Like all Jewish young boys, my father went to the local *cheder*. Since under the Czar he was not allowed to attend the local school, he was tutored privately in both English and German.

Eventually Grandfather Samuel was able to send for his family. They arrived in New York City in 1873. My father on arrival, aged nine, could already speak English, a great asset in those days for an immigrant boy. He was conscious of having had a Russian or Yiddish accent, which he was later largely to overcome. His given names in America became Bernard Manuel. My grandfather, who during these years and later ran a small grocery store on the Lower East Side of New York, became a naturalized citizen on October 9, 1876. At that time my father was eleven years old.

Excerpted from *Rhode Island Jewish Historical Notes*, Volume 6, Number 1 (November 1971): 83–116.

My father attended public school in New York, probably completing two years of high school. He presumably attended a Talmud Torah as well. After school he ran errands, sold matches and newspapers on the streets, and delivered groceries, possibly from his father's store. During these years he studied avidly and read voluminously. My father described how he would read until the wee hours, squatting cross-legged on top of the family ice-box, to avail himself of the uncertain flicker of a nearby gaslight. He was all his life wedded to strong eyeglasses. In those days of primitive ophthalmology (when eyeglasses were sold from pushcarts) the punishing effect on his eyes of this voracious reading almost blinded him.

He learned to read and write Hebrew fluently, and in later years he could quote the Talmud at length from memory. When it came time to make his own way in the world, this traditional learning was of no help to him in job hunting. He had a natural talent for drawing and decided to make his living as an artist, doing portraits in crayon. He could not, however, pursue this career because of his poor vision. His doctor advised him to give it up if he did not want to become blind.

He then tried his hand at the sewing machine business. My father was facile with his hands and undoubtedly could make the necessary repairs himself. This venture, however, did not thrive.

In the mid 1890s he determined to seek his fortune in Texas, where his younger brother Moses had already settled and would prosper in the drygoods business. He tried his luck in Denison, a busy railroad, industrial, and farming community in northeast Texas. He sold goods from door to door (a salesman or peddler), but presumably did not do well. He was, in fact, not talented in either business or selling. He returned to New York sometime about 1899.

In answer to a blind "help wanted" advertisement in a New York newspaper, he found himself applying for a job with the Pinkerton Detective Agency. An unlikely prospect, small in stature and obviously Jewish, he was nevertheless promptly hired. A shrewd manager saw something more in this modest little man than met the eye. Shortly after getting his feet wet in his new venture as a detective operative, he was transferred to the Boston office.

Before his Texas interlude he had boarded in New York with a German Jewish family named Lotary. At home was a pretty and lively daughter, named Antoinette, by whose brown hair, yellow eyes, and fair skin he was bewitched. He fell in love with her and asked for her hand in marriage. Since she was only sixteen when they met and his prospects for supporting a wife and family were nil, her parents took a dim view of the undertaking and told him to come back later when Tony was a little older.

Some ten years later after his transfer to Boston, now with the prospect of a steady job, he again at long last asked for her hand. They had kept up a courtship and correspondence over the years. She was now twenty-six and he thirty-five. If her family still had reservations, she had none. They were married on October 15, 1899. My father's residence was given as Chelsea, Massachusetts, where he had boarded with his first cousin.

The Lotarys came to America from Germany in 1879, when their eldest daughter Antoinette was six. My mother always claimed that she was born in New York, but we knew otherwise. My mother had two brothers and two sisters. One brother, said to be affected with the "wanderlust," disappeared without a trace in 1906, probably a victim of the San Francisco earthquake. Her two beautiful sisters created a song-and-dance sister act in vaudeville. Her remaining brother was, like my mother, a more solid citizen.

My mother left school after the eighth grade and went to work. Until her marriage she worked most of her years in a necktie factory, rising to the rank of "forelady." A bright young man named Harry Schwartz, who had a knack for magic tricks, worked at a nearby bench. He later became the great magician, Harry Houdini.

My parents' honeymoon was a train trip to Somerville, Massachusetts, where my father had rented an apartment in a two-family frame house. They started their life together with eleven dollars, one week's wages from the celebrated Pinkerton agency.

While my father's career with the Pinkertons was brief, he was early respected by his superiors for his cleverness and ingenuity. He had at last found a career for which he had a natural talent and which was both challenging and rewarding. While working for the Pinkertons in Boston he was employed on one occasion as a machine operator in the shoe industry. It is possible that this involved anti-union activity, in which the Pinkertons had had a long tradition and experience.

While conducting an investigation for the Pinkerton agency in Providence, he met and earned the admiration of Patrick ("Patsy") Parker, chief of detectives of the Providence police. Providence was then the world's jewelry manufacturing center. The loss of even small amounts of precious metals (gold, silver, and platinum) to inside thievery created serious problems for the industry. Parker introduced my father to several of the industry's leaders and recommended him highly. They induced my father to transfer his activities to Providence to undertake the solution of their problems. Among his early clients in the business were such firms as Theodore Foster and Brothers, Chapin and Hollister, and Ostby and Barton. He later became fast friends with William P. Chapin.

In 1901 my father with his bride and infant daughter, Eleanor, moved to Providence where he was to make his career and live out his life. They rented a flat, again in a two-family frame house, at 595 Broadway near Olneyville, across the street from St. Mary's Catholic Church. The house in later years was removed for the Roberts Expressway. This was an Irish neighborhood, and my family made fast and lifelong friendships with some of their neighbors. My sister Beatrice and I were both born in this house (November 11, 1904, and June 6, 1907, respectively.)

My father could not immediately establish an agency since he had to be licensed and bonded, and this required a year of residence. Meanwhile he worked as a claims agent for the street railway company and did some free-lance work for the Pinkertons, which he also continued later. He established his own agency, the National Detective Agency, in about 1902. He first appeared in the 1903 city directory as "agent." The agency is listed by name for the first time in 1906. His office was in the old Industrial Trust Building at 49 Westminster. The agency survived until his death, although in 1923 the name was changed to the Goldowsky Detective Agency.

In 1906 a group of jewelry manufacturers banded together to form the Jewelers Protective Association, a subsidiary of the New England Manufacturing Jewelers and Silversmiths Association, which had its headquarters in Providence. This new organization retained my father for investigative services. He became highly expert in this special field and particularly knowledgeable about individuals who preyed on the industry. He kept detailed card files on all jewelry employees and working jewelers. Over a period of years he was able drastically to reduce the losses and prevent recurrence. He always maintained that the worst scourges were the fences, the receivers of stolen goods, and that without them the crime of theft could not exist. In this industry the fences usually operated loan or secondhand shops. He put a few out of business and kept the others under constant surveillance.

The Goldowsky family at Rocky Point Amusement Park, Warwick, ca. 1917. Left to right: Seebert, Eleanor, Bernard, Antoinette, Maurice Adelman (Eleanor's husband), and Beatrice.

During the years before World War I, my father maintained a branch of his business in Newark, New Jersey, because it was the second jewelry center of the United States, and much expensive jewelry was made there. It was operated by my uncle, Alfred Lotary, but was closed upon his untimely and premature death.

In 1908 my parents purchased a single family house at 64 Baker Street (later changed to 224 Baker Street), near the Broad Street entrance to Roger Williams Park. This was a Victorian cottage, later enlarged. They moved there in August during the second year of my life. It was the family home until it was disposed of after my mother's death in November of 1940. It was surrounded by grape arbors and a small grove of fruit trees which yielded a copious harvest of apples, pears, cherries, and peaches.

My father bought the first family automobile, a new Willys Overland touring car, in the spring of 1915 at the attractive price of 750 dollars. My father, then fifty years of age, a somewhat middle-aged novice driver, took the family on an early summer Sunday drive. The car turned completely over on the Boston Post Road opposite Apponaug Pond in Warwick. Fortunately, the car spanned a deep roadside ditch, for the phaeton top was completely crushed. Injuries were not serious, but that ended my father's driving career. After extensive repairs were completed, he foreswore ever driving again and hired a student, then a junior at Brown University, to drive the family car. This young man [Maurice Adelman] later married my elder sister.

In my father's obituary in the Providence *Evening Bulletin* of March 31, 1936, appeared the following comments: "Mr. Goldowsky . . . was well known among the police and private detectives throughout the country. During the World War he gave liberally of his services to the Government in aiding the intelligence service." There is little else upon the record of those eventful years, for the episodes were top secret and my father was tight-lipped. Even my mother was not privy to his secrets.

While my father during this period had some pro-German sentiments and, in fact, read the *Fatherland*, George Sylvester Viereck's propaganda organ, he was not deterred from engaging in intelligence activities designed to help his beloved country. He was always an enthusiastic patriot. The work fell roughly into two parts: first, the period between the outbreak of the war in Europe in August 1914 and the entry of the United States in April 1917, and, second, the period of our involvement from April 1917 to the Armistice in November 1918. During these activities he operated under the pseudonym or alias of "Mr. Brown."

He received no remuneration for his intelligence work either before or after our entrance into the War. These were acts of patriotism, and he felt that they somehow substituted for his being unable on account of age to offer himself for military service.

His professional activities extended beyond the jewelry trade. He did investigations for other industries. The B. B. and R. Knight Company of West Warwick, manufacturers of Fruit Of The Loom products, is one example of a textile firm with which he did business. He had a long and productive relationship with the company, and Webster Knight, owner of the business at the time, was a close friend and patron. He did investigations for retail firms and various other types of businesses. He refused divorce cases, which he considered an unsavory and unethical type of investigation, but he was not averse to becoming involved in family problems if the investigations would lead to constructive results.

At times he would affect a disguise. He spoke of an investigation in downtown New York for which he dressed up as a rabbi in a big black hat and long black coat, which he had rented from a theatrical costumer. There is no doubt that in this outfit he blended into the surroundings and appeared not at all like the traditional flatfoot. His small stature (five feet, six inches in height) later modified by a rotund corpulence, his prematurely gray hair, Jewish features, and unassuming mien made him a most unlikely and unsuspected person when engaged in suspicious activities. He himself thought that much of his success depended on his uncharacteristic appearance. He had great endurance, could stand or walk for along periods, and could go without sleep for many hours. He often disappeared from home for days or weeks at a time. We were trained in our childhood never to discuss his absence among our associates, and we never inquired of his whereabouts. Discretion was our daily lesson. As lifestyles became more complicated, my father foresaw the end of the truly productive days of the "private eye." The automobile made surveillance difficult and expensive. He felt that only organizations with the resources and manpower of the F.B.I. and the police had a future in larger investigations.

His politics were conservative, and he was a lifelong Republican. Anti-union and anti-strike activity in the jewelry industry were a substantial portion of his activity. In the days before the Wagner Act this was an eminently respectable pursuit. It is quite probable that he learned the methods when he was a Pinkerton man in Boston. One of his operatives, surprisingly, was a union official, having infiltrated the union hierarchy.

He was feared by the criminal element and respected by the police, juries, and lawyers. His cases were always meticulously prepared and were not brought to trial until the evidence was conclusive. He generally let the police make his arrests, although he was a legitimately sworn constable. He never lost a case that had been brought to trial. His interrogations were clever and demanding. I remember his being called an obscenity and then attacked by a criminal whom he had once brought to justice. This occurred in the lobby of the old Fay's Theater, where we as a family were attending a movie. Fearlessly, my father swung his umbrella at the culprit until the two combatants were separated by bystanders before serious consequences had occurred.

His religious philosophy in contrast to his politics was sharply liberal. He was for half his life a secular Jew without affiliation. He was turned from religion, despite his Jewish background, sympathies, and education, by what he felt was a pervasive hypocrisy. During our childhood, however, through the urging of my mother, my parents joined Temple Beth-El (Congregation of the Sons of Israel and David). My mother's religious training was inconsequential or nonexistent, but she felt that an affiliation was necessary if they were to be buried respectably. My parents are buried in the Temple Beth-El cemetery on Reservoir Avenue.

My father has been described as a little man with a big brain. He was that, but also a little man with a big heart—generous to a fault. He always loved children, and his first organized charitable interest was the Lakeside Home for Children in Warwick, to which he had been introduced by his warm friend, William P. Chapin. Later he became very actively involved in fundraising for the Jewish Orphanage of Rhode Island and, at a still later period, the Jewish Home for the Aged. He ran charity balls on several occasions for both of these organizations.

During the period after World War I he was deeply involved in organizational and fundraising activities for various Zionist undertakings. My father and mother were entertained and given a silver bowl on the occasion of their twenty-fifth wedding anniversary by the Providence Keren Hayesed Committee. On his seventieth birthday my father was again entertained, this time by the Zionist District of Rhode Island, and was presented with a silver pitcher bearing the inscription, "For his faithful services to the cause of Zionism."

Though my father's profession made him of necessity a stern realist in judging people, their character, and their works, he was paradoxically to the end of his life an unfailing romantic. During my parents' troubled years he admired and appreciated my mother's steadiness, patience, and goodness, but his irrepressible sense of humor was never below the surface.

In his later years with the conversion of the Rhode Island jewelry industry largely to costume jewelry and the premature depression in that industry even before the financial crash of 1929, my father's business became anachronistic and slowly deteriorated, although it survived until his death in 1936. This, together with his disproportionate generosity, drained his resources seriously. Feeling that he could leave his family no material patrimony, he composed this testament, handwritten in his beautifully ornate and clear script, meant to be opened after his death. Rabbi William G. Braude, then a relative newcomer to Providence, read it at my father's funeral:

> To my children, Eleanor Lillian, Beatrice and Seebert Jay.
> This is not a legally executed document because I have no worldly goods to leave my family.
> I have all my life striven to win that which money cannot buy and which no stock market could wipe out, to wit, a good name. So if I have also failed in that, my life was a complete bankrupt.

I hardly know anything more despicable than selfishness. I despise the man who lives only for himself. So if you, my good children, wish to cherish my memory, do not fail to discharge the debt you owe to God's distressed children in the way of alleviating their suffering.

 Your loving father,

  Bernard M. Goldowsky

  Providence, R.I.

   July 5, 1934

189

S. Goldowsky

Bernard Manuel Goldowsky

My Life at the Jewish Orphanage of Rhode Island

SAUL BARBER

A DEATH IN THE FAMILY

I was six when my father died, and it changed my whole life. He was thirty-six, my mother thirty-four, and they were raising a family of four children, with me as the youngest. My parents were Jewish immigrants from the Russian Ukraine. My father came to the United States in 1910, at the age of eighteen, and sent my mother her ticket a year later. They had been married only shortly before he left for America, partly at least to avoid service in the Czar's army, which was an extreme hardship for Russian Jews.

He settled in the Boston area because he had relatives there, and went to work in one of the many immigrant sweat shops. Five children were born but the eldest, a son, died in infancy. The two oldest were girls; they were thirteen and eleven years old, my brother and I being eight and six at the time of my father's death.

He had moved from sweatshop employment to independent work peddling fruit and vegetables from a horse and wagon. From peddling he saved enough to open, with a partner, a neighborhood fruit and vegetable store, which appeared to be successful. But his partner eventually absconded with the funds, apparently after having skimmed weekly receipts for several months before disappearing. This left my father without the resources to continue the business, but he was able to connect with a cousin in Providence, and start a business with him buying live chickens from the central markets and selling them store-to-store to the kosher butchers in the area.

The whole family moved to Providence when he had the business going well a few months after starting it. The business he was in was a marginal sort of thing. There was a lot of physical labor involved in loading and unloading the stock but each of them was young and strong and thought nothing of it. That is, until my father became ill.

He had complained for some weeks of greater than usual fatigue as well as a slight numbness in his extremities. The doctor had recommended soaking alternately in hot and cold water, but that did not relieve the symptoms. One afternoon my father came home early very short of breath, almost gasping for air, and unable to continue working. The doctor diagnosed him as having pneumonia and advised bed rest for at least several days. But the next day my father was breathing normally and felt much better. So, feeling the pressure of the need to earn his day's receipts, he went back to work, although my mother, fearing the worst, pleaded with him to remain home. Her fears were well-founded because he came home early again, this time truly gasping for air, and was quickly hospitalized with the diagnosis of double pneumonia. He died within twenty-four hours.

My most vivid, and last, recollections of my father were seeing and hearing him gasping for breath on each of the days when he came home early from work and was immediately put to bed. I never saw him again, although I do recall the stretcher being

Excerpted from *Rhode Island Jewish Historical Notes*, Volume 13, Number 3 (November 2001): 451–477.

The Barber family, ca. 1926. Left to right, Betty, Nathan, Ida, Frances, and Saul at age six. Like many children of his era, Saul was placed in an orphanage when his family was unable to support him.

wheeled to the waiting ambulance. In school on the day of his death, I remember being called out of class to the principal's office with my brother, who had also been called out; we were told to go home immediately without being told why, although the pitying looks on people's faces filled us both with a sense of foreboding. When we got home we didn't have to be told the news. We saw my mother seated in the kitchen along with a number of neighbor women. My mother was crying, as were some of the neighbors. I ran to her and buried my face in her lap. The whole family, of course, was devastated by my father's death. In later years I have felt that my brother and I, more so than our sisters or even our mother, suffered the most.

As a young girl in Russia, my mother helped her mother in a Jewish bakery shop. With this background, my mother was able to obtain employment in a local Jewish bakery. The hours were long and the pay very little, but it was just enough to support us while we children continued our schooling.

When we first moved to Providence our parents had enrolled us boys in a *cheder* (Hebrew school), which we attended for an hour or so every day after public school, but after my father's death we could not afford the small tuition and we were withdrawn. However, it was decided that as the males in the family, my brother and I were to say the *Kaddish* (mourner's prayer) which custom required be said by adult male survivors, morning and evening, daily for a year following any death in the immediate family.

My father died in October of 1926 and for the rest of the school year we continued to live as a nuclear family. As the year progressed, however, it became clear to my mother that my brother Nathan and I were not being properly supervised. We lived in a run-down and unsavory neighborhood and without more supervision by our sisters we were beginning to run a bit wild. Neither sister, at ages eleven and thirteen, was quite mature enough to manage two normal, high-spirited young boys. We wouldn't go to bed when told and after supper insisted on going out to hang around the neighborhood until our mother came home. Since, during the winter months, she often came home from work after dark she worried about what might happen to us.

One of my father's older brothers, Uncle Shlaymie, also lived in Providence, so my mother consulted him. He recommended that she apply to the local Jewish Orphanage of Rhode Island (JORI), which had been started a number of years earlier under the auspices of Jewish philanthropic organizations. It had moved to a brand new building just a few years earlier, and my uncle had been impressed by it. They looked into it further and decided to approach the superintendent regarding us. A decision was finally made that we were to be admitted to the orphanage until circumstances changed or until we were old enough to care for ourselves responsibly. It was my admission to the orphanage, and the years I spent there, that changed my life so drastically.

I spent nine years there, from the age of six to fifteen. Nathan was two years older, thus not traumatized quite as much as I was, and he was at JORI two years fewer than I. Our sisters remained at home with our mother and did not suffer displacement trauma. Their lives did change for the worse. Neither was graduated from high school, despite the fact that both were excellent students. They chose instead to leave school at age sixteen in order to help out with home finances. My older sister Betty, in particular, was devastated by our father's death. Nevertheless, my sisters did not suffer the effects of a complete change in their lives, whereas my brother and I did.

THE "HOME"

My mother never told Nathan and me that she was putting us in an orphanage. My vision of such an institution would have been like something out of a Dickens novel. She realized that we would have objected strenuously to any notion of leaving home permanently for another residence; consequently, she broached the subject of our going away to camp for the summer, and that was what we thought was to happen.

One beautiful day in June of 1927, after school was over for the academic year, my mother and Uncle Shlaymie walked with us to the orphanage, carrying with us only a few belongings. I was almost seven years old. It was about a two mile walk, from the north side to the east side of the city, but it was a lovely day and an enjoyable trek, especially since we thought we were going to camp and were looking forward to the playground facilities which had been promised to us.

We did not become aware of the true situation for many days after our arrival. What we saw on arrival was a two-story red-brick building with a central portion, two wings and an ell off each wing. It was only a few years old, still impressive looking, and located in what I suppose must have been a lower middle-class neighborhood, directly across the street from a public grammar school. The latter had an extensive playground with swings, hammocks, a large slide, and a roundabout. My mother pointed this out to us as fulfilling her promise of a playground and we were mollified despite the strange appearance of the "camp."

I don't recall the process of being admitted to the orphanage, or of meeting the superintendent or the boys' supervisor. I do recall being fed supper separately because the children had already been fed. The supper included my first experience with chocolate pudding. It looked delicious, but when I tasted it, it was bittersweet and I didn't like it. To this day, I don't like bittersweet chocolate.

The building fronted on Summit Avenue; Fifth Street on the left, as one faced the structure, separated that side from the Summit Avenue Grammar School and its playground. Otherwise, it was surrounded by single family residences or two-story houses with a family on each story. The orphanage building had three stories.

The living room was where we usually gathered after supper, if it was dark out, until it was time to go to bed. Bedtime was in three shifts according to age groups. During summer, of course, we played outside as long as it was light. We younger children went to bed then when it was still light, a hardship we resented as children everywhere do. In the living room we also listened to certain programs of the radio, especially on Sunday nights, when Eddie Cantor, Jack Benny, and Edgar Bergen (with his puppet, Charlie McCarthy) were on. Otherwise, the room was used for reading, although quiet conversation was allowed. During summer months we were all required to spend one hour there directly after dinner (noon) as an enforced rest period.

The library contained perhaps several hundred books, mostly for juveniles. It was there that I found an almost complete series of the Rover Boys, Tom Swift, Ralph of the Railroads, the Boy Allies, and others. I was an avid reader, and over the years I read them all. When I was older, in the high school years, ten or so desks were added to the room and assigned to each of us who regularly had homework from school.

On the second floor each wing contained the dormitories, three rooms on each side of the superintendent's apartment, the girls on the left and the boys on the right. A door at each end of the apartment connected with each dormitory.

In my early years there, we didn't use the living room as a social hall. Rather, the playroom was designated for that purpose as well as for play. The girls had a similar room in the other wing, thus keeping the sexes largely separated during indoor leisure hours. Basketball was the favored sport for the boys during the winter months. Beyond the basketball court, at the end of the gym, was a semicircular stage. The backstage area was used to store remnants of sets from productions put on only infrequently for relatives, friends, and members of the Jewish community of Rhode Island. No doubt these were part of fundraising efforts.

The backyard was large and spacious. The section closest to the back doors was almost completely sandy with perhaps an occasional patch of tall grass and weeds. There was, in this area, a large sandbox that could easily accommodate a dozen children at a time. For several years there was also a horseshoe pitching area, and we used to spend long hours at that game during the summer. The tennis court was much used, not only for the game itself but also for roller skating.

The portion of Fifth Street separating our yard from that of the adjacent grammar school was still a dirt road, and we had free access to the equipment in the school yard during the summer months. One of the chief attractions there, once we tired of the swings and slides, was a tall wooden fence separating the boys' side of the yard from the girls'. During the summer, access to either side was not prohibited. We boys enjoyed the fence because climbing it was something of a challenge, as was walking along the top, which required some of the skill of a tightrope walker.

The neighborhood boys and girls used the playground facilities as much as we did and we interacted with them easily, in part because we went to school with them as well. The local boys also used the vacant lot for baseball and football, and sometimes we played with them there and sometimes on our field. The rivalries, when they existed, were entirely friendly, often overseen by our boys' supervisor, who might also be the only available umpire for the game.

I BECOME AN ATHLETE!

I don't remember precisely when I was disabused of my notion that Nathan and I were in camp, but it must have been within a few days and it was surely told to us scornfully by one or more of the older boys. Most of the kids (we were always called, and we always referred to each other as, kids) were, in fact, not orphans, but like Nathan and me, had lost one parent by death, or, in some instances, had lost the care of one parent for an extended period of time due to illness or marital separation.

The truth of our registration in the orphanage rather than camp, and for a period extending far beyond that summer, became evident within the first few weeks and was a cruel blow. Our mother used to visit us once a week in the early years on Saturdays or Sundays, depending on which day she had off. I used to beg her to take us home but she always responded with excuses that she couldn't afford to. I remember particularly promising her that I would work to help bring in money by selling newspapers on the street corner. I even demonstrated how I would do so by mimicking the calls of the boys who, in those days, were common sights in business districts selling their papers with loud cries of "Hey, get your morning papers!" My mother thought I was real cute doing this and called my behavior to the attention of one of the other mothers. I, of course, immediately desisted and never tried that tactic again. Eventually, when school started, I and Nathan as well stopped begging to be brought home, accepted our fate, and became thoroughly integrated into the life of the orphanage.

Life at the "Home," as we soon called it, was generally benign and enjoyable, but there were instances of cruelty toward us younger boys by the older boys. These took place primarily when the boys' supervisor, Mr. Wiseman, had his day off and left the supervision of the routine to the oldest boy, whom I shall call Frank. He seemed to be particularly sadistic and I was always afraid of him. One of the things that he, and some of the older boys following his lead, used to do was to hold us younger kids under the cold shower much longer than necessary, after lifting us up so that our faces were very close to the shower nozzle. This latter gambit, in particular, was frightening to me because the full force of the nozzle on my face took my breath away, and I used to struggle to free myself. I recall crying because of this mistreatment, but because I was the only one of the smaller boys doing so, I was then ridiculed for being a softie.

Those daily showers were frightening to me in another way. We were, it is true, very dirty by the end of a summer's day, and were required to scrub, with fairly stiff brushes, to get the dirt out of all our crevices. I had particular trouble getting the insteps of my feet thoroughly clean and was often sent back to re-scrub them when I was inspected.

Once I remember that Frank sent me back so often, and I scrubbed so hard, that I abraded the skin and drew blood. I think that the practice stopped when I had to be bandaged for the injury and the reason for it came out. I'm sure, however, that I named no one as responsible because revenge on me would have been swift and terrible.

Those early summers when I was a "little kid" were spent mostly at free play, in the sandbox in our yard, or on the play equipment in the school yard. Sometimes we had roller skates available to us, the kind that clamped onto the soles of shoes, and we would skate on the sidewalks and driveways of the school. For some of my early and middle years we also used to go swimming three times a week, weather permitting, at Woodville, a freshwater pond in the woods somewhere north of the city. We generally arrived in mid-morning in time for a swim before lunch. The beach was a typical stony one and not conducive to sunbathing, but in back of the beach was a small meadow in which we had lunch and occasionally played some games. Mostly, however, we just swam, or rather the older kids swam and we little ones pretended in the shallow water. There was no "buddy" system to keep track of everybody, and neither was there any attempt to teach us even the rudiments of swimming. Nevertheless, there were no drownings or near-drownings. And I did learn to swim there on my own.

Besides the Woodville trips, there were sometimes special outings. One of these was a visit to the forty-acre farm of one of the members of the board of directors (we kids called each one of them a "board of director"). The estate was in Barrington, and included a beach on Narragansett Bay or one of the bodies of water opening onto the bay. I remember all the kids got special outfits for the outings and I, along with the other little kids, received a special sailor outfit with bell bottom trousers which I thought was particularly beautiful. All I remember from that trip, and I believe we went there only once or twice, was running from field to field and swimming on the beach. The waters there were abundant with crabs, probably blue crabs, because several of the kids got nipped, and I was afraid to go in.

The other outing that I remember well, and which got to be an annual event, was the trip near the end of the summer to Narragansett Pier. This is a large public beach in the town of Narragansett heavily used in those days by the Jewish people of Rhode Island. It also was on Narragansett Bay but much farther south than and across the bay from Barrington, thus much closer to the open ocean and less prone to pollution. It had a heavy surf and fine beach sand—as fine as anywhere I have encountered. This trip we took in a genuine bus; it was thirty or forty miles from the Home and thus too far to go in those makeshift trucks we used for the Woodville trips.

The trips to Narragansett Pier had to be planned well in advance and our greatest fear, as the date approached, was that it might be rained out. It never was. Playing in the heavy surf, making castles in that wonderful sand, and running along that hard-packed beach at the water's edge were like heaven to us. On one of these trips everything went just right and I remember thinking, as we rode the bus back to Providence, that I had experienced a perfect day, just as it said in the song that we sang in school: "When you come to the end of a perfect day." It remains in my memory as perhaps the happiest day of my childhood.

Sports played a large part in our leisure activities. During the summer, baseball was the favorite game. As I grew older I, and most of the other boys in my age group, gradually gave up the sand box and other "babyish" activities and emulated the older boys by playing baseball among ourselves as often as we could. Equipment for baseball was generally sparse and not in good condition. Usually only one baseball at a time was available for our use. That was used long enough so that the original cover was knocked off, but its continued use for weeks longer was accomplished by wrapping it in black electrician's tape.

The diamond area was a heap of hard-packed sand liberally endowed with stones. The stones and the general roughness of the surface made fielding ground balls a challenging and often painful experience. We had no regular bases and made do with heavy stones. The bases were also the only markers we had for foul lines; consequently, close decisions over whether a hit ball was fair or foul were often decided only after prolonged argument, the decision largely dependent on which side had more convincing, or domineering, arguers. The outfield sloped a bit downhill and the grass was never cut. In early years "cow flaps" from a neighbor's wandering cow were a minor hazard in the outfield, but that stopped within a few years when cows were no longer kept in what was fast becoming an expanding urban area.

We also played tennis a lot once the court was constructed and tournaments were occasionally arranged. We also did a certain amount of organized track and field competing: the 100-yard dash, running broad jump (now called the long jump), high jump, relay racing, and others. Also, one year, Mr. Katz organized an intramural track meet.

During the winter months we played a lot of basketball. George Katz was a good player and had played with a local adult YMCA team before becoming our supervisor. He taught us the fundamentals of set-shooting, lay-up shooting, and other maneuvers. Even when I was a little kid we always had an orphanage team which played the local Jewish Community Center and YMCA teams. The whole Home would turn out to watch these games, although chairs had to be strung along the sidelines since the depth of the offside areas could accommodate only one row of chairs without jeopardizing the safety of the spectators. Initially we little kids were only spectators at these events. But as we matured we were organized into a team and occasionally played neighborhood teams. Later, as big kids, we played a fairly busy schedule of games over the winter months, perhaps one a week.

One year, perhaps when I was eleven, I won a secret ballot for most valuable player; for that outstanding accomplishment, which I was very proud of, I was given a very good baseball glove. It was the first glove I had ever owned and I kept it for many years, through college and graduate school. It was also the best glove I had ever used, since the gloves we usually had were pretty beat up and rarely was there one to fit into the right hand for a left-handed thrower.

All the athletic competitions I played in at the Home were not only enjoyable but they also helped me compete later on. During my senior year in high school, when I had finally left the Home and was living with my mother and stepfather, I not only made my school's basketball team, but I was a regular starter. To be sure, my brother Nathan had paved the way for me. He had been a member of the junior varsity team at Hope High School in Providence during his sophomore year and then, when he left the Home to live with my mother and stepfather two years before I did, he made the starting team at Aldrich High School [in Warwick], to which I came in my senior year. We were not a very good team. We finished last in our league with only two victories, including a loss at season's end to our traditional rivals, but I loved every minute of it. After all, here I was, no longer an "orphanage kid," but instead on equal footing with all the other kids in the school and, indeed, even a bit of a star because of my basketball playing.

Back at the orphanage we also played a lot of touch football during the fall months. These were always just pickup games among ourselves. We had no goal posts so kicking played no significant role in the games. Usually each team would try to make a touchdown with its allotted four downs, because the field was short enough to make that a reasonable possibility. Occasionally a team might be backed up far enough to elect to kick on a fourth down but that was rare. Passing plays were the main weapons in those games. When I was younger we also played tackle football occasionally. I excelled at this game because of my agility and because I was the play caller of our age group. As the one who called the plays, I was also the quarterback and passer even though my hands were too small to hold the ball in one hand.

THIS WAS OUR LIFE

Those first few years in the Home are often hazy in my memory. One incident stands out in my mind during those early years, however. I still longed to return to my home on Black Street with my mother and sisters and had romanticized the place in my mind. Those summer trips to Woodville Pond used to pass close to my old Black Street neighborhood, and I was on the lookout for my house there each time. Once we passed by the corner of Chalkstone Avenue and Black Street and I actually saw my house quite clearly. I jumped up and cried, very excitedly, "There it is, there it is." Older boys asked what I was making such a fuss about and when I explained, ridiculed me for getting excited over nothing. I looked at my brother Nathan, and saw that he had not reacted as I had. I sat down feeling very chastened and foolish. I think that incident may have finally broken my yearnings to return home, and I accepted my lot with greater equanimity.

There were close to fifty kids in the home with, perhaps, twice as many boys as girls. Besides the superintendent and the boys' and girls' supervisors, there was a full-time cook, a full-time kitchen assistant, and a full-time janitor who was also a jack-of-all-trades. All of these people lived in the home in single bed-sitting rooms except, of course, the superintendent and his family, who had a suite.

Once, a number of years later when I was about thirteen, four of us in the thirteen to fifteen age group broke the rules rather flagrantly and we thought the cook, Mrs. Brown, had caught us at it. It had been arranged for the four of us to join a club at the Jewish Community Center about a mile and one-half away. The club met once a week at night and we went regularly and found it very enjoyable. One week, however, when Jack Dempsey was opening in person at the Fay Theater in downtown Providence, we decided to go see him instead of going to the club. I believe we had asked permission to go see him on another night but were refused on the grounds that it wasn't proper entertainment for us, and anyway we'd get back too late from the show. The Fay Theater was a movie theater but also had an abbreviated vaudeville show accompanying each film. This was in the waning days of vaudeville throughout the country, but when Jack Dempsey made his tour he was a big attraction.

We decided that week to see Dempsey instead of going to the club. I think we felt we could easily be caught but not until after we came back, and seeing Dempsey would be worth any punishment we might get. When we came back, much later than usual, everyone seemed to be asleep and we walked very quietly along the back of the building on our way to the back door on the boys' side. It was dark there initially, but suddenly the yard became much lighter, and when I looked back I saw Mrs. Brown in her window overlooking the back yard. She had apparently just entered her room and had put the light on and was looking out of the window. I thought she surely had seen us, and so did the others, yet we got in the building and upstairs to bed without any other encounters. As we waited for the ax to fall we thought for sure she had seen us and would report us. She never did. I don't know to this day whether she had not seen us because she was looking from a lighted room into a dark yard, or having seen us did not think anything of our coming in so late.

The daily routine at the home still has some highlights of remembrance for me. We were awakened by the boys' supervisor, then we washed, dressed, and went down to breakfast. In early years we used to line up to go into meals but that was abolished at least by the time Stollie (Mr. Stollerman) became superintendent. The dining room had six or seven tables seating eight kids each, three on each side and one on each end. We each had an assigned place at a given table. The seating was not segregated by sex or age. At one end, an older kid, male or female, sat and was more or less in charge of that table. The two supervisors would carry the food out from the kitchen and distribute it to the different tables, and the head kid at each table would do any further distributing. I don't remember if it was served family style at each table or if the dishes were carried out already served with food. Bread and butter were certainly family style since one of my clearer memories of those meals was hearing individual kids call out, "Please pass the bread" loudly enough to be heard several tables away. The supervisors worked pretty hard during these meals responding to requests for more bread or milk, or even seconds when those were available. They ate either before or after us, I don't recall which, at a smaller table at the front of the room. The superintendent and his family ate in an adjoining room, and the other workers undoubtedly ate in the kitchen.

Our meals were strictly kosher and we started each one with a prayer. Initially the prayer for each meal was recited in unison in Hebrew, as was the traditional "Hamotzie," which translated into thanks to God for giving us "bread from the earth." Later, the prayer at supper was different. It was recited in English and started out "Our God and God of our fathers, another day has passed away and night is soon approaching. Before we, however . . ." For the life of me I can't remember another word of that prayer, even though I recited it every day of my life for at least four or five years.

The food was generally good and adequate for our needs, probably standard fare for lower-middle-class American Jews of the time. Mrs. Brown was, of course, Jewish and probably cooked in a manner typical of the times. I don't remember, for example, that my mother's meals were much different from those I got in the Home. To be sure, Stollie was always praising Mrs. Brown's cooking, and often on certain holiday meals he would call her out of the kitchen to receive accolades from us for her special efforts for that feast.

During my first few years there were, however, certain meals which I dreaded. Those were the meals that included certain cooked vegetables which I could not, for the life of me, stomach. We were required to clean our plates before being allowed to eat dessert. If we lingered too long over unpalatable things we even forfeited dessert and, in fact, were not allowed to leave the table until our plates were cleared. For me, the three hardest vegetables to swallow were cooked spinach, cauliflower, and brussels sprouts. The spinach in particular was just boiled in water and came out as a green glop, but none of them was easy for me. I can remember sitting there interminably, dessert taken away from me, with all the other kids gone from the dining room, still not able to get the hated stuff down. Finally, what I did was to put the stuff in my pocket (imagine boiled, wet spinach!), bring my dish into the kitchen and scurry away to empty my pocket outdoors as quickly as possible. I got to be pretty good at pocketing the stuff (brussels sprouts and cauliflower were easier to do than spinach) without being noticed and even in time to have dessert and leave with everybody else.

A number of us little kids had our tonsils out at Miriam Hospital during one of those early summers. They took six of us the time I went, and we were all together in one children's ward, including the one girl of the group. The tonsil operation was a traumatic experience for me. They used ether as the anesthetic, and the smell was not only over-whelmingly obnoxious but I had the terrifying feeling of being smothered. People were kind to us, however. I recall a number of them coming in to see and comfort us. I suppose six tonsillectomies in a row, on a bunch of little orphanage kids, was something of a phe-nomenon and people were curious about it. Some of them gave us a few coins apiece, but the room was darkened and I couldn't see what they were. Even in the darkness and in my misery I tried to figure out what denomination the coins were. The smaller ones I hoped were dimes and the larger, nickels (larger denominations were unthinkable), so I was dis-appointed the next morning to discover only five pennies and one nickel. Nevertheless, it was a mini-bonanza for me since I almost never had any money of my own to spend.

We kids at the Home had our daily and weekly chores which generally took the form of cooperatively sweeping our dormitory and play rooms periodically, but I don't recall that these chores intruded significantly on our free time. During my first year the little kids used to take turns helping the kitchen man out after supper. This usually consisted of wiping the cutlery after he had washed them and putting them away in an orderly fashion. I had two work experiences during my last two years in the Home. One was running errands for a Jewish tailor, Mr. Gilstein, whose shop was only a few blocks away. The next year the superintendent got me a job at the Outlet Company, Provi-dence's largest department store. This was a step up for me because I worked only one day a week, Saturday, albeit for eight hours, and was paid the magnificent sum of two dollars. This was during my junior year in high school and my last year in the home.

SUPERVISORS AND SUPERINTENDENTS

My first superintendent was a short but athletic looking man who, though stern in punishment, was friendly and kindly most of the time. His ideas for running the Home were perhaps a bit old-fashioned because I seem to remember that there was a lot of reg-imentation, such as lining up for this or that. He left for a New York job within a year or two of my arrival and was succeeded by a man who was married to a Gentile woman. He was not as kindly and kept himself, as well as his wife and small daughter, aloof from us residents. He was apparently something of a scholar with a Ph.D. degree in classics. I re-member, for example, that he occasionally read Latin literature for his own amusement.

He was succeeded as superintendent by Mr. Stollerman, who remained in that post until the home was disbanded during World War II. "Stollie" (as we kids always called him, but not to his face) was a New Yorker, with bachelor and law degrees from New York University. He never practiced law, since lawyers were starving in New York during the Depression, but came to us from a similar position in a smaller institution in New York. He was a short man with a pot-belly, a round face, a gift of gab, a pretty wife and a pre-school daughter. He quickly showed that he genuinely liked the kids and the Home and that he had progressive ideas about how the institution should be managed. The kinds of regimentation we were used to were gradually done away with. There was, for example, no more lining up to go into meals, to get ready for bed, or to receive clean clothes. The atmosphere, although it had never been repressive, became much more like that of a family than an institution. Indeed, Stollie eventually had the official name changed in 1939 from "Jewish Orphanage of Rhode Island" (JORI) to "The Rhode Island Jewish Children's Home." This was a small thing, to be sure, but it illustrates Stollie's more progressive way of thinking.

Stollie was an interesting case. He had progressive ideas about how to run an orphanage. As near as I can remember his ideas were to make life for us as home-like as possible. He was genuinely fond of the kids, and they returned his affection. His wife and children mingled with us kids readily, although they still ate in their private dining room. His children often played with the Home kids as they grew to an age that was compatible with the youngest of us. I didn't know them well because they were all girls and the oldest of the three was five or so years younger than I. The youngest was born while I was still a resident, and I remember Stollie answering the phone after the birth with the greeting "Eddie Cantor speaking." He had a good sense of humor and was, of course, referring to the fact that the famous comedian also had a family of all girls (five, I believe, in Cantor's case).

Stollie was a great talker and he loved it when a number of us older kids would corner him in the living room or on the stairs going up to his apartment and get him started telling stories. We would sit around him on the floor or stairs, and he would tell us stories about his growing up in New York. His gift of gab served him in good stead because he used it effectively to raise money for the Home or to get projects funded from public funds. He was always raising funds to improve the furniture in the living room, or to improve the interior decor of the rooms, and so forth. During his regime the WPA was prevailed upon to build a series of sidewalks in part of the backyard. They also planted grass there and built our tennis court. He expounded ideas about care for kids like us (whom we would now call "underprivileged") in occasional talks around the state and eventually, I am told, wrote a small book on the subject. I am also told that he received enough recognition so that he was awarded an honorary degree by Rhode Island State College [later known as the University of Rhode Island].

Stollie was particularly fond of me and I liked him in return. He encouraged me to apply to college, even after I had left the Home, and raised funds privately to help me a little financially. For the first two years of college he raised the money for my fees and even contributed something to my room and board. Later, even though beginning in my sophomore year I earned enough during the summers and school year to cover all of my room and board, Stollie continued to help me with college fees and books. He also had his eye out for me as a possible son-in-law and said as much to my mother, but I never got to know any of his daughters very well because the war and graduate school took me out of the state for many years. When I was in town I often paid him a courtesy visit but he died at a fairly young age (62). His family moved back to New York, and I lost track of them.

During World War II the Home was disbanded (1942). The number of kids had shrunk markedly and those who remained could, with the new prosperity, be taken in by some member or members of their family. Stollie was made head administrator of the only Jewish hospital in the state, the Miriam Hospital. The buildings and grounds of the orphanage were transferred by title to the hospital, and over the years a new Miriam Hospital was built on the old orphanage site. The old hospital had outgrown its building on the west side of town, and our much bigger building was converted to the hospital. Wings were added and the hospital is now much bigger, by several times, than our original building. I do remember once visiting my sister in that hospital where she had undergone cardiac surgery. The room she was in was in the oldest section of the hospital and therefore was in the part that had been the Children's Home. I believe I recognized her room as one of the boys' dormitory rooms. Something about the appearance and even the smell, over and above the hospital smells, brought me back to my childhood days there.

WE WERE EDUCATED TOO!

During my first autumn in the Home I entered the third grade in the school across the street. I think it was in the third grade that I read my first novel. It was probably no more than a long short story but I loved it so much that I then started to explore the books in the library at the Home.

Most of the kids my age or younger didn't read for enjoyment as early as I did, and I loved the stories so much that I wanted to share them. I was able to do this when we went to bed. As the youngest boys in the Home at that time, our bedtime was perhaps an hour before the next group. We were, of course, not supposed to get out of bed or talk after lights were out, but once we felt that we were unobserved we took our chances in disobeying those rules. Talking was almost impossible to curb and this we did almost freely. During those times I started telling the others about the stories I had read. I never remembered them very accurately but I followed them as best I could and improvised the rest. I don't believe I was very good at improvising but the other kids seemed to enjoy my storytelling almost as much as I enjoyed telling them.

One of the series of adventure novels I told them about was the Boy Allies, several teen-aged boys caught in Europe in the first World War. I remember having difficulty ending the stories properly. Their adventures always ended when they beat the Germans at something or other, but I always felt that some sort of ending needed to be tacked on to that in order to end the story properly. I finally used the device of each of them getting a medal from a high official as a reward for their daring deeds. But after a couple of times that was too repetitious so I used the device, first of making the medal bigger and bigger and, finally, of increasing the number of medals, each receiving "a whole roomful of medals."

After the lights went out, we used to try to outdo each other in the tricks we could do on our beds. Our favorite was to see who could jump the highest, using the bed springs for an assist. These were iron bedsteads with flat, metallic straps crisscrossing the underside, and the straps hooked to very strong springs attached to the frame of the bed. The mattresses were like thick quilted pads, since innerspring mattresses (not to mention box springs) were unknown to us. So those beds took a terrific beating from our shenanigans but as far as I know they withstood them admirably.

After elementary school, we went to a new junior high school [Nathan Bishop] which had been open only about two years before I reached seventh grade. The junior high concept had only just been developed and adopted in Providence.

The junior high had a wonderful new gym equipped with parallel bars, horizontal bar, horse bars, rings, climbing ropes, a special device for teaching kids to do flips, and so forth, without danger to them, and I looked forward eagerly to using these devices. I was to be bitterly disappointed because I only got to use them for fleeting moments.

We did get into the beginnings of literature, however, and that was very interesting. I also took beginning Latin in the second half of the eighth grade and all of the ninth. I took to Latin immediately and the teacher was a good one. It was in Latin class that I finally began to understand English grammar more fully; over the years as I read and wrote more, the transference from Latin to English enabled me to become reasonably proficient in grammar and, I hope, clarity of expression. I do know that during my thirty plus years as a professor I had no trouble with manuscripts submitted for publication in scientific journals, and my colleagues in the biology department generally regarded me as the one to turn to for critical reading of their graduate students' theses and papers.

My religious education was continued in the Home in two ways. First we went to a Jewish Sunday school at a nearby Conservative temple, Temple Emanu-El. Thus, with my entry into the Home I changed over from an Orthodox environment to a Conservative one. I enjoyed Sunday school because it was another classroom situation of the sort in which I excelled, yet the pace and requirements of learning were slow and undemanding. They taught us Bible tales and, later, about Zionism and anti-Semitism and other issues of Judaic history and contemporary events. The Temple itself was an imposing, granite building situated close to both middle- and upper-middle class neighborhoods with a significantly high percent of Jewish occupancy. My Sunday school classmates were, I could see, from families that were far better off than mine and they were, consequently, living the kind of life I would have liked to live. I was never completely comfortable with them for that reason, although none of them ever alluded to our differences in status.

We kids in the Home also received Hebrew lessons at the Home by a Hebrew teacher, Mr. Shoham, who came there once or twice a week for that purpose. I remember the teacher very well because he could have been a good father figure for me if I had gotten to know him better. He was of average height, neither heavy nor slender, with a small full black moustache, and he was a kind and friendly man. He had lived in what was then called Palestine for a few years so he brought with him the aura of an unusual experience, because we had been studying about Jewish settlements there in Sunday school and they seemed, to me at least, to be a dangerous and adventurous way of life. Because of my natural bent toward foreign languages I did extremely well in his classes, and he appeared to be very fond of me. I retain, to this day, a pleasant memory of my association with him.

The teaching of Hebrew within Conservative Judaism at that time was restricted to learning the alphabet and their sounds, and then learning to pronounce the words as they appeared in the standard prayer book. In this manner we became proficient in reading printed Hebrew without understanding the meaning of a single word. Learning Hebrew without being able to translate it was, to me, a great waste of time and boring.

The main purpose of teaching Hebrew the way I learned it was to prepare boys for their bar mitzvah ceremony (there was no corresponding bat mitzvah for girls when I was growing up) at the age of thirteen, at which they are required not only to recite a few prayers but also to read a passage from the Torah. I was bar mitzvahed in the Home, but instead of a single ceremony for me, which would normally occur, a group of six of us Home residents shared the same ceremony, each of us performing part of the ritual in turn. It is interesting that in my bar mitzvah class of six kids, two of us earned Ph.D. degrees and one became moderately wealthy as a stockbroker.

Although we went to Sunday school at the local Conservative temple, we did not go to Sabbath services there. Instead we held our own Friday night services at the Home, usually presided over by the superintendent or the boys' supervisor. There was a special room available for this purpose, a long narrow one with a dais and pulpit to simulate a mini-synagogue. It was separated from one end of the main living room by a set of folding walls which, to my recollection, were never opened. It was also the room in which Mr. Shoham gave us our Hebrew lessons. Occasionally Friday night services were led by one of the older boys; I seem to remember my brother Nathan having done so for a while.

During my first year at the Home I was introduced to the Conservative version of the Passover seder. It consisted of a short religious service recounting the events and significance of the Exodus of the Bible, followed by a holiday feast at which matzos instead of bread were eaten, and this was followed by another short service also relating to the story of Exodus. It was a jolly occasion with much singing of traditional, joyful songs reserved for just this event. One of the major events of the seder is the asking of the "four questions" by the youngest child sufficiently proficient in Hebrew to do so. I was chosen to do them, but because I had never participated in a group seder before, I missed my cue and one of the slightly older boys who had been through it before filled in the gap before I realized my error. It was, at the time, a significant disappointment to me.

I remember that during my very early years the boys at the Home put on an old-fashioned "minstrel show" that was attended by family, friends, and donors. This was done in blackface and consisted of a chorus and a series of skits, songs, dances, and so on, done by those who had any talent for it. It was put on in the gym, which had a stage for just such a purpose. I don't remember whether or not we little kids were part of the chorus, but I do remember it was an exciting night with all the outside people arriving and all of us staying up much later than usual. Minstrel shows were at that time a common form of variety show, but, of course, tended to perpetuate the myth of Blacks as good natured but shiftless ne'er-do-wells whose only accomplishments lay in song and dance. I hope those shows are no longer done.

Years later we kids put on a Purim play in which I had one of the leading roles. It was not a traditional Purim play that re-enacted the events in Jewish history leading to this holiday. Rather, it was a play within a play, in which a group of orphanage kids who were quarantined in the hospital section of the Home because of an infectious but not debilitating condition and were consequently kept out of the normal celebration of the holiday, decided to put on their own Purim play just for themselves. I believe Stollie put it together by combining a play written about orphanage kids with the more traditional holiday play. I played one of the quarantined kids and the role of King Ahasuerus in the play within the play.

The gym was packed for the performance (folding chairs were used for all performances there) and it seemed to go off very well. I was surprised, in particular, by how well my performance was received. I recall being praised by Mr. Shoham for my part in it. It was a gratifying moment in my life, and I never lost my interest in theater.

THE LAST WORD

Walking to junior high, about a mile away, was my first extended experience with a larger world outside of the Home and its near neighborhoods. The grammar school, after all, was just across the street. That part of the street was, in fact, unpaved for most of my tenure at the Home so that the school playground was like an extension of our own back yard and playing field. In fact, the kids who lived in the neighborhood located on the other side of our playing field generally used it as a shortcut to their homes. We Home kids thus had a goodly amount of interaction with kids outside of the Home, in school, in the school playgrounds, and in our own playing field.

But these contacts were limited to the vicinity of the Home, and our segregation from the rest of society was obvious to us. This sense of being different from all of the other kids bothered me a lot, and I always yearned to be like everybody else. Walking those streets to school through middle-class neighborhoods awakened in me my sense of being different, identified by the rest of the world as an "orphan" living in an orphanage. I saw those houses and looked in their backyards and living rooms and yearned for the day when I could live like that. I suppressed these feelings and admitted them to no one—perhaps not even consciously to myself—but they were very strong and persisted in me for many years after I had left the Home.

I believe many, if not most, of the other kids in the Home harbored similar feelings of social inferiority and longing to be like everyone else. One of my friends once remarked to me long after we had both become adults that it had taken him many years to get over what he called his orphanage complex. I knew instantly and without further explanation what he meant by that. I don't think I ever got over it fully. Once I left the Home, during my senior year in high school (in Warwick rather than Providence), and then during college, I never mentioned to any of my friends my years as a resident in an orphanage. To this day I mention it only very rarely to friends and acquaintances, so I suppose I will carry some of the "complex" with me to the end of my days.

Perhaps I felt this difference most keenly during the Sunday school classes. Most of the kids in these classes lived in upper-middle-class areas because the Temple was situated in such a neighborhood and because it was the relatively more affluent Jews who gravitated to Conservative (rather than Orthodox) congregations. Thus the kids of my Sunday school class had similar backgrounds to mine, parents or grandparents who were immigrants from Eastern Europe, but whose lifestyle was so much more desirable than my own only because I had the misfortune to have my father die before I had reached a more mature age. I should emphasize that none of the other kids ever mentioned my lower social status, or even behaved in any way that could have been interpreted as "lording it over" me because of my status, neither those in secular or religious school. I don't think this was true just for me because I was a good student and respectable athlete. I had no sense that any of the other kids in the Home, including some who were backward in school or athletic play, felt as if they were looked down upon because of their social status. Nevertheless, I repeat, many of us felt this difference keenly, and in my case certainly, never got over it completely.

Perhaps it should be emphasized again that none of these feelings carried over into our behavior in the Home. There, within our own confines and with our own peer group, we felt secure and content. Our lives were actually not that much different from those whose lifestyles we envied so much. We had no lack of playmates and activities and "enjoyed" an extended family of over forty other kids. The food we ate and the clothes we wore were not that much different from those of our neighbors. We were loyal to our institution and carried with us, when we left the Home permanently, as much nostalgia for our childhood days as anyone else did. I left the Home in 1936, at the age of fifteen.

Our Rabbi with the Rainbow Division
A World War II Reminiscence

RABBI ELI A. BOHNEN

Not long after the United States became involved in World War II, and many Jewish young men were being drafted into the Armed Services, it was clear that there would be a need for Jewish chaplains. The Rabbinical Assembly called a conference of its members to discuss steps to be taken to provide Jewish chaplains for the several branches of the military. At this conference, held at the Jewish Theological Seminary in New York, the assembly voted to institute a draft of its own, since the law did not permit clergymen to be drafted by the government.

First to be called would be single rabbis, then married rabbis with no children, then men with one child. The opportunity was given to choose the branch of service. I indicated that I would want to be in the Navy.

When my turn came, I found that my orders were to report to the Army Chaplain School at Harvard University. It surprised me to learn that I was not being sent to the Navy. However, I proceeded to put my affairs in order, to arrange for a rabbi to replace me in my pulpit in Buffalo, and to find housing for my wife and daughter, who was then three years old.

Some time later, I discovered why I had not been sent to the Navy. The Jewish Welfare Board had been designated as liaison between the Jewish community and the Armed Forces. I became aware of the fact that there were many army divisions with hundreds of Jewish men without Jewish chaplains. Milton Steinberg, of blessed memory, was appointed by the JWB to make a tour of the military units to convince the generals to request Jewish chaplains. One of the divisions that Steinberg visited was the 42nd Infantry (Rainbow) Division, which had over four hundred Jewish enlisted men.

As Steinberg reported the conversation with General Collins, he quoted him as saying that before he became a general, Collins had served with another division which had a Jewish chaplain. This chaplain caused so much trouble that he determined never to have one if it could be avoided.

Milton Steinberg and I were good friends; in fact he had officiated at my wedding. It was he who convinced Collins of the need for a Jewish chaplain, and I was ordered to report to the 42nd Division, with a rank of first lieutenant, to train in Muskogee, Oklahoma.

Harry Collins looked like a general. He was tall, handsome; indeed he became known to the troops as "Hollywood Harry." I could not have asked for a more understanding general. He responded to my requests on behalf of the Jewish Displaced Persons whenever a matter concerning them was involved. He became a good friend. Some time after my arrival in Muskogee, I was summoned by him. In the course of the interview, he said rather sternly: "I know that there exists, in some divisions, what your people call anti-Semitism. It will not be tolerated in my division. Should it crop up, I will

Originally published in *Rhode Island Jewish Historical Notes*, Volume 8, Number 2 (November 1980): 81–90.

Rabbi Eli Bohnen, president of the Rabbinical Assembly, flanked by Rabbi Abraham Joshua Heschel and the Reverend Martin Luther King, Jr., at its annual meeting in New York City, March 1968. On April 4th Reverend King was assassinated in Memphis. Temple Emanu-El.

hold you personally responsible if I am not made aware of it immediately. If it does occur, I will hit the S.O.B.s so hard they will not know what struck them."

I recall a case where a Jewish soldier was going to be court-martialed. The soldier was not a native American; he was a German refugee and was serving in the division as an interpreter who interrogated German prisoners. The charge brought against him was that he had gambled with enlisted men, which was against the rules. He was tried by the Judge Advocate General, who was, I suspected, an anti-Semite. The Jewish soldier was put in the stockade as a prisoner, to await trial, and he sent for me. I went to the general and asked him for leniency. The general said he would personally attend the hearing, to which he asked me also to come. As the hearing progressed, it became evident that the young man was indeed guilty. The Judge Advocate General asked for a sentence of six months and a day in prison. The general turned to me and asked if there was anything I wished to say in rebuttal. "Sir," I said, "there is no doubt that the soldier is guilty but the 'Judge' is advocating an unreasonable punishment. According to the law, if the punishment were as advocated, it would mean he would be sent back to Germany, the land of the Nazis. It would disqualify him from ever becoming an American citizen. In effect, it would be a life sentence." The general thought for a moment and then said: "Chaplain, you are right. We will give the soldier the minimum sentence. We won't prevent him from becoming an American."

When the time came to go overseas to join the Seventh Army, the Division was divided into two parts. One was to remain behind for a few weeks, and the other would proceed to France.

I was with the unit that would not leave immediately. This assignment gave me the opportunity to celebrate Chanukah with our Jewish soldiers in the U.S.A. The Jewish community of Tulsa was most generous and sent us a large supply of gifts to distribute to our soldiers. Our division had a portable press, so we were able to print beautiful Chanukah greeting cards in color for the men to send home, something they greatly appreciated.

I was then informed that our unit would be onboard trains going to the port of embarkation on Christmas Day. I would be the only chaplain for all faiths on the train. I realized that this meant we would have a very unhappy and miserable passenger list. To be away from home, going to war, on Christmas Day was enough to destroy anyone's morale. Again I turned to the Tulsa Jews and asked for Christmas gifts. Once again they responded with an unbelievable amount of items. The problem now was, how could a rabbi handle Christian services? Fortunately, I found a Catholic soldier who was able to conduct a service and a Protestant who could lead the members of his faith. The prayers were more meaningful than ever before, because many of us wondered who would return home and who would lie in a military cemetery in Europe. These services were conducted in an open area alongside the train tracks, after which the soldiers returned to the train. The Division band was in my car. I had the men come to this central car, sing carols, and receive the Christmas gifts given by the Tulsa Jews. They were distributed by my assistant, Eli Heinberg, who had managed to find a Santa Claus suit, which raised the morale of the men.

We embarked for France. The voyage was uneventful. Soon after our arrival, the assistant Division chaplain left for medical reasons and I was asked to take his place, with a promotion to the rank of major, something that came as a complete surprise to me. I heard that the chaplains of the four battalions in the Division objected to my appointment. They claimed that it should go to a Christian chaplain since the Christians were in the great majority. I went to the Division chaplain and told him that I had no ambitions for an army career and that I would be perfectly willing to have one of the other men given the post. He was taken aback and asked me how long I had been in the army, and said that by now I should know that a promotion is not an invitation to be accepted or declined. It was an order from the general.

Later I was told that the general had called in the colonels who were the commanders of the four chaplains. He said that he had heard they had threatened to complain to Catholic hierarchy about the Jewish chaplain's promotion. The general told the colonels that if such a complaint were made, he would have them court-martialed for insubordination. The general went on to say that he had confidence in me that the interests of all faiths would be served. The Division chaplain later told me that the general had heard of how Christmas was observed on the trains and of the gifts that each soldier had received and of the services which were held for all three faiths en route.

One of the highlights of our experience in Germany was the Passover seder held in the town of Dahn. Preparations had been made for the observance of the holiday. However, the Haggadahs which the Jewish Welfare Board had ordered for us did not arrive in time because our army was advancing rapidly. Fortunately, we had one copy of a JWB Haggadah. We used the Division's offset press to print portions of the seder for the men. A copy of this "Rainbow Haggadah" is now at the Seminary Museum in New York. It was included in Professor Yerushalmi's collection of Haggadahs published by the Jewish Publication Society in 1975—because it was the first Hebrew publication in Germany since the beginning of the war.

One of my unforgettable memories of my army days concerns a soldier whom I will call Captain Fields, although that was not his real name. It was my custom, while in Germany, to pay regular visits, together with my assistant, to the men in the front lines. We would talk to the men and we felt it made them feel good that someone of their own faith was interested in their well-being.

As we spoke to a group of Jewish soldiers, they asked us if we knew Captain Fields. I told them I did not know him. They said he was the bravest man they had ever known. He did not send them into battle; he led them. They asked me if I knew if Captain Fields were a Jew. I told them that I did not know, for I had never seen him at services.

The next time we visited the company, we found the men deeply depressed. Their beloved captain had been killed in action. After each battle, the Protestant chaplain, the Catholic chaplain, and I would visit the temporary cemetery in which the recent casualties were buried. We were given a list of the names of these men. As we approached the grave of a man who was of our faith, we would step forward and recite a prayer, while the other two clergy would step back and wait. The graves were marked by wooden slabs upon which were attached the soldier's "dog tags" indicating his name, serial number, and religion.

As we looked down our list, the name Fields soon appeared, and I said, "I believe this is one of my boys," bending down to look at the dog tags. To my surprise, I saw a "P" for Protestant where I had expected to see an "H" for Hebrew. "My mistake," I said, and the Protestant chaplain came forward and read a prayer.

Whenever a soldier was killed in action, a letter would be sent to his parents informing them that their son was buried in a military cemetery and that a reverent service had been conducted by a chaplain of his faith. The letter said that it was hoped that this fact would bring some measure of consolation to the bereaved family. The general had assigned me the task of writing these letters for his signature. Thus a letter was sent to the mother of Captain Fields indicating that her son had received a Christian burial.

Several weeks had gone by when I found in my mail a letter from Mrs. Fields. She wrote that her son was a Jew, that he had become bar mitzvah in his temple, and that she would want a correction made on the dog tags. She went on to conjecture that while her son was a brave man and was not afraid of dying, he did fear capture and torture by the Nazis because he was a Jew. I responded to her letter assuring her that I would see to it that a Jewish service would be held for her son and that the designation on the dog tag would be changed to "H" for Hebrew.

The 42nd fought its way from Marseilles across France, into Germany, and then Austria. We moved from one town to another until on May 8, 1945, the Rainbow Division, with the 3rd Division, took Dachau. My assistant, Eli Heinberg, and I entered the notorious concentration camp immediately after its surrender. As I wrote to my wife, what I saw there gave me material for nightmares for the rest of my life. The living survivors looked worse than the corpses, which were piled up ready for the crematorium.

After the surrender of the German forces and the end of the war, I was given leave to go to Switzerland for a brief vacation. On the train, I met a young lieutenant who had recently arrived from the United States. He told me he had been assigned to Dachau in command of the German P.O.W.s who had not yet been sent home. Their job was to maintain the grounds. I asked the lieutenant if the gas chambers and crematoria were still there or if they had already been dismantled. He looked at me as if I were a little child, and in a very patronizing tone said: "Come, come, Chaplain. Surely you don't believe that there were ever gas chambers in Dachau! You know, we had our propaganda just as the Germans had theirs." I couldn't believe what my ears were telling me.

As soon as I returned from Switzerland the first large contingent of Jews arrived in Salzburg. The general summoned the commanding officers of the medical battalion, a Jewish captain, who was the general's personal physician, and me. He told us that he had just come from the D. P. camp where the Jews were in the majority and found it in a very chaotic state. It was filthy and not fit for human habitation. He then assigned me to work with the Jewish Displaced Persons and ordered us to go to the camp and make up a list of what would be needed to make the place livable. The three of us proceeded to that camp and found that the general had not exaggerated. We drew up a list of what was needed and brought it to the general, who handed it to his G4, the supply officer. The officer turned pale and said: "Sir, how can I get all these things? Austria has collapsed; its economy is in chaos. How can I get all this?" The general said, "I have Jewish friends back home. I know that they live clean lives in clean homes. I am ordering you to get the items on the list." The officer snapped to attention, saluted, and said, "Yes, Sir."

At first the Jews and the Yugoslavs were herded together. There was no love lost between the two groups because the Jews had good reason to believe that the Yugoslavs had collaborated with the Nazis.

One day I received a shipment of candies from the United States which I had requested for the D. P. children. I was standing and distributing the candies indiscriminately when the mother of one of the Jewish children pointed to a Yugoslav child and said: "Don't give him any candy. He's a Yugoslav." I answered rather sharply: "But he's only a little child. What harm is there in giving him candy?" The woman responded with bitterness: "It's easy for you to talk like that. Your wife and children are safe at home in America. Look over there at the child's mother. Look closely at her skirt. What do you see?" "Why, it's a *tallis*," I exclaimed. "Of course," she cried, "it's a *tallis*, and you can be sure that the Jew who wore that Tallis was murdered by a Yugoslav who wanted to bring home a gift for his wife. The little boy to whom you gave the candy will grow up and be a murderer of Jews like all the rest of the Yugoslavs."

A large proportion of the Jews had come to Austria as a way station to Italy, which was regarded as a stepping-stone to Palestine. One of the problems that we had to cope with was boredom. Eli Heinberg, my assistant, was very innovative. In civilian life, he was an industrial engineer. Before long, he had set up a trade school with classes in English and classes in Hebrew.

I had called upon the Jewish soldiers in the Division to write to their families to send me food, clothing, cosmetics, books, and so forth, to be distributed to the D. P.s. Credits were given for work in the camp, for tailoring, for shoe repairing, and so on. With these credits the D. P.s could go to the shop we set up and purchase the items which had been received from America.

The response to the requests by the soldiers for items for the D. P.s was overwhelming. One day three freight cars addressed to me came to Salzburg. Indeed the goods arrived in such quantities that I was visited by a colonel of the Inspector General's department, who was investigating the possibility that a black market project was under way. I convinced him that I was working with General Collins's blessing. He then told me that he himself was a Jew and that I should keep on doing what I was doing.

It would be a mistake to assume that everything went smoothly. When a Jewish Palestinian, a member of Haganah (the Underground), visited the camp, he told me I had been accused of diverting new clothing for my own use and substituting torn and used clothing. I found some solace in the thought that Moses had to protest that he had never stolen anything that belonged to his people. It was not a bed of roses and there were many evenings I came home drained and discouraged. But in retrospect, I thank God that I was able to be there when my people needed me.

We were indeed fortunate that General Collins was in command. I had to meet with him frequently to solve the many problems which continued to arise. While I tried to keep the general informed about every aspect of the Jewish situation, there were many times when I did not tell him everything that was taking place.

One of the problems was that of cleanliness. The Jews were housed in abandoned barracks and crowded together. The result was that none of the inhabitants of the barracks took responsibility for keeping the rooms clean. I recall one episode that left me completely frustrated and on the verge of despair. A young lieutenant knocked on my door. I asked him to come in and saw that he was distraught. He told me that he was in charge of the Jewish barracks and that the general was coming to inspect the quarters. He said that he had never seen such filth. There was excrement on the floors, on the walls, and even on the ceilings. He said the general would accept no excuse for such a situation. "Chaplain, it will be my neck. Please help me."

That very morning the general had awarded me the Bronze Star medal for meritorious service. I was still wearing my dress uniform with my new medal. I told the lieutenant that I would gather the Jews together and try to have the place cleaned up. I called a meeting in front of the barracks and told the D. P.s that the general was coming and they owed it to him to clean up the area since he had been so good to them. Their answer was: "We worked enough when we were in the concentration camps. We won't work any more." Nothing I could say would move them. As a last resort I told them of how I had been honored with a medal by the general. It called for a celebration. I was going to celebrate by cleaning their barracks and wiping up the excrement, myself. I proceeded to take off my dress jacket and began to walk to the barracks when two young D. P.s ran out from the crowd and seized me. They shouted: "No rabbi of ours is going to clean our filth. We will do it."

One of the things a soldier learns, regardless of his rank, is that you do not just walk in upon a general. The procedure is that you go to the office of the chief of staff, which is next to the general's, and ask permission to speak to the general. The chief would then ask you what your business is. If he thinks the matter needs the general's attention, he will give you permission to knock on the general's door. If he thinks someone else can handle the matter, he will direct you to that person.

When Collins realized that the Jewish D. P. problem was a serious matter that needed careful attention, he gave me special instructions. If I had a problem concerning Jewish D. P.s, I was to walk through the chief's office, into the general's office, without asking for permission. I mention this fact to indicate how seriously General Collins treated the matter of Jewish D. P.s.

Since problems came up almost every day, I was a frequent visitor to Collins's office. I had the feeling that whenever I went through the chief's office without asking permission that he was looking daggers at me.

The military authorities had established strict orders that there were to be no unauthorized parades or demonstrations in the D. P. camps. We were able to restrain some of the hotheads in the camp who wished to protest the conditions under which they lived. When we heard that an Anglo-American commission was being sent to survey the conditions, we anticipated trouble. I was sure that the D. P.s would ignore the rule against demonstrations. I felt that if a demonstration were held and ignored, nothing serious would happen. The general became aware of the situation and summoned me to meet with him. I pleaded with him to look the other way and let a Jewish captain handle the situation. The general said: "Chaplain, do you realize what you are suggesting? You are asking that I turn over a general's responsibility to a captain. I can't do that." However, he did take my advice to ignore the demonstration and ordered his men to be calm and do nothing to bring about a confrontation. The next day the general summoned me again. He spoke in very sad tones. He said that he was doing everything he could in behalf of the Jews and he expected them to appreciate it and not create additional problems for him. Fortunately, after a few days the situation became less tense and we breathed more easily for a while.

The Jews of Austria had been divided into two camps: One was in Salzburg, where I was stationed, and the other was in Linz. The headquarters were in Vienna, under the jurisdiction of General Mark Clark. General Collins of the 42nd was in command of the Salzburg area, and another general was in command of the 3rd Division in the Linz area. There was a distinct difference in the way the 42nd Division operated and the way the 3rd Division operated. General Collins had his finger on the Jewish situation. He knew what the problems were and he had his staff officers keep him informed. In Linz the general let his subordinates handle everything, while he paid little or no attention to the day-by-day problems that arose. In the 3rd Division there was no contact with a Jewish chaplain as there was with the 42nd Division.

The inevitable riot broke out in the Linz camp. Mark Clark was furious. He saw it as a reflection on his leadership and he decided to call together all the officers in charge of the Jewish camps in Austria. We were called at midnight and told that we were going to be traveling to Vienna. Everyone in the division who had anything to do with the Jewish D. P.s was ordered to join a caravan of military vehicles. The general and his aide were in the lead. As we proceeded, the general sent his aide back to each car in turn, to bring the officer in it to join him. Each officer was closely questioned on everything he knew about the Jewish D. P. situation. The general extracted every bit of information he could get. This process went on throughout the night until we arrived at Mark Clark's headquarters. We were given a little time to freshen up. The meeting took place in the board room of the Rothschild Bank. Mark Clark came into the room and we all jumped to attention. He apologized for making us drive through the night. Then his voice became harsh. He said he had deliberately made us travel all night because we had disobeyed his orders about the D. P.s. "I know why you have not obeyed my orders. It is because you are not in sympathy with them. I want you to know that I don't give a damn whether you approve or not. You will obey them." He then proceeded to question the officers of the 3rd Division about their knowledge of the D. P. situation. Most of them could not answer his questions. They did not know how many D. P.s there were in their area. They did not know what the conditions were. In short, they had not familiarized themselves with the situation in their camp. After interrogating the officers of the 3rd Division, Clark turned to General Collins. My general knew all the answers. What he had not known before the riot in Linz he had learned as he questioned his officers on the midnight ride. Twice he turned to me to amplify his answers. Mark Clark made no secret of his displeasure and annoyance with the officers of the 3rd Division. He called out to General Collins, "Harry, come with me," and putting his arm around the shoulders of the general, he walked with him into his private office leaving the officers of the 3rd Division like beaten dogs. It was a great day for General Collins, and it was a great day for the Rainbow!

The general asked me to have lunch with him together with the general of the 3rd Division. I was most uncomfortable during the luncheon because the general of the 3rd Division was obviously angry. I did not understand why he was so bitter. It wasn't until I returned to Salzburg that I was told that while General Collins was commended for his handling of the D. P. program, the general of the 3rd Division, whom I choose not to name, was relieved of his command and demoted in rank.

As a result of the meeting in Vienna, the lot of the D. P.s was greatly improved. D. P.s were moved into decent housing, food was better, barbed wire was removed, and they were treated with greater consideration.

My last official act before leaving for the U.S.A. was to make preparations for the observance of Passover. A delegation of bearded Jews approached me and asked to have the general give them a field of wheat, a mill for grinding the wheat, and a bakery for baking matzot. I told them I had made provisions for matzot and had already made all the plans for Passover. There was no need to bother the general. They objected to this, saying that they could not use machine-made matzot. I confess I was annoyed by what I regarded as nit-picking and told them they would have to make do with the matzot I had arranged for. I left for the port of embarkation believing I had done everything necessary for the holiday. Some weeks later the chaplain who replaced me wrote that the bearded gentlemen had not accepted the idea of using the matzot for which I had arranged. Somehow, they had gotten to General Collins and he had given them the field, the mill, and the bakery. When I read the letter I could not help saying to myself, "Never underestimate a stubborn Jew."

As I bring this report to a close, I want to pay tribute to my assistants, Eli Heinberg and Joseph Samelson, who worked alongside me in my efforts on behalf of the Jews in the D. P. camps. Their tasks were not easy but their dedication to their Jewish brethren overcame all the difficulties with which they were confronted.

Recollections of a Septuagenarian

RABBI WILLIAM G. (GERSHON ZEV) BRAUDE

ATTEMPTS TO LEAD A CONGREGATION, TO FIGHT FOR CAUSES, AND STUDY TORAH

My first home in Providence was in an apartment house at 90 Whitmarsh Street. Being very close to the old Temple Beth-El on Broad Street, the location seemed ideal. The tenants in the apartment house were elderly people who at first rejoiced at the arrival of a rabbi in their midst. Within a few months, however, the Armenian proprietor called on me, and said that the neighbors were unhappy with me and would I move elsewhere. Why was I asked to leave? Because I disturbed the peace at night walking to and fro in my apartment as I memorized my sermons, all of which were written out in full, so that rehearsing them took considerable time; understandably this distressed those below my apartment.

Fortunately, Mattie Pincus, who lived a block down the same street, came to the rescue of the new rabbi so soon declared *non grata*. Her father, Newman Pincus, secretary of the congregation and a Civil War veteran, had just died, leaving her and her mother Adelaide with limited means in a house bigger than they needed. So with an eye on me as tenant, she rebuilt her dwelling into two adjoining apartments, one of which was to become "the parsonage." Mattie was a woman of great energy and even greater soul. She worked as a bookkeeper at Greene Anthony, a wholesale shoe firm, and gave all her spare time to the congregation. She preserved its records. It was she who had bound and kept *The Organ*, the Temple bulletin, and who edited it with such skill. She ran the Temple Alumni Association, a youth group; she served as volunteer librarian; she gave a hand in the religious school, whose expenditures and enrollment she meticulously kept. She aspired to serve on the congregation's board, but in those days being a woman and possessed of no wealth, that honor was not given her.

When Rabbi Henry Englander came to Providence to install me, he told her, "You take care of this boy," and she did so to the last day of her life. She died shortly before the dedication of the Temple of Orchard Avenue, about which she dreamt for years.

Mattie and her mother Adelaide would hover over me, frequently inviting me to meals and overseeing all sorts of household chores in my two-room ménage, and did not bat an eyelash when they found books in the refrigerator or in the kitchen cabinets.

The first task I set for myself was to get to know the people of the congregation. Although at that time a Chevrolet cost only $600, I could not afford to purchase one. My salary of $4,000 a year had to be used in part to help my mother and sister and relatives in Palestine. So having decided to call on and get to know each and every member of the congregation, I set out on street cars, or on foot, frequently trudging through the streets of the East Side. One night, what began as a mild snowfall turned into a blizzard. As I

Excerpted from *Rhode Island Jewish Historical Notes*, Volume 8, Number 4 (November 1982): 401–441. The first part of this series appeared in Volume 8, Number 3 (November 1981): 345–372.

Rabbi William G. Braude on the third floor of his home in Providence, ca. 1975. His private collection of Judaica, one of the largest in New England, was acquired by Stanford University. Temple Beth-El.

was looking for shelter somewhere, the sight of a mezuzah on a doorpost encouraged me to ring the bell.

My pastoral tour elicited a favorable response, and for some time many people came to Sabbath eve services. My being new was, of course, also helpful. I felt that good turnouts should continue, and that a brief decree from me printed in the Temple bulletin, "Friday night was Temple night," would clinch the matter. It did not quite happen that way. Before long I heard that on a Friday night there had taken place a big dinner party, hosted by two monied men of the congregation, one of whom had been on the search committee that brought me to Beth-El. I called him first to ask him not to plan parties on a Friday night in the future. He was noncommittal, but polite. The second unceremoniously told me to mind my own business.

Undaunted I set out to "do" other things. In my inaugural talk (October 18, 1932), I said, "All Jews are held together by invisible and enduring bonds that make Israel a people eternal." Well, one of these bonds is the Jewish calendar. Beth-El's practice of holding confirmation services on the Sunday before or after Shavuot seemed to threaten disunity among our people. And so I began to plead that confirmation be held on the day the festival fell. Though at the time my reputation was high, neither the president nor the board would introduce the change I requested, but put it up to the congregation's annual meeting. The good sense of the congregation moved them to accept my plea. Ever since 1934, confirmation at Beth-El has been held on Shavuot, now the prevailing pattern in Reform congregations throughout the land.

Shavuot was at least given a courteous bow. But Purim was regarded as a barbaric observance. One very fine lady argued that "in this day and age someone like Haman who would set out to destroy the entire Jewish people was inconceivable." The lady's remark was made with Hitler already ruler of Germany. Tu Bishvat, Jewish Arbor Day, being connected with Palestine, was contraband. The present Sisterhood's calendar, I am glad to say, lists all special days in the Jewish year.

During the years that followed, not only Shavuot, but Sabbath morning services, all evening and morning festival services, even Rosh Hodesh, New Moon, became part of the congregational calendar. Since the seventh of November 1955 we have had a daily minyan, meeting even when blizzards struck.

In my inaugural talk I spoke of "the ideals of lore and learning that have ever been luminous in the darkest of centuries." Well, in practical terms it meant that a congregation is to have a *Jewish* library.

Beth-El did have a library. It was founded in 1892 by Rabbi David Blaustein and Mattie Pincus, but it was in a state of neglect, its relatively few items of Judaica being overwhelmed by castoff sets of public school textbooks, of the Rover Boys, Horatio Alger, and such. Without asking permission from anybody, Mrs. George Nathanson, president of the Sisterhood, and I went through the shelves and discarded all volumes extraneous to a Jewish library. All such books we distributed among rural libraries or turned over to the state board of education. Feverishly, I set about building up the collection. Thus, in the 1930s, when the Soncino translation of the Talmud began to appear, I remember standing on a Sunday morning in front of the Temple soliciting from parents or grandparents ten dollar contributions—ten dollars was the cost of each of the volumes.

To enlarge the library, I conceived a three-fold barter: Beth-El had a surplus of ordinary Judaica, which Brown University did not possess. Brown had a surplus of books on science and biology, which Yeshiva College in New York did not possess. Yeshiva had a surplus of certain Hebrew books, which Beth-El did not possess (in fact Beth-El had no Hebrew books). So with me at the wheel of my car, which by this time I acquired, Beth-El's books went to Brown, Brown's books to Yeshiva, and Yeshiva's books to Beth-El.

Whenever something which I regarded as particularly un-Jewish occurred in the congregation, I let off steam by buying Hebrew books for the library.

Through the years the people of Beth-El have been very good in contributing to the library, which now numbers approximately 21,000 volumes, and is said to be the foremost congregational library in the United States. Our library's resources are made use of throughout the state and in nearby Massachusetts.

In this connection, not only Hebrew books were of concern to me, but also Hebrew names for our people, giving such names to newly born children when named during the Friday night service—a practice now widely observed. In the school we began calling children by their Hebrew names.

My personal library also deserves mention. In 1945, when we moved from 160 Brown Street to our own home on 93 Arlington Avenue, the collection had become so large that it could no longer be accommodated in one room. So we broke down a partition on the third floor, built bookcases in the interior of the enlarged space, and what was left of the walls was panelled with California redwood and birch. Presently the collection spreads into the hallway, then into another room, and into what had been a storage area, even into drawers in which cloth and linen used to be kept. The entire third floor is now a library, all of it—books, pamphlets, periodicals, offprints and separata numbering well over eight thousand items—catalogued.

In my inaugural talk I pledged loyalty to the people of Israel "whatever they be, whether adorned with patriarchal beards or clean of visage." Among other things I took this to mean reaffirming that Yiddish, not infrequently treated as a stepchild, was bone of our bones and flesh of our flesh; it meant reaching out to our Orthodox brethren; it meant also avowing Zionism and working for its goals.

By way of reaffirming Yiddish, I subscribed to a Yiddish newspaper and was not self-conscious about reading it while traveling on street cars. In my sermons at Beth-El, I frequently used Yiddish expressions, and to make a point, even sang Yiddish ditties. Yiddish flowed naturally from my being, and so I resorted to it to add color and drama to my talks. Many members of the congregation loved it because Yiddish evoked precious memories. To those who objected, it meant an unwelcome reminder of the poverty and humiliation which Yiddish represented to them.

On the second day of Rosh Hashanah I used to attend Orthodox synagogues, and now and then lectured from their pulpits in Yiddish. In those days brotherhoods of Reform congregations liked confrontations of Reform, Orthodox, and Conservative rabbis meeting on a dais and setting forth the elements which set them apart. I resisted suggestions for such meetings, feeling instinctively the need to assert Israel's commonalty—*Kelal Yisrael*, our people's togetherness.

Through the years I felt that Temple Beth-Israel on Niagara Street and Temple Emanu-El on Morris Avenue were collaborators and not competitors, that Conservative and Reform congregations and their rabbis should work together—should be partners, not rivals. I affirmed Zionist convictions, and at services that called for the anthem, had the Hatikvah sung, causing displeasure among some in the congregation.

In my inaugural address I pledged "my loyalty to the traditions of our people . . . to the customs and practices that have ever been our ethnic and ethical integrators." Well, among other tasks, this meant Judaizing or Hebraizing the music of the service, which needed it badly, as I was to discover when soon after my arrival I visited the choir loft. I was appalled by its collection of music, made up in the main of anthems with "Jesus, Son of God" crossed out and "our Father in heaven" written in. For the High Holidays, Sigmund Schlesinger's German Protestant music flavored by tunes from Italian operas was the mainstay.

I turned for counsel to Rabbi Jacob Singer of Chicago, with whom I spent an entire day. It was he who introduced me to the High Holiday music of Edward Stark with "cantor solos, form and choruses based upon traditional themes."

In 1943 we engaged Heinrich Schalit, renowned composer of synagogue music, as director of the choir, and after a period of intense and at times bitter struggle, the cantorate was restored to Beth-El's congregational worship.

In my inaugural talk I pledged loyalty to "the conceptions of justice and righteousness, which have ever been the foes of oppression and misdoing." In the 1930s, I was captivated by Gandhi, and became an ardent pacifist. I failed to understand that, whereas Gandhi confronted the British *Raj*, which, despite backslidings, remained civilized, we Jews and the world confronted the German Nazi, cruel and committed to denial of all precepts of behavior associated with the word "civilization." And so, in my callow pacifism, I did foolish things. Thus, I opposed the call by Jewish organizations to declare a boycott against Germany, asserting that such a boycott was an act of war. I wrote to Dieckhoff, the Nazi ambassador in Washington, saying that unless his government would relent in its hostility to Jews, I might advise my friends not to use the German liner, *The Bremen*. I was naive enough to believe that my pebbles of disapproval might move the Nazi monster.

In those days I was intimately associated with liberal ministers such as Everett M. Baker, a Unitarian, Arthur E. Wilson, a Congregationalist, and Robert H. Schacht, a Unitarian, and Jewish and Quaker ladies in promoting pacifism and "social justice," as it was then called.

We were in the midst of the Depression, and our small group clamored for increased support for the poor. In 1939 we founded the Providence Urban League—I became its vice president—and on my own I went from office to office, from bank to bank, from hospital to hospital, pleading that Negroes be engaged for tasks other than those that are menial. To little avail.

A few years later in an anguished sermon entitled "Confessions in a Grave Hour," I recanted my pacifism, and in 1939 or 1940 endeavored to enlist in the Navy as a chaplain. The medical examiner rejected me because of my severe myopia.

When the refugees began coming to Providence, I threw myself into the work of providing all kinds of help for them. The morning after November 10, 1938, Crystal Night, I all but ran for a week or so, from one office to another, from one store to another, trying to get people to sign affidavits of support for families clamoring to flee the Nazi death trap.

To counteract the horror of Crystal Night, the congregation set aside a Friday night to welcome the new arrivals. A few minutes before the service was to begin, the man who was then president of the congregation rushed into the rabbi's small study in the rear of the synagogue, and in a stentorian voice demanded, "Did you tell those people that they could wear hats?" Cowed by the bullying attack on me, I stammered whatever I stammered in reply. That Sabbath eve was for me an eve of mourning—mourning not only the Nazi atrocities, but mourning also the insensitivity of that man to the feelings of our guests.

Soon after my arrival at Beth-El, I felt that the religious school should have a full-time head and persuaded the board to engage Mordecai I. Soloff. Ours was the first and only midsized congregation to have a professional director. During his two years in Providence, he tightened discipline, introduced regular weekday instruction in Hebrew, and began developing an orderly curriculum. Unfortunately, while I was away during the summer, the arbitrary decision of one individual resulted in Mordecai Soloff's abrupt dismissal. Not until my return to Providence did I learn of it.

This incident brings me to the position of the rabbi vis-à-vis the president and the board. Within a few months after my coming to Providence, the man who was then president let drop a hint that as president he had the right to read in advance and presumably censor my sermons. I told him politely but unmistakably that I rejected his notion.

That give-and-take between myself and the president on freedom of the pulpit and incidents such as the dismissal of Mordecai Soloff led me on August 26, 1937 to set down in my diary a defiance: "Some men are determined to possess my soul, and I shall never permit it."

In this ongoing struggle I was helped for a while by John Jacob Rosenfeld, a friend, who in 1942 left his estate—it ultimately reached $270,000—to the congregation for the building of a school. The bequest enabled my friends to rally around me, and among other things relieved me of a president whom I found intolerable. For a spell I was allowed "to possess my soul."

In 1936 after Mordecai Soloff was asked to leave, Mattie Pincus took over the running of the school. But I kept pressing for a full-time director. Albert Bilgray, who in 1937 had completed a term as rabbi in Springfield, Ohio, decided he wanted to devote himself altogether to education, and was willing to come to Beth-El. Albert Bilgray, who was to serve in Providence for seven years, was able, conscientious, and gentle. He was the only rabbi to serve as president of the Rhode Island Association of Ministers.

During the years that followed, after we moved to Orchard Avenue, the membership of the congregation quadrupled, and we needed two rabbis. We were fortunate in the young men who came to serve: Jerome Gurland and I became so close. His presence—his tact and understanding—helped immensely during several congregational crises. Then, too, we not only studied *Chumash* and *Rashi* together, but also read through the *Pesikta Rabbati*. Then Herman Blumberg, able and loyal, resourceful and imaginative in the school, and profoundly concerned with social issues.

Finally, Leslie Y. Gutterman, whom I met at Hebrew Union College in 1970. I found myself captivated at once and invited him to Providence. It soon became obvious that he would be my successor. His charm, wit, and rare pastoral talent have won for him the esteem and affection of the congregation and of the larger community.

Each of these rabbis has been for me a source of strength and inspiration. The companionship of friends in the congregation, a few of whom I would single out by name, has also meant much. Their support and understanding heartened me in difficult days. There was, as already stated, Mattie Pincus. There were Irving J. Fain, Beryl Segal, Abe Klein, and Dr. Samuel Pritzker—their devotion was that of brothers. I might mention many, many other men and women whose friendship and loyalty sustained me as I moved from controversy to controversy. Never, never, however—even in dark days—did I doubt the worth of the congregation or the genuineness of its people.

PURSUING STUDY OF TORAH IN THE FACE OF CRITICISM AND BUILDING THE NEW TEMPLE

For a number of years certain members of the board began to be impatient with my pursuing studies at Brown University, a matter agreed upon at my arrival in Providence. I was admitted to Brown's Graduate School and for my M.A. thesis decided to go over the secondary sources treating Jewish attitudes to converts and conversion. The only place to do the reading required was the library of Harvard's Divinity School. So during my vacation in the summer of 1933 I rented a room in Wigglesworth Hall. I spent my days in the Divinity School library struggling through German essays on Jewish attitudes toward converts and conversion—essays suffused with anti-Semitism, which indicated that Nazism in Germany was not a Johnny-come-lately phenomenon.

[But I had a] growing awareness that some people of the congregation were increasingly displeased by my obsession with studies and by what they regarded as "truancy" from my duties as a rabbi. Still, despite criticism, I persisted in my studies at Brown. I found myself in classrooms with Samuel Belkin, who was to become president of Yeshiva University and one of my closest friends.

Robert P. Casey, head of the department of religious studies, appointed me lecturer in 1937 after I received my Ph.D. Pearl Finkelstein registered in the elementary class in Hebrew. I first met her in June 1937, near the Van Wickle gate of Brown University. Her smile captivated me at once, so that during that summer I wrote to her. On the sixteenth of September I took her to Boston for dinner, and on the eighth of December I knew that I wanted her to be my wife.

In June, 1938, in the garden of the home of her parents Joseph and Rose Finkelstein in Johnston, Rhode Island, Rabbi Morris Schussheim of Temple Beth-Israel, where she was confirmed, Rabbi Jacob K. Shankman, and Rabbi Samuel Belkin officiated. As the procession of the wedding party moved out of the house toward the tree which was to provide the *chuppah* (wedding canopy), birds began to sing.

Even while courting Pearl, I took to calling her Peninnah (Hebrew for "Pearl"), which I shorted to "Pen." Before *Kiddush* (Sanctification of the Sabbath) on Sabbath eve, when I serenade her with *Eshet Chayil*, and sing the words "Her price is far above rubies," it is in tribute to what she has meant to me through the years.

A year or two later, I was to meet Knute Ansgar Nelson, a Benedictine monk from the Portsmouth Priory, Portsmouth, Rhode Island. When he came to my class at Brown University, he knew no Hebrew at all. At the end of the year he mastered so much Hebrew that he was able to memorize *Pirke Abot*. So we started the second year by reading the Book of Psalms. I used Rashi's commentary, and Brother Ansgar would bring a folio volume of St. Augustine. Later Brother Caedmon Holmes, whom Brother Ansgar taught Hebrew, was to join us in the reading of our sacred texts. Both men are filled with "awe of God and love of Torah."

Subsequently I encountered similar reverence in Fr. Pierre Lennard, head of the Ratisbonne Monastery in Jerusalem, who studied Talmud. At first, he said, its passages were baffling, unintelligible. But he persisted until the apparently disparate parts came together, and then he experienced joy—the thrill and privilege of meaning, pellucid meaning shining forth.

My immersion in Psalms led me to give talks on them to the School for the Jewish Woman, an ambitious venture in adult education, sponsored jointly by Temple Beth-El and the Conservative Temple Beth-Israel. Beneficent Congregational Church invited me to give a series on the Psalms during Lent; and the downtown Grace Episcopal Church invited me to be one of the Lenten noon-hour preachers—during those years a prestigious series.

John Jacob Rosenfeld's bequest to the congregation for the building of a school was to mean much for the future of the congregation, located as it was then on Broad Street in an area from which Jews had begun to move. The new site presently acquired was on Orchard Avenue on the East Side of Providence, which was rapidly becoming the center of the Jewish community. At the time we decided we had to build elsewhere, a sum even larger than Rosenfeld's had become available from the bequest of Alphonse Joseph Lederer, who, like Rosenfeld, was a close friend.

The issue we faced at the beginning was the style of architecture. The majority of the board and I, too, felt it should be colonial. Here my wife's knowledge and determination were to prove decisive. Her minor at Pembroke College in Brown University was the history of art. She began by persuading me that significant structures are rarely evocative or nostalgic, but are in an idiom which is contemporary. She did more. She went to a conference on synagogue architecture convoked in New York City by the Union of American

Hebrew Congregations. At that conference, plans of synagogues were displayed. She found Percival Goodman's designs most exciting.

Percival Goodman believed that a synagogue should have organic unity, so that its exterior would reflect the activities within it. He also believed that a synagogue plan should provide settings for great works of art which would reflect our religious aspirations and loyalties.

During Goodman's subsequent visit with the building plans committee he made a very good impression. Still, our decision to build in the contemporary style was made final only after Albert Simonson, professor of architecture at Rhode Island School of Design, advocated it before the board. During construction I gave counsel to the different artists. Thus I explained to Ibram Lassaw that the two pillars flanking the Ark, *Jachin* ("Fire") and *Boaz* ("Cloud"), were meant to reflect God's explicit and implicit powers. Lassaw's columns, upon being unpacked, were at first dubbed "Jungle-gyms," but after the Museum of Modern Art asked permission to have our Pillar of Cloud exhibited at the Biennale in Venice as one of the three best examples of American sculpture, the scorners and name-callers grew silent. I should add that the artists were accorded full freedom in the execution of their works.

Pen's gifts found varied expression during the building of the Temple. She worked on the color schemes and made the final choice of fabrics. She did the silk-screened draperies for the rabbi's study and worked closely with Dorothy Liebes, the weaver. The colors were to be those of the hangings in the Tabernacle—scarlet, purple, blue, gold thread and fine linen. She put together the colored stripes of varying widths. She made the *Mappah*, the coverlet for the Cantor's lectern, and the *Mappah* for the chapel out of Indian saris. She designed and with the help of women of the congregation sewed by hand the Torah mantles—gold for the year round and white for the High Holy Days.

In 1954 as we were reaching the end of construction, we had the "war" of the Hanukkah lamp, a sizable installation which was to be lit by children and adults during the week of Hanukkah. A few were against such public display and wanted the lamp set up in the rear of the Temple. Others, including Pen and myself, wanted to have it stand in the open—a way of saying, "We are what we are—the lights represent affirmation of our faith." We won—the Hanukkah lamp is at the Temple's façade. The dedication of the new Temple, a magnificent series of events, took place in April 1954.

In the middle 1940s I began to feel the need for chairs of Jewish studies at American universities. On his own, Henry M. Wriston, president of Brown University, approached Jewish alumni to have them endow a chair for Jewish studies at Brown but with no success. Wriston indicated the low esteem accorded to Jewish studies in those years.

From time to time I approached people in Providence to give money to Brown to endow a chair of Jewish studies, but succeeded only in raising money for one-year stands. We thus had Gershom Scholem, Leon Roth, Zvi Werblowsky, Raphael Loewe, and Yigael Yadin come to Brown as visiting professors for a year.

My increasing concern with Jewish studies led me to support the struggling Providence Hebrew Day School under the auspices of Torah Umesorah. All of Providence's Jewish "leadership," and, it goes without saying, the leadership of my own congregation, were opposed to such a school. Nevertheless, in November 1948 I gave a sermon in which I backed the idea; and, I should add, Pen and I sent our children to the Day School.

At that time the very idea that a Reform rabbi send his children to a Hebrew day school—a parochial school as it was disdainfully designated—was not just preposterous, it was scandalous. This decision as well as other actions of mine persuaded some people that I was "Orthodox." So much so that in 1954, a few years later, when the Beth-El on Broad Street was sold to Shaare Zedek, an Orthodox congregation, there circulated the quip, "Braude was determined to turn Beth-El into an Orthodox shul, and by golly he had his way."

I was scared. So before deciding to send our children to the Day School, I turned to my guru, Professor Harry A. Wolfson of Harvard University, whose instant response was, "Send them, send them. They'll learn to eat *trafe* on their own. But Hebrew never." What in 1948 appeared to be preposterous has now become accepted. In cities where there is a day school, the local Reform rabbis generally send their children to it.

In those years Pen and I also decided to have a kosher home, and I, intermittently, resumed putting on tefillin for *Shaharit*. The wish to enable visiting Jews who observe *Kashrut* to eat at our table motivated in part our decision. Like tefillin, *Kashrut*, once a no-no in Reform circles, is now observed in the homes of many Reform rabbis throughout the land.

About that time I went to see Harry Wolfson to discuss with him the idea of chairs of Jewish studies at American universities. But he proceeded to another matter: A great university was about to launch a series of translations of classic Jewish texts. Would I be interested? I suggested the *Midrash on Psalms*, the principal source of Rashi's commentary on the Psalms. Shortly thereafter, under Wolfson's guidance, I began working on the text. The work became such an obsession that my wife began calling it her husband's mistress.

Professor Harry A. Wolfson was not the only scholar who helped. Rabbi Menahem Mendal Kasher introduced me to Professor Saul Lieberman of the Jewish Theological Seminary, who gave me many, many hours during which he shared with me his enormous learning in Rabbinica.

The *Midrash on Psalms* in two volumes was finally published by Yale University Press. It did not set the world on fire as I dreamt. Not even members of my own family were overwhelmed except for one, my oldest son, Joel Isaac, who at the time was studying at the Hebrew University.

The *Midrash on Psalms*, a work of twelve hundred pages, required infinite preparation and concentration. So unless there was an emergency, I shut myself off mornings in my study and was "unavailable" for chitchat on the phone. But when there was genuine need, I left my desk and immediately went to help. The grumbling in the congregation rose. More and more people felt that they did not hire a rabbi to write books. My job was on the line. Nevertheless, if I had been confronted with an ultimatum, "Give up your 'obsession' or resign," even though I had no financial resources, and three children to support, I would have resigned. This too I would not have dared to do but for Pen's support.

Fortunately for me there were enough people who felt that to serve his congregation properly a rabbi should continue to study Torah. My twenty-fifth year was celebrated with much éclat. I was granted a year's leave, which our family spent in Israel, and was given life tenure. Our twenty-fifth wedding anniversary was celebrated by the congregation's purchase of a Torah scroll in our honor. In 1967, the seventy-fifth anniversary of the library, it was renamed the William G. Braude Library of Temple Beth-El. Through the years, the majority of the people of Beth-El have supported me in ever so many ways.

Instinctively, they felt that no rabbi, including myself, had only one facet in his work. The nature of the rabbinate is such that a rabbi must engage in a multitude of concerns as I endeavored to do. If he is worth his salt, he comes to excel in one area, whether it be social action, Zionism and Israel, matters ecumenical, pastoral or administrative, or scholarship. In my reaching out for the world of Jewish learning, the majority of the people of the congregation not only saw nothing wrong in it—they believed it to be admirable.

Nevertheless, in earlier years, the criticism of some in the congregation, particularly certain officers, as well as my growing reverence for the tradition made me begin to think that I should not continue as a Reform rabbi—perhaps change to a Conservative or even an Orthodox pulpit.

I remember going to consult Rabbi Samuel Schulman, the retired rabbi of Temple Emanu-El, New York. He, too, he said, shared my reverence for tradition. From time to time he wanted to stand up on a Sunday morning in Carnegie Hall with *tallis* and tefillin on his head. Nevertheless, Rabbi Schulman advised me to remain in the Reform rabbinate. So did Samuel Belkin.

I am glad I listened to their advice. I should add that the Centenary Statement of Reform Judaism, published in the middle 1970s by the Central Conference of American Rabbis, made me feel no longer an "outsider," but one in the mainstream of the movement.

During the 1950s and early 1960s "social action" was of passionate concern to me, as it was to Ernest Nathan, then president, to Irving Jay Fain, to Stanley Grossman, and to many others. And so in tandem with Rabbi Saul Leeman I joined Martin Luther King's march to Montgomery, Alabama. But it was in Montgomery that I began to have a more sober view of the entire problem. It happened while visiting a Sephardi synagogue during the repast following a Thursday morning bar mitzvah. The woman seated next to me, who, of course, knew that I was one of the marchers, all but turned her back upon me. Finally she faced me, glowering, "When are you going home?" I told her I would go the next day. And she went on: "Why did you come here? Helicopters and the U.S. Army have been protecting you along the route. Then you will go back North, denounce us, and make like a big hero while we remain here and take upon ourselves the mischief you wrought. These people, the whites of Montgomery, have been good to us, and you make our life here so very difficult."

Then and there, I realized that I was indulging in heroics with impunity, blissfully unaware and unconcerned that others, specifically my brothers in the South, would have to pay the bill. Still, I do not regret my participation in the march and remain a liberal in the classic sense, espousing equality and very limited interference by government.

During my march to Montgomery I noted that many blacks, and whites too, wore *yarmulkes* (skull caps), which they called "freedom caps." So many Jews with yarmulkes on their heads participated in the march that the yarmulke became a symbol of freedom.

The impact of the yarmulke as a "freedom cap" and my growing respect for Jewish tradition led me to give in 1965 the Rosh Hashanah sermon, "What I Learned in Alabama about Yarmulkes," at the end of which I put on a yarmulke as I pronounced the *she-heheyyanu*. I was told afterwards that during the sermon some people wept. A few dared to applaud, and quite a number took yarmulkes out of their pockets and put them on their heads. Since no one in the congregation knew that I was about to cover my head—until that morning I always appeared in the pulpit with my head uncovered—the emergence of yarmulkes on men's heads was a complete surprise to me. Apparently some men setting out for Beth-El, because of their childhood memories, put yarmulkes in their pockets.

In my various affirmations of respect, indeed reverence, for tradition I, in fact, came to realize that I voiced the convictions of many people in the congregation.

VENTURES

My incursion into politics: Upon my return from a trip during the summer of 1943, Pen, my wife, reported that Lillian Potter had telephoned and told the following: Gordon Mulvey, who worked for City Hall as a plumber, circulated petitions and secured the required number of signatures to be a candidate in the forthcoming election for the School Committee. Since no other candidate had himself qualified, he was a shoo-in, and the cause of good government in Providence would suffer irreparably, unless a strong counter-candidate be nominated. The League of Women Voters felt that my reputation as an intellectual might tip the balance in the ballots, particularly since Brown University was in our school district. With such flattery from a bevy of women, reinforced as it happened by my wife's quondam liberalism, how could I resist? I consented to run, little realizing what I was letting myself in for. I did not stand a chance. For, despite the supposedly nonpartisan character of the elections for the School Committee, they were in fact strongly partisan—Gordon Mulvey represented the Democrats, who at that time were in absolute control of the city, and his opponent was automatically Republican.

Besides, in those days, a clergyman's incursion into politics was a no-no, disapproved of by quite a number of people in my congregation. Hence, when I tried to explain during a Rosh Hashanah sermon what a "valiant knight" I was, one of those who disapproved, a "pillar," got up and solemnly walked out of the Temple. He was quoted later as saying that he did not wish to have the pulpit polluted by politics. His demonstrative departure made Pen and me even more determined to proceed. We tried hard. We had ads inserted in the *Providence Chronicle*, the African American weekly. Here is the text of one such ad:

YOUR CANDIDATE FOR THE SCHOOL COMMITTEE
District G
WILLIAM G. BRAUDE

A few days before the recent School Committee caucus, my wife asked an African American friend of many years' standing to vote for me. He promised he would. The day after the caucus he happened to pass our house. My wife hailed and asked: "Did you vote for my husband, Tom?" He was then halfway down the street. Slowly he wheeled around and came back to her. "I have a confession to make. I did not vote yesterday because I am not a citizen of the United States." "But, Tom," my wife was surprised, "how long have you been here?" "Practically all my life," Tom answered. "I was brought here as an infant from a French island possession. When I grew up I applied for my first papers. That day I learned that to become a citizen I had to swear off all allegiance to the Republic of France. I came home and wept most of the night. In the morning I made my resolution: I would never swear off the French Republic. There they treat the colored man like a human being. There the colored man has equal opportunity to share in the life of the community."

I happened to come along as Tom was finishing his story. This straightforward confession by an honest and sensitive man moved me deeply.

If the people elect me as a member of the School Committee I shall dedicate my best energies to the end that the colored people of our community be given the right to teach, to work and to share as equals in the schools of Providence.

For the Man Who Will Represent YOU Vote For

WILLIAM G. BRAUDE

Vote on Tuesday, November 2nd at Your Nearest Polling Place

Pull the First Lever

For Transportation Call De. 9533

We distributed fliers in Italian. We turned our home into campaign headquarters. Our three-year-old son, Joel Isaac, walked around, saying: "Back Braude for Better Schools." Republicans, of course, provided money. In the end, it goes without saying, we lost.

Did the cause of good government suffer irreparably? Not at all. The "plumber," the unspeakable plumber, was to become an invaluable member of the school committee, in time to serve with distinction as its chairman. So much for the prescience of the League of Women Voters.

In retrospect, do I regret the effort which took so much out of Pen and me? Not at all. As a result of the campaign I came to realize the complexity of Providence, made up as it was of so many ethnic "islands" which lived unto themselves. Although at the time I had already been in Providence eleven years, there were many Jews in my district who had never heard the name "Braude," and neither knew nor cared about my very existence—chilling but wholesome medication.

I learned, too, to entertain a healthy respect for a "politician." His severest critics would have to admit that getting elected was no "cinch." A political campaign, even in a School Committee election, is a grueling ordeal.

Suppose I had been elected. I would then have given myself to the problems of the School Committee, whose crucial decisions I could not possibly have affected. I would have had to cut sharply into the time given to congregational duties. Besides, I would not have been able to devote myself to rabbinic studies which I was to begin under Professor Wolfson in 1945.

So, in defeating me, the voters acted, if I dare say so, as unconscious instruments of God's will: by voting against me they directed me to the world of Jewish lore.

STILL ANOTHER ENDEAVOR

Quite a number of years ago my teacher Harry A. Wolfson suggested to me that I should translate Bialik and Rawnitzky's *Sefer ha-Aggadah*. Then when I visited him at the Stillman Infirmary on Wednesday September 11, 1974, he asked me again—his last words to me—whether I had started on the *Sefer ha-Aggadah*, and he told me I was the one to do it. On September 23, 1974, the day after Harry Wolfson's funeral, I began to work on the translation.

Sefer ha-Aggadah, "The Book of Jewish Lore," a work of 687 pages, was published by Dvir in 1908, and since then was reprinted frequently. It is the most comprehensive anthology of Jewish lore extant, and is widely regarded as a masterpiece. When published, the work may appear in four volumes. May God permit me to see this ongoing endeavor to its conclusion. [The magnificent translation was published posthumously by Schocken Books in 1992.]

My forty-two years as active rabbi of Temple Beth-El have not always been easy, often quite stormy, filled as they were with controversy, and crises, during the worst of which I never doubted the decency, the judgment, the good will of the people in the congregation. A rabbi and a congregation who stay together are, to quote Marie Presel, like an old married couple. They have their fallings out, but they always come together. So, on balance, my decision to come to and stay at Beth-El was right. In time, even critics will, I hope, come to feel that my years at Beth-El have served some purpose, God's purpose, I trust, which none of us can presume to chart or fathom. We are Congregation of the Sons of Israel and David. Both Israel and David have had tempestuous careers, and thank God, both Israel and David's symbols are alive, even as with God's help, this congregation will stay alive long after all of us are gone, and will continue to meet in a Beth-El, which it will strive to make truly a House of God, so that beneath its halls for worship, study, and assembly there will be God's everlasting arms.

APPENDIX A
Editors of Rhode Island Jewish Historical Notes

David C. Adelman	1954–1961
Seebert J. Goldowsky	1962–1978
Albert Salzberg	1979–1982
Seebert J. Goldowsky	1983
George H. Kellner	1984
Michael Fink	1985–1987
Judith Weiss Cohen	1988–1997
Leonard Moss	1998–2003

APPENDIX B

Letter from the Hebrew Congregation of Newport to President George Washington, 1790, and the Reply of President Washington (undated)

George Washington received many letters of congratulations upon his election as first President of the United States in 1789. The Newport Jewish community was one of three American Jewish communities that sent their greetings. Drafted by synagogue hazan Moses Seixas, the Newport letter was written in 1790 in conjunction with Washington's visit to the city. Seixas's letter expressed gratitude for the new nation that granted Jews "the invaluable rights of free citizenship," and he penned the memorable phrase, "a government which to bigotry gives no sanction, to persecution no assistance."

In his reply to the Newport Jewish community, Washington took Seixas's phrase and extended its meaning. In America, Washington asserted, "all possess alike liberty of conscience and immunities of citizenship." These rights are not given by the government as a matter of "indulgence" or "toleration," but are the inherent, natural rights of all its citizens—including its Jews. The government requires only that "they who live under its protection should demean themselves as good citizens" and give their nation "on all occasions their effectual support."

The Seixas and Washington letters offer important language for American religious rights and freedoms. A public reading and celebration of the letters takes place annually at Touro Synagogue.

ADDRESS OF THE NEWPORT CONGREGATION TO THE PRESIDENT OF THE UNITED STATES [AUGUST 17, 1790]

Sir: Permit the children of the stock of Abraham to approach you with the most cordial affection and esteem for your person and merit, and to join with our fellow-citizens in welcoming you to Newport.

With pleasure we reflect on those days of difficulty and danger when the God of Israel, who delivered David from the peril of the sword, shielded your head in the day of battle; and we rejoice to think that the same spirit which rested in the bosom of the greatly beloved Daniel, enabling him to preside over the provinces of the Babylonian Empire, rests and will ever rest upon you, enabling you to discharge the arduous duties of the Chief Magistrate of these States.

Deprived as we hitherto have been of the invaluable rights of free citizens, we now—with a deep sense of gratitude to the Almighty Disposer of all events—behold a government erected by the majesty of the people—a government which to bigotry gives no sanction, to persecution no assistance, but generously affording to all liberty of conscience and immunities of citizenship, deeming every one of whatever nation, tongue, or language, equal parts of the great governmental machine.

This so ample and extensive Federal Union, whose base is philanthropy, mutual confidence and public virtue, we cannot but acknowledge to be the work of the great God, who rules in the armies of the heavens and among the inhabitants of the earth, doing whatever seemeth to Him good.

For all blessings of civil and religious liberty which we enjoy under an equal and benign administration, we desire to send up our thanks to the Ancient of days, the great Preserver of men, beseeching Him that the angels who conducted our forefathers through the wilderness into the promised land may graciously conduct you through all the difficulties and dangers of this mortal life; and when, like Joshua, full of days and full of honors, you are gathered to your fathers, may you be admitted into the heavenly paradise to partake of the water of life and the tree of immortality.

Done and signed by orders of the Hebrew Congregation in Newport, Rhode Island.

Moses Seixas, Warden

Newport, August 17, 1790

WASHINGTON'S REPLY TO THE HEBREW CONGREGATION IN NEWPORT, RHODE ISLAND [UNDATED]

Gentlemen: While I received with much satisfaction your address replete with expressions of esteem, I rejoice in the opportunity of assuring you that I shall always retain grateful remembrance of the cordial welcome I experienced on my visit to Newport from all classes of citizens.

The reflection on the days of difficulty and danger which are past is rendered the more sweet from a consciousness that they are succeeded by days of uncommon prosperity and security.

If we have wisdom to make the best use of the advantage with which we are now favored, we cannot fail, under the just administration of a good government, to become a great and happy people.

The citizens of the United States of America have a right to applaud themselves for having given to mankind examples of an enlarged and liberal policy—a policy worthy of imitation. All possess alike liberty of conscience and immunities of citizenship.

It is now no more that toleration is spoken of as if it were the indulgence of one class of people that another enjoyed the exercise of their inherent natural rights, for, happily, the Government of the United States, which gives to bigotry no sanction, to persecution no assistance, requires only that they who live under its protection should demean themselves as good citizens in giving it on all occasions their effectual support.

It would be inconsistent with the frankness of my character not to avow that I am pleased with your favorable opinion of my administration and fervent wishes for my felicity.

May the children of the stock of Abraham who dwell in this land continue to merit and enjoy the good will of the other inhabitants; while every one shall sit in safety under his own vine and fig tree and there shall be none to make him afraid.

May the father of all mercies scatter light, and not darkness, upon our paths, and make us all in our several vocations useful here, and in His own due time and way everlastingly happy.

G. Washington

APPENDIX C

Map of Rhode Island

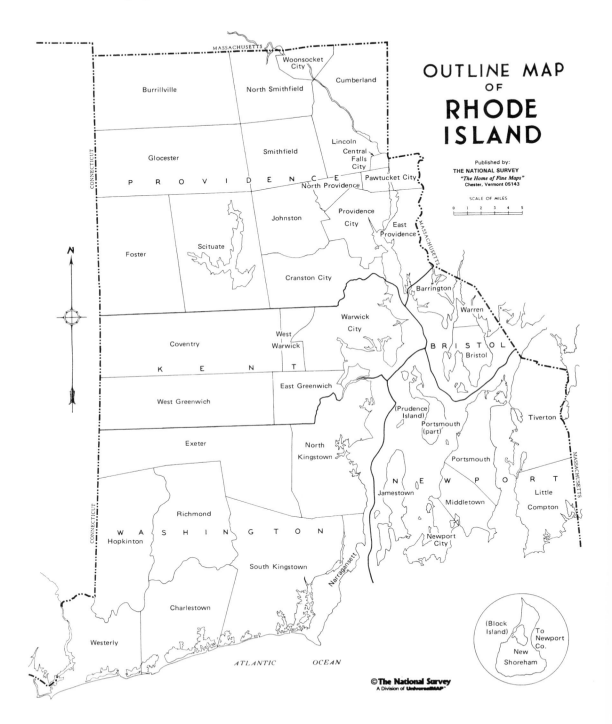

OUTLINE MAP
OF
RHODE
ISLAND

Published by:
THE NATIONAL SURVEY
"The Home of Fine Maps"
Chester, Vermont 05143

SCALE OF MILES

© The National Survey
A Division of UniversalMAP

The Jews of Rhode Island: A Timeline

1636	Providence established by Roger Williams on land belonging to the Narragansetts.
1638	Anne Hutchinson and her followers settle Pocasset (renamed Portsmouth in 1643) on Aquidneck Island; Aquidneck is the basis for the colony's official name, "Rhode Island and Providence Plantations."
1639	Founding of Newport by a break-away group from Pocasset; Both Williams and Hutchinson left Massachusetts to seek religious freedom; their settlements attract other religious dissenters during the colonial era.
1658	Small Jewish community probably established in Newport by ca. fifteen Jewish families from Barbados; no permanent community develops until mid-eighteenth century.
1677	Establishment of Jewish cemetery on Griffin (later Touro) Street.
1690s	Small Jewish community in Newport, possibly bolstered by Jewish immigrants from Curaçao.
1712	Jews Street recorded on John Mumford's map of Newport.
1740s–50s	Newport develops an organized Jewish community with emigrants from New York City and Europe, peaking at around thirty households in 1770.
1750	Newport's Redwood Library opens; includes books and funds donated by Jewish community.
1752	Aaron Lopez arrives in Newport from Portugal.
1756	Newport congregation Jeshuat Israel (Salvation of Israel) organized; later known as "Touro Synagogue."
1759	Land purchased and ground broken for synagogue building.
1761	United Company of Spermaceti Chandlers established with two Jewish firms among its nine founding members; the Company partially succeeds in controlling the price of whalehead matter used in making candles.
1763	Dedication of Newport synagogue building, designed by eminent Newport architect, Peter Harrison.
1764	Rhode Island College (later Brown University) opens in Warren under Baptist auspices but with no religious "test" for admission.
1773	Rabbi Haijim Karigal's "A Sermon Preached at the Synagogue in Newport, Rhode-Island," printed in Newport, became the first published Jewish sermon in America. Karigal, from Hebron in the Holy Land, delivered the sermon in Spanish, which was translated into English by Abraham Lopez.
1774	Joseph Jacobs is elected deputy to Rhode Island's General Assembly.
1776	British occupy Newport for three years; most Jews—patriots and loyalists—flee the city.
1781	George Washington's first visit to Newport synagogue, when it housed Rhode Island's General Assembly and Supreme Court.
1790	George Washington's second visit to Newport; replicating language in a letter from the Newport Jewish community, Washington writes that the United

States government "gives to bigotry no sanction, to persecution no assistance."

1822   Departure of Moses Lopez, last Jew in Newport, for New York City; ownership of synagogue and cemetery retained by descendants of colonial families but entrusted to New York's Shearith Israel, "The Spanish and Portuguese Synagogue."

1822   Death in Boston of Abraham Touro, son of Newport's first *hazan* (reader), Isaac Touro. Abraham's will provided funds to preserve the synagogue, Jewish cemetery, and road connecting them. Earliest reference to "Touro Synagogue" recorded in 1823; Touro Street and Touro Park are named in 1824 in Abraham's honor.

1838   Solomon Pareira probably first permanent Jewish settler in Providence.

1840s   Services held in Providence homes.

1849   Pareira and others establish Jewish cemetery on New London turnpike in Cranston; when deeded to Providence's first congregation it becomes known as "The Reservoir Avenue Cemetery."

1850   Touro Synagogue, maintained by Christian caretakers, reopened for summer services and visitors.

1852   Henry Wadsworth Longfellow writes poem, "The Jewish Cemetery in Newport," which is published in 1854.

1854   Death in New Orleans of Judah Touro, younger son of Isaac. His landmark will leaves funds to the Newport synagogue, Newport institutions, and Jewish and non-Jewish organizations and charities throughout America and the Holy Land. Abraham and Judah Touro both buried in Newport Jewish cemetery.

1854   B'nai Israel (Sons of Israel), first congregation established in Providence primarily by immigrants from Western and Central Europe.

1867   Emma Lazarus writes poem, "In the Jewish Synagogue in Newport," which is published in 1871 with the line "the sacred shrine is holy yet."

1870   Sons of David, Providence's second congregation, organized; establishes Moshassuck Cemetery in Lincoln, which later becomes part of Central Falls.

1870   Haggai Lodge 132 of B'nai B'rith established in Providence.

1874   Merger in Providence results in formation of Congregation Sons of Israel and David.

1875   Sons of Zion organized; in 1892 it becomes known as "The Orms Street Shul" in Providence's North End.

1877   Congregation Sons of Israel and David accepts "Moderate Reform" and joins Union of American Hebrew Congregations; hires Jacob Voorsanger, Rhode Island's first rabbi ordained in America (at Hebrew Union College), who organizes Ladies Hebrew Benevolent Association.

1883   Touro Synagogue reconsecrated and its Torahs returned from Shearith Israel in New York.

1884   Isaac Hahn of Providence is elected first Jewish state representative.

1880s and 1890s   Building on textile industry founded in late eighteenth century, Rhode Island's "modern" textile and jewelry industries lead the nation by early twentieth century; attract Jewish and other immigrants to Rhode Island's factories.

1888   Redwood Lodge of Masonic Order established in Providence.

1890   Sons of Israel and David dedicates "The Friendship Street Synagogue," the first built in Providence; Rabbi Isaac M. Wise, father of America's Reform movement, participates in ceremonies.

1893   Congregation Ohawe Shalom (Lovers of Peace), later known as B'nai Israel (Sons of Israel), founded in Woonsocket; land for cemetery purchased.

1894   Ownership of Newport synagogue officially transferred to Shearith Israel in New York City.

1894   Israel Strauss is first Jew known to have graduated from Brown University; in 1897 Clara Gomberg is first Jewish graduate of Women's College (founded 1891), later known as Pembroke College.

1896   Rabbi David Blaustein of Sons of Israel and David attempts organizing the United Hebrew Charities; another attempt in 1900 is made by Associated Hebrew Charities.

1896   Congregation Sons of Jacob organized; in 1906 it dedicates its synagogue, which will be the last to survive Providence's North End.

1896   YMHA established in Bristol.

1897   Women of Miriam Lodge 13, Order of B'rith Abraham, care for sick and envision a Jewish hospital; in 1907 Miriam Hospital Association founded.

1898   YMHA established in Providence; YWHA established two years later.

1903   Providence's Gemilath Chesed, Rhode Island's first Hebrew Free Loan Association, established.

1908   Congregation Machzeka Hadas opens Home for Jewish Orphans in South Providence; a year later Rhode Island Home for Jewish Orphans is dedicated in North End; following merger in 1910, Orphanage moves to North Main Street; in 1924 building is dedicated on Summit Avenue.

1908   Congregation Sharah Zedeck (Gates of Righteousness) organized in Westerly.

1908   Marian Misch elected national president of National Council of Jewish Women.

1909   Arbeiter Ring (Workmen's Circle) founded in Providence.

1910   Women lead kosher meat boycott in South Providence.

1911   Sons of Israel and David dedicates its new synagogue in South Providence; it becomes known as "Temple Beth-El."

1912   Ladies Hebrew Union Association, after caring for sick and elderly for two decades, opens the Jewish Home for the Aged on Orms Street in North End of Providence.

1913   YMHA established in Newport.

1915   Former President William Howard Taft, invited by Harry Cutler, speaks at Passover services at Temple Beth-El.

1915   Menorah Society chapter established at Brown University; first Jewish fraternity, Phi Epsilon Pi, founded in 1916 but disbands three years later.

1917   Harry Cutler elected national president of Jewish Welfare Board; also a member of the American Jewish Congress's delegation to Paris Peace Conference at end of World War I.

1919   Rhode Island's first Jewish newspaper, the *Providence Jewish Chronicle*, begins publication, followed briefly by Yiddish paper, *Rhode Island Jewish Review*.

1920   Providence's Vaad Hakashrut (Committee on Dietary Laws) organized; reorganized 1969.

1921   Congregation Ohawe Shalom (Lovers of Peace) dedicates its synagogue in Pawtucket.

1925	Miriam Hospital is dedicated on Parade Street in Providence.
1925	Providence Jewish Community Center organized; occupies former quarters of Hebrew Education Institute on Benefit Street; in 1940 building renovated.
1926	Touro Synagogue acquires and transports Levi Gale House, built in 1825, to serve as its community center.
1927	Temple Emanu-El, Rhode Island's second Conservative congregation, dedicates its synagogue, the first built on Providence's East Side.
1929	Jewish Family Service established in Providence.
1929	*The Jewish Herald* begins publication.
1931	J. Jerome Hahn, first Jewish judge of Superior Court in 1919, elected first Jewish justice of Rhode Island Supreme Court; later Jewish justices are Alfred Joslin and Victoria Lederberg.
1931	Justice Hahn donates Roger Williams Spring to Providence in memory of his father, Isaac.
1931	Lincoln Park Cemetery dedicated in Warwick.
1932	Jewish Home for the Aged is dedicated on Hillside Avenue on East Side.
1936	In honor of Rhode Island's Tercentenary, Zionist Organization of America holds national convention in Providence.
1936	Lawrence Spitz, labor activist, becomes secretary general of Independent Textile Union in Woonsocket.
1937	Jewish Orphanage of Rhode Island dedicates JORI summer camp at Point Judith.
1938	Hurricane wreaks massive damage in New England; downtown Providence is submerged and coastal communities are flooded; 262 lives are lost in Rhode Island.
1942	Jewish Orphanage closes; two years later Miriam Hospital purchases facility; in 1952 new hospital is dedicated.
1945	Providence organizes General Jewish Committee, a forerunner of the 1970 Jewish Federation of Rhode Island; the 1948 fundraising campaign first to exceed $1 million.
1946	Touro Synagogue designated National Historic Site by Department of Interior; Society of Friends, founded a year later, requires annual reading of Washington letter.
1946	Israel Kapstein, Class of 1926, becomes first Jewish professor to gain tenure at Brown University; Kapstein's undergraduate friends and fellow writers were Nathaniel (né Weinstein) West and S. J. Perelman.
1947	Providence Hebrew Day School opens on Waterman Street in Providence.
1947	Hillel Foundation established at Brown University.
1950	Hillel Foundation established at University of Rhode Island in Kingston; moves to Christopher House in 1980.
1951	Rhode Island Jewish Historical Association founded in Providence.
1952	Cranston Jewish Center, later known as Temple Torat Yisrael, dedicates its synagogue; first suburban congregation in West or East Bay.
1952	Jewish Community Center moves to former police station on East Side of Providence; in 1966 it becomes Jewish Community Center of Rhode Island.
1953	Jacob Temkin appointed first Jewish United States Attorney for District of Rhode Island.

1953	Bureau of Jewish Education established in Providence.
1953	Professor Ernest Frerichs begins expansion of Judaic studies at Brown University, which attracts other leading scholars, including Professor Jacob Neusner in 1968.
1953	Selma Pilavin elected national chairwoman of United Jewish Appeal; later Rhode Islanders in that office are Sylvia Hassenfeld and Roberta Holland.
1953	Martin Chase opens Ann & Hope, in Lonsdale, pioneering the national development of discount department stores.
1954	During its centenary, Temple Beth-El dedicates its third synagogue, on Providence's East Side; designed by Percival Goodman, it is one of the earliest and finest examples of modern synagogue architecture in New England.
1954	American Jewish Tercentenary celebrated in many venues throughout the state; bronze plaque is dedicated in Providence City Hall.
1954	George Wein of Boston produces Newport Jazz Festival; his Newport Folk Festival, featuring numerous Jewish artists, follows in 1959.
1958	During Rosh Hashanah, President Dwight D. Eisenhower participates in Washington letter ceremony at Touro Synagogue.
1959	Milton Stanzler founds Rhode Island affiliate of American Civil Liberties Union; many cases involve religious liberty and separation of church and state.
1961	Leonard Holland begins twenty-two-year tenure as Adjutant General and Commander of Rhode Island National Guard.
1962	B'nai Israel dedicates its new synagogue in Woonsocket, an outstanding example of modern synagogue architecture and decoration.
1963	Restoration of Touro Synagogue completed.
1963	Brown University Hillel dedicates Rapaporte House.
1963	Stanley Aronson appointed founding dean of Brown University's Medical School.
1964	General Jewish Committee publishes its first demographic study of Rhode Island Jewish community.
1964	Milton Stanlzer and other theater enthusiasts from Jewish Community Center found Trinity Repertory Company, which becomes Tony Award–winning, professional company.
1964	Irving Fain, a trustee of Mississippi's historically black Tougaloo College, helps establish exchange program with Brown University; also champions Rhode Island's passage of fair housing legislation.
1965	Rabbis William Braude, Saul Leeman, and Nathan Rosen participate in civil rights march from Selma to Montgomery, Alabama.
1965	Daniel Robbins appointed first Jewish director of Museum of Art at Rhode Island School of Design; develops Albert Pilavin Collection, Museum's first collection of modern and contemporary art.
1966	Miriam Hospital dedicates new complex on Summit Avenue.
1967	In aftermath of Six Day War, Federation raises record $2.6 million.
1968	New England Academy of Torah established in Providence.
1968	Last Jewish steam bath closes in Providence.
1969	Frank Licht first Jew elected governor; reelected 1971; in 1987 Providence County Courthouse named in his honor.

1969	Federation establishes Jewish Community Relations Council.
1970s	Soviet Jews begin settling in Providence, assisted by Jewish Family Service and other communal agencies.
1971	New Jewish Community Center of Rhode Island dedicated on East Side.
1971	Richard Israel first Jew elected attorney general; reelected 1973; other Jews later elected to this office are Julius Michaelson and Jeffrey Pine.
1971	Brown University appoints Richard Marker as first Jewish chaplain in the Ivy League.
1971	Aaron Siskind, a master photographer from Chicago, begins teaching at Rhode Island School of Design; lives in Providence until his death in 1991.
1973	In aftermath of Yom Kippur War, Federation raises record $3.5 million; Federation begins publication of a newspaper, *The Federation Voice*.
1975	Federation moves from offices in downtown Providence to Alperin Building, connected to Jewish Community Center on East Side.
1978	Solomon Schechter Day School established under auspices of the Conservative movement within Temple Emanu-El; in 1989 name changed to Alperin Schechter Day School.
1978	Maurice Glicksman, a physicist, becomes first Jewish dean of faculty and provost at Brown University.
1978	Blizzard paralyzes Providence and much of state.
1979	Ralph Semonoff elected president of Rhode Island Bar; as the son of Judah, who served in 1957, he is the Association's only second-generation president.
1980	Shalom Apartments for Jewish seniors opens in Warwick; expanded 1996.
1982	Bruce Selya appointed first Jewish judge of United States District Court for Rhode Island; in 1986 is elevated to First Circuit Court of Appeals.
1982	United States Postal Service issues Touro Synagogue stamp to commemorate Washington's 250th birthday.
1983	Mikveh dedicated at Jewish Community Center.
1984	Chabad House dedicated on Hope Street in Providence; in 1994 Chabad of West Bay established in Warwick; in 2003 Chabad of College Hill established in Providence.
1985	Richard Licht first Jew elected lieutenant governor.
1988	Rhode Island Holocaust Memorial Museum dedicated at Jewish Community Center.
1988	Sylvia Hassenfeld elected national president of Joint Distribution Committee.
1988	Susan Miller, first woman congregational rabbi in Rhode Island, appointed at Temple Beth-El.
1991	Bruce Sundlun elected governor of Rhode Island; re-elected 1993; in 1997 terminal at T. F. Green Airport in Warwick named in his honor.
1992	U.S. Supreme Court upholds ruling in favor of the Weisman family and against the Providence School Committee; in 1989 family had objected to rabbi's prayer at a middle school graduation.
1993	Jewish Home is closed in Providence; Jewish Seniors Agency established to assist residents of retirement and nursing homes.
1994	Hasbro Children's Hospital dedicated at Rhode Island Hospital; Miriam Hospital merges with Rhode Island Hospital to form Lifespan.
1995	Federation celebrates its 50th anniversary.

1995   Norman Tilles, former national commander of Jewish War Veterans, becomes
        national president of Hebrew Immigrant Aid Society.
1996   David Gitlitz becomes first Jewish dean of arts and sciences, then provost, at
        University of Rhode Island.
2000   These rabbis have served Rhode Island congregations or organizations for
        twenty or more years: George Astrachan, Alan Flam, Wayne Franklin, Peretz
        Gold, Leslie Gutterman, Marc Jagolinzer, Abraham Jakubowicz, Philip
        Kaplan, Alvan Kaunfer, Yehoshua Laufer, James Rosenberg.
2001   Jewish War Veterans dedicate new memorial in Lincoln Park Cemetery in
        Warwick.
2003   Camp JORI dedicates new facilities at Worden's Pond in Wakefield.
2003   Jewish Seniors Agency dedicates Tamarisk assisted living residence in
        Warwick.
2004   Brown University Hillel dedicates Weiner Center, a complex of federal,
        Victorian, and new buildings.
2004   Celebration of 50th anniversary of *Rhode Island Jewish Historical Notes*.
2004   Celebration of 350th anniversary of the Jewish arrival in North America.

CONTRIBUTORS

SAUL BARBER was born in Boston in 1920 and graduated from the University of Rhode Island in 1941. After serving as a communications officer in the Pacific theater during World War II, he earned his doctorate in biology at Yale in 1954. Barber was a professor of biology at Lehigh University from 1956 until his retirement in 1985. He served as chair of his department, was dean of arts and sciences, and was a visiting professor at Oxford. Barber received numerous grants from the National Institutes of Health and the National Science Foundation for his studies of animal physiology. He died in 1998 at his retirement home in Yarmouth Port, Massachusetts.

ELI A. BOHNEN, born in 1909, was reared in Toronto. A 1931 graduate of the University of Toronto, he was ordained at the Jewish Theological Seminary, New York City, in 1935 and received his doctorate in Hebrew literature from the Seminary in 1955. Rabbi Bohnen served as assistant rabbi of Congregation Adath Jeshurun in Philadelphia and as rabbi of Temple Emanu-El in Buffalo. During World War II he served as chaplain of the "Rainbow Division" in Europe and remained after the war to work with displaced Jewish survivors. He was rabbi of Temple Emanu-El in Providence from 1948 until his retirement in 1974. Also president of the Rhode Island Board of Rabbis and national president of the Rabbinical Assembly, he died in 1992.

WILLIAM G. BRAUDE, a son and grandson of Orthodox rabbis, was born in Lithuania in 1907 and emigrated to America at 13 years of age. He grew up in Colorado and Ohio, graduated from the University of Cincinnati in 1929, and was ordained at Hebrew Union College in 1931. After serving Temple Beth-El in Rockford, Illinois, he was called to Providence's Beth-El in 1932, which he led until his retirement in 1974. Having earned his doctorate in religious studies at Brown University in 1937, he devoted much of his life to teaching and scholarship. He was largely responsible for building Beth-El's new home on the East Side of Providence, and its impressive library was named in his honor in 1967. Rabbi Braude, who passed away in 1988, rallied support for victims of Nazi oppression, sought racial equality, and promoted intra-Jewish and interfaith understanding.

PAUL M. BUHLE has taught, since 1997, in the American civilization department at Brown University. A native of Champaign-Urbana, he earned his bachelor's at Illinois and his doctorate in history at Wisconsin in 1975. He has also taught at Tufts University and Rhode Island School of Design. For more than a quarter-century, he has built the Oral History Collection of the American Left at New York University's Tamiment Library. Buhle has authored or co-authored more than twenty books, including *C. L. R. James: The Artist as Revolutionary* (1989), *Encyclopedia of the American Left* (1990), *A Very Dangerous Citizen: Abraham Lincoln Polonsky and the Hollywood Left* (2001), and *Radical Hollywood: The Untold Story Behind America's Favorite Movies* (2002).

STEVEN CULBERTSON graduated from Brown University with a major in religious studies in 1986 and earned a master's in city planning from the University of Pennsylvania in 1988. He serves as executive director of the Frankford Community

Development Corporation in Philadelphia. He and his family live in a Victorian home they renovated.

GERALDINE S. FOSTER graduated from Pembroke College in 1949 and earned a master's in teaching at Brown in 1965. For many years she taught English at Nathan Bishop Middle School in Providence as well as Yiddish and Jewish literature at synagogues throughout Rhode Island. A frequent contributor to *The Notes*, she has also created several pictorial histories of Rhode Island's Jewish institutions. Foster has been president of the women's division of Jewish Federation of Rhode Island, the Bureau of Jewish Education, Na'amat, and the Rhode Island Jewish Historical Association. She is the mother of four and the grandmother of eight.

SHALOM GOLDMAN is associate professor of Hebrew and comparative literature in the department of Middle Eastern studies at Emory University. He earned his bachelor's at New York University, his master's in Arabic and Islamic studies at Columbia University, and his doctorate in Hebrew Bible and Judaica at New York University in 1986. From 1987 to 1996 he taught at Dartmouth College, and he has been a visiting professor at the University of Tel Aviv. His books include *Hebrew and the Bible in America* (1993) and *The Wiles of Women/The Wiles of Men: Joseph and Potiphar's Wife* (1995). Goldman's forthcoming book is *Holy Language/Holy Land: Hebrew, the Bible, and Christian Zionism in American Culture*. With the composer Philip Glass he wrote the libretto of *Akhnaten*, which was first performed in 1984 and has become a classic of modern opera.

SEEBERT J. GOLDOWSKY, a native of Providence, graduated from Brown University in 1928 and from Harvard Medical School in 1932. During World War II he was a surgeon in the Pacific theater, and later served as chief of surgery at the Miriam Hospital and as medical director of Blue Cross and Blue Shield of Rhode Island. For twenty-seven years Dr. Goldowsky was editor-in-chief of the journal of the Rhode Island Medical Society. For seventeen years he also was editor of *The Notes*. He wrote numerous scientific papers, *Yankee Surgeon: The Life and Times of Usher Parsons* (1988), and a history of Temple Beth-El (1989). Dr. Goldowsky had a profound influence on Rhode Island and Jewish history. He died in 1997.

CALVIN GOLDSCHEIDER is the Ungerleider Professor of Judaic Studies and professor of sociology at Brown University. He has also taught at Hebrew University of Jerusalem, Brandeis, Berkeley, and the University of Southern California. He earned his bachelor's degree at Yeshiva University in 1961 and his doctorate at Brown. Goldscheider's major publications have focused on sociology and demography of ethnic populations with a particular emphasis on family and immigration. Some of his major books include: *The Ethnic Factor in Family Structure and Mobility* (1978), *American Jewish Community: Social Science Research and Policy Implications* (1980), *Jewish Continuity and Change: Emerging Patterns in America* (1986), and *Israel's Changing Society* (2002).

GEORGE M. GOODWIN, who grew up in Los Angeles, studied art history at Lake Forest College and Columbia University and earned his doctorate at Stanford in 1975. He has taught art history at many levels, organized exhibitions and archives, and conducted extensive oral history interviews. Having earned a master's in Jewish communal studies at Hebrew Union College, Goodwin has also worked for Jewish federations. He has written on modern Jewish culture for such journals as *American Jewish Archives*, *American Jewish History*, *Faith & Form*, *Modern Judaism*, and *Rhode Island History*. A photographer and a collector of folk art, he lives with his family in Providence's youngest plaque house, built in 1920.

ELEANOR F. HORVITZ, a Providence native, studied at Pembroke College before earning her bachelor's in English and psychology at Washington University in 1941. She completed a master's in teaching at Brown in 1969. Beginning in 1974, Horvitz served thirty years as the librarian-archivist of the Rhode Island Jewish Historical Association. While the most prolific contributor to *The Notes*, she was also a columnist for the *Jewish Federation Voice* and the *Jewish Herald*. Horvitz has been active in the League of Women Voters, the women's auxiliary of the Rhode Island Medical Society, and the Providence Heritage Commission.

MARILYN KAPLAN, a native New Yorker, received her bachelor's in history from Vassar in 1960. She earned a master's in teaching at Yale, a master's in history at Brown, and an M.B.A. from the University of Rhode Island. After teaching history in high schools and community colleges, Kaplan assumed administrative and fundraising responsibilities at the Dayton Foundation in Ohio and at the State University at Buffalo. She and her husband have recently returned to Rhode Island to be close to family and friends.

KAREN M. LAMOREE earned a bachelor's in political science and history at Clark University in 1983 and a master's in information science at the State University at Albany in 1986. While on the staff of Brown University's Hay Library, she authored *Research Guide to the Christine Dunlap Farnham Archives* (1989) and contributed an article to *The Search for Equity: Women at Brown University, 1891–1991* (1991). Formerly on the staff of the State Historical Society of Wisconsin, she is currently archivist of St. Andrew's Episcopal Church, Madison. Though a resident of Sun Prairie, Wisconsin, she still considers herself a New Yorker.

RICHARD A. MECKEL is an associate professor of American civilization and history at Brown University. He grew up in Norwalk, Connecticut, and earned a bachelor's in American literature at the University of Notre Dame in 1970. His doctorate is in American studies from the University of Michigan. He has contributed to such anthologies as *Allocation of Resources to Children* (2000) and *Formative Years: Children's Health in America, 1880–2000* (2001). The author of *Save the Babies: American Public Health Reforms and the Prevention of Infant Mortality, 1850–1929* (1990), he is currently preparing a history of child welfare in America.

JOEL PERLMANN is the Levy Institute Research Professor of History at Bard College. He earned his bachelor's in history at Hebrew University of Jerusalem and his doctorate at Harvard. He has taught at Harvard's Graduate School of Education and has been a member of the School of Social Science at the Institute for Advanced Study at Princeton. Perlmann has written numerous articles for such journals as *William and Mary Quarterly*, *Historical Methods*, *The Public Interest*, and *American Jewish History*. Some of his major books are *Ethnic Differences: Schooling and Social Structure Among the Irish, Italians, Jews, and Blacks in an American City, 1880–1935* (1988), *Teaching and Gender in the United States: A Social and Economic History* (2000), and *Women's Work? American School Teachers, 1650–1920* (2001).

JONATHAN D. SARNA is the Joseph H. & Belle R. Braun Professor of American Jewish History at Brandeis University and chairs the academic advisory and editorial board of the Jacob Rader Marcus Center of the American Jewish Archives in Cincinnati. Trained at Brandeis and Yale, he previously taught at Hebrew Union College—Jewish Institute of Religion. He has also taught at Yale, University of Cincinnati, and the Hebrew University of Jerusalem. Sarna has written, edited, or co-edited twenty books, including *The American Jewish Experience; JPS: The Americanization of Jewish*

Culture; *The Jews of Boston* (with Ellen Smith); and *Women and American Judaism* (with Pamela Nadell). His most recent book, *American Judaism: A History*, has just appeared.

ELLEN SMITH is chief curator of the new National Museum of American Jewish History in Philadelphia; principal of Museumsmith, a firm specializing in museum exhibitions and historic site interpretations across the country; and associate director of the Gralla Fellows Program for Religion Journalists at Brandeis University. Co-editor with Jonathan Sarna of *The Jews of Boston* (1995), she was chief historical consultant to the Emmy Award–winning WGBH television documentary of the same name (1996). Her recent publications are on early American Jewish portraits (1997 and 2003) and Jewish New Year's postcards (2001); her recent major exhibitions are on Seattle Jewish women (2003), Yiddish theater (1999) and *Facing the New World: Jewish Portraits in Colonial and Federal America* at the Jewish Museum in New York (1997). She has taught American Jewish history and material culture at Northeastern and Brandeis universities and lives with her family in Newton, Massachusetts.

HOLLY SNYDER is archivist of the John Nicholas Brown Center for the Study of American Civilization, in Providence. A fifth-generation New Englander, she earned her bachelor's at Hampshire College and master's degrees in history and library science at Catholic University of America before receiving her doctorate in American civilization from Brandeis University in 2000. She has written for many journals and contributed articles to *Women and American Judaism: Historical Perspectives* (2001) and the *Encyclopedia of New England Culture* (2003). From 2001 to 2003 she was a postdoctoral fellow in modern Jewish history at Hampshire College. Snyder's first book, a comparative study of Jews in early America, is forthcoming from the University of Pennsylvania Press.

ERWIN STRASMICH, a former president of the Rhode Island Jewish Historical Association, is a Providence native. He graduated from Brown University in 1946 and for many years served as his class secretary. He was vice president of a textile manufacturing company and an industrial real estate company both in Fall River, Massachusetts. Now retired, Strasmich and his wife live in New York City where they enjoy music and theater. They are also collectors of American prints and drawings.

BIBLIOGRAPHIES

THE JEWS OF RHODE ISLAND

The Jews of Rhode Island bibliography is organized in four sections. The first, a "General Bibliography," includes books and articles, excluding articles that have appeared over the past fifty years in *Rhode Island Jewish Historical Notes*. A few titles on general American Jewish history are also included to provide context and background for the Rhode Island Jewish experience.

The second, "Bibliographic Resources Published in the *Rhode Island Jewish Historical Notes*," directs readers toward archives, libraries, and organizations with important material on the Rhode Island Jewish community.

The third bibliography, "Selected Articles in *Rhode Island Jewish Historical Notes*," extends the topics of the first two bibliographies and this volume. *The Notes* remains the key resource for secondary articles on the Rhode Island Jewish community.

The fourth bibliography, "Demographic and Statistical Studies," cites the major works of demographic research published on the Rhode Island Jewish community over the last forty years.

Each of these four bibliographies provides the key scholarly and popular readings within their categories. While not intended to be comprehensive scholarly bibliographies, they will encourage additional research, suggest new areas of inquiry, and enable deeper learning and appreciation of the Jews of Rhode Island.

Rhode Island Jewish Historical Notes appears as RIJHN

I. General Bibliography

GENERAL AMERICAN JEWISH HISTORY

The following titles are good places to start within this large bibliography.

Feingold, Henry L., ed. *The Jewish People in America.* 5 vols. Baltimore: Johns Hopkins University Press, 1992. [For the Jewish community of colonial Newport, see the first volume of the series, *A Time for Planting: The First Migration*, by Eli Faber.]

Marcus, Jacob R. *United States Jewry: 1776–1985.* 4 vols. Detroit: Wayne State University Press, 1989.

Sarna, Jonathan D. *American Judaism: A History.* New Haven: Yale University Press, 2004.

RHODE ISLAND JEWISH HISTORY

Adler, Emily S. and J. Stanley Lemons. *The Elect: Rhode Island's Women Legislators, 1922–1990.* Providence: League of Rhode Island Historical Societies, 1990.

Barquist, David L. *Myer Myers: Jewish Silversmith of Colonial New York.* New Haven: Yale University Press, 2001.

Barry, Jay. *Gentlemen Under the Elms*. Providence: Brown Alumni Monthly, Brown University, 1982.

Bigelow, Bruce. "The Commerce of Rhode Island with the West Indies, Before the American Revolution." Ph.D. diss., Brown University, 1930.

Bridenbaugh, Carl. *Peter Harrison: First American Architect*. Chapel Hill: University of North Carolina Press, 1949.

Buhle, Paul M. *Working Lives: An Oral History of Rhode Island Labor*. Providence: Rhode Island Historical Society, 1987.

Chiel, Arthur A. "Ezra Stiles and the Jews: A Study in Ambivalence," in *A Bicentennial Festschrift for Jacob Rader Marcus*, ed. Bertram W. Korn. New York: KTAV, 1976. Reprinted in Shalom Goldman, ed. *Hebrew and the Bible in America: The First Two Centuries*. Hanover and London: University Press of New England, for Brandeis University Press and Dartmouth College Press, 1993: 156–167.

Chyet, Stanley F. *Lopez of Newport: Colonial American Merchant Prince*. Detroit: Wayne State University Press, 1970.

Conforti, Joseph. "Irving Fain and the Fair Housing Movement in Rhode Island, 1958–1970." *Rhode Island History*, Vol. 45 (February 1986): 23–35.

Conley, Patrick T. *Liberty and Justice: A History of Law and Lawyers in Rhode Island, 1636–1998*. East Providence: Rhode Island Publications Society, 1998.

Conser, Jr., Walter H. "Ethnicity and Politics in Rhode Island: The Career of Frank Licht." *Rhode Island History*, Vol. 44 (November 1985): 97–107.

Coughtry, Jay A. *The Notorious Triangle: Rhode Island and the African Slave Trade, 1700–1807*. Philadelphia: Temple University Press, 1981.

Crane, Elaine Forman. *A Dependent People: Newport, Rhode Island in the Revolutionary Era*. New York: Fordham University Press, 1985.

Dexter, Franklin B., ed. *The Literary Diary of Ezra Stiles, D.D., LL.D., President of Yale College*. 3 vols. New York: Charles Scribner's Sons, 1901.

Eisenmann, Linda M. "Women at Brown, 1891–1930: Academically Identical, But Socially Quite Distinct." Ed.D. diss., Harvard University Graduate School of Education, 1987.

Faber, Eli. *Jews, Slaves, and the Slave Trade: Setting the Record Straight*. New York: New York University Press, 1998.

Foster, Geraldine S. *The Jews in Rhode Island: A Brief History*. Providence: Rhode Island Heritage Foundation and the Rhode Island Publications Society, 1985.

Foster, Geraldine S., Eleanor F. Horvitz, and Judith Weiss Cohen. *Jews of Rhode Island: 1658–1958*. Dover: Arcadia Publishing/Chalford Publishing Corporation, 1998.

Gilkerson, John S. *Middle-Class Providence, 1820–1940*. Princeton: Princeton University Press, 1986.

Goldman, Shalom, ed. *Hebrew and the Bible in America: The First Two Centuries*. Hanover and London: University Press of New England, for Brandeis University Press and Dartmouth College Press, 1993.

Goldowsky, Seebert J. *A Century and a Quarter of Spiritual Leadership: The Story of the Congregation of the Sons of Israel and David (Temple Beth-El), Providence, Rhode Island*. Providence: The Congregation of the Sons of Israel and David, 1989.

Goldstein, Sidney and Calvin Goldscheider. *Jewish Americans: Three Generations in the Jewish Community*. Englewood Cliffs, N.J.: Prentice-Hall, Inc., 1968.

Goodwin, George M. "The Design of a Modern Synagogue: Percival Goodman's Beth-El in Providence, Rhode Island," *American Jewish Archives* Vol. 44 (Spring–Summer 1993): 31–71.

Goodwin, George M. "Woonsocket's B'nai Israel Synagogue," *Rhode Island History* Vol. 58 (February 2000): 3–20.

Gutstein, Morris A. *The Story of the Jews of Newport.* New York: Bloch Publishing Company, 1936.

———. "A Newport Ledger, 1760–1770." *Publications of the American Jewish Historical Society,* Vol. 37 (1947): 163–169.

———. "To Bigotry No Sanction": A Jewish Shrine in America 1658–1958. New York: Bloch Publishing Company, 1958.

Hawk, Grace E. *Pembroke College in Brown University: The First Seventy-Five Years, 1891–1966.* Providence: Brown University, 1966.

Horvitz, David E. *Temple Emanu-El: The First Fifty Years.* Providence: Temple Emanu-El, 1974.

Hühner, Leon. *The Life of Judah Touro (1775–1854).* Philadelphia: Jewish Publication Society, 1946.

Kaufman, Polly W., ed. *The Search for Equity: Women at Brown University, 1891–1991.* Providence: Brown University, 1991.

Kohler, Max J. "Judah Touro, Merchant and Philanthropist," in Abraham J. Karp, ed. *The Jewish Experience in America: Selected Studies from the Publications of the American Jewish Historical Society (Vol. II: In the Early Republic).* Waltham: American Jewish Historical Society, 1969: 158–76. Originally published in *Publications of the American Jewish Historical Society* 13 (1905): 93–111.

Lamoree, Karen M. *Research Guide to the Christine Dunlop Farnham Archives.* Providence: Brown University, 1989.

Lewis, Theodore, "Touro Synagogue, Newport, R.I." *Newport History* Vol. 48 (Summer 1975): 281–320.

Lieberman, Terry, ed. "One Hundred Years: A History of Miriam Hospital Women's Association." Providence: The Miriam Hospital Women's Association, 1997.

McLoughlin, William G. *Rhode Island: A History.* New York: W. W. Norton & Co., 1986.

Miller, G. Wayne. *Toy Wars: The Epic Struggle between G.I. Joe, Barbie, and the Companies that Make Them.* New York: Random House, 2002.

Mitchell, Martha. *Encyclopedia Brunoniana.* Providence: Brown University, 1993.

Morgan, Edmund S. *The Gentle Puritan: A Life of Ezra Stiles, 1727–1795.* New Haven: Yale University Press, 1962.

Perlmann, Joel. "Beyond New York: The Occupations of Russian Jewish Immigrants in Providence, R.I. and in Other Small Jewish Communities 1900–1915." *American Jewish History* Vol. 37, no. 3: 369–394.

Perlmann, Joel. *Ethnic Differences: School and Social Structure Among the Irish, Italians, Jews, and Blacks in an American City, 1880–1935.* Cambridge: Cambridge University Press, 1988.

Pestana, Carla G. *Liberty of Conscience and the Growth of Religious Diversity in Early America, 1636–1786.* Providence: John Carter Brown Library, 1986.

Platt, Virginia Bever. "'And Don't Forget the Guinea Voyage': The Slave Trade of Aaron Lopez of Newport." *William and Mary Quarterly,* Vol. 32 (1975): 610–618.

Publications of the American Jewish Historical Society. (Readers should consult the Indexes to the *Publications,* later renamed *American Jewish Historical Quarterly* and now *American Jewish History,* for the many articles on Newport's colonial Jewish community that have appeared, especially in the early volumes.)

Rhodes, Irwin S. "References to Jews in the *Newport Mercury,* 1758–1786." Monographs of the American Jewish Archives, No. III. Cincinnati: American Jewish Archives, 1961.

Rudolph, Richard. "The Merchants of Newport, Rhode Island, 1763–1786." Ph.D. diss., University of Connecticut, 1975.

Sarna, Jonathan D. and David G. Dalin, eds. *Religion and State in the American Jewish Experience*. Notre Dame, Indiana: University of Notre Dame Press, 1997.

Smart, Samuel C. *The Outlet Story, 1894–1984*. Providence: Outlet Communications, 1984.

Smith, Judith. *Family Connections: A History of Italian and Jewish Immigrant Lives in Providence, Rhode Island, 1900–1940*. Albany: State University of New York Press, 1985.

Snydacker, Daniel Jr. "Traders in Exile: Quakers and Jews of Colonial New York and Newport." Ph.D. diss., Johns Hopkins University, 1982.

Snyder, Holly. "A Sense of Place: Jews, Identity, and Social Status in Colonial British America, 1654–1831." Ph.D. diss., Brandeis University, 2000.

Stanzler, Milton. "Trinity Repertory Company: Creating a Professional Theater in Providence. *Rhode Island History*. Vol. 53 (May 1995): 19–35.

Stern, Malcolm H. *First American Jewish Families: 600 Genealogies, 1654–1988*. Third edition. Baltimore: Ottenheimer Publishers, 1991.

Urofsky, Melvin I. *Newport Jewry and the Touro Synagogue*. Newport: Friends of Touro Synagogue, 2004.

Wein, George, with Nate Chinen. *Myself Among Others: A Life in Music*. Cambridge, Mass.: Da Capo Press, 2003.

Weisberg, Nadia D., ed. *Diamonds Are Forever, but Rhinestones Are for Everyone: An Oral History of the Costume Jewelry Industry of Rhode Island*. Providence: The Providence Jewelry Museum, 1999.

Withey, Lynne. "Household Structure in Urban and Rural Areas: The Case of Rhode Island, 1774–1800." *Journal of Family History* Vol. 3 (1978): 37–50.

Withey, Lynne. *Urban Growth in Colonial Rhode Island: Newport and Providence in the Eighteenth Century*. Albany: State University of New York Press, 1984.

II. Bibliographic Resources Published in *Rhode Island Jewish Historical Notes*

The editors of *Rhode Island Jewish Historical Notes* have published many important, detailed bibliographies. Freda Egnal's three magisterial bibliographies remain unsurpassed (through the time of their publication) in presenting and annotating the printed and archival resources. Other bibliographic essays update and supplement her work. The archives and libraries of the American Jewish Historical Society (New York City); the Newport Historical Society; and the Rhode Island Historical Society should also be consulted for their most current acquisitions. Local Jewish institutions, especially synagogues, also hold useful information.

Egnal, Freda. "A Guide to the More Important Printed Sources Concerning the History of the Jews in Rhode Island Based on Materials in the Brown University Library." Volume 4, Number 1 (May 1963): 78–99.

———. "An Annotated Critical Bibliography of Materials Relating to the History of the Jews in Rhode Island Located in Rhode Island Depositories (1678–1966)." Volume 4, Number 4 (November 1966): 305–506.

———. "A Catalogue of All Rhode Island Jews Mentioned in Materials Relating to the History of the Jews in Rhode Island Located in Rhode Island Depositories (1678–1966)." Volume 5, Number 1 (November 1967): 7–80.

Frost, Carol J. "An Annotated Bibliography of Materials Relating to the History of the Jews in Rhode Island, Located in Rhode Island Depositories (1967–1989)."

Jacobson, Jacob Mark. "Bibliography of Sources for Rhode Island Jewish Materials": Volume 5, Number 4 (November 1970): 338–369.

Wax, Bernard. "Rhode Island Materials in the American Jewish Historical Society Collections." Volume 7, Number 1 (November 1975): 171–174.

III. Selected Articles in *Rhode Island Jewish Historical Notes*

Rhode Island Jewish Historical Notes is the most important source for articles on Rhode Island Jewish history. To help insure that these studies become more easily available to a broader public and scholarly audience, selected articles are listed below by topic and author. This list is not intended to replace the following indices:

Rhode Island Jewish Historical Notes: Cumulative Index, Vols. 1–7, 1954–1978. Providence: Rhode Island Jewish Historical Association, 1984.

Rhode Island Jewish Historical Notes: Second Cumulative Index, Vols. 8–11, 1979–1994. Providence: Rhode Island Jewish Historical Association, 1997.

For the sake of space, short-title citations appear below. Please consult the original articles for the full titles.

Topic	Author	Vol./No./Year
CEMETERIES		
Reservoir Avenue/Beth-El		1/4/1955
Early burials in Providence,		3/1/1958
Lonsdale-Central Falls, Lincoln,		
Warwick		
Newport	Bernard Kusinitz	9/1/1983
		9/3/1985
		9/4/1986
COMMUNITY HISTORIES		
Bristol	Steven Culbertson and Calvin Goldscheider	9/4/1986
East Greenwich	Eleanor Horvitz and Geraldine Foster	12/4/1998
Local Jewish History	Jonathan Sarna	12/1B/1995
Narragansett Bay	Geraldine Foster and Eleanor Horvitz	11/1/1991
		11/3/1992
		11/3/1993
Newport		
Merchants	Jacob Jacobson	5/4/1970
Merchants	Marilyn Kaplan	7/1/1975
American Revolution	Andrea Lobson	7/2/1976
Blacks and Jews	Joshua Rotenberg	11/2/1992
Decline	Jay Eidelman	12/1B/1995

Topic	Author	Vol./No./Year
Hidden Jews	Holly Snyder	12/4/1998
Rebirth (19th cent.)	Benjamin Brown	13/3/2001
Pawtucket and Central Falls	Eleanor Horvitz	9/2/1984
		9/3/1985
Providence		
Early Days		3/3/1960
Italians and Jews	Stefano Luconi	13/4/2002
Jewish Life	Bessie Bloom	5/4/1970
Last steam bath	Noel Rubinton	12/4/1998
North End	Eleanor Horvitz	8/1/1979
Russian Jews in Rhode Island	Stephanie Miller	13/3/2002
Sabbath Tour	William Braude	9/4/1986
South Providence	Eleanor Horvitz	7/2/1976
Suburbs	Geraldine Foster and Eleanor Horvitz	13/2/2000
West Warwick	Paul Streicker	5/2/1968
Westerly	Ella Soloveitzik	3/3/1960
	Rebecca Twersky	7/3/1977
Woonsocket	Eleanor Horvitz	9/4/1986

EDUCATION AND CULTURE

Topic	Author	Vol./No./Year
Brown University		
Brown University's Jewish Fraternity	Eleanor Horvitz and Benton Rosen	8/1/1981
First Jews at Brown	Seebert Goldowsky	11/3/1993
Jews at Brown	Martha Mitchell	11/3/1993
Pembroke College	Karen Lamoree	10/2/1998
Hebrew language	Shalom Goldman	11/3/1994
Newport Folk Festival	George Goodwin	12/3/1997
Performing Arts	Zita Brier	12/3/1997
Rhode Island School of Design	George Goodwin	12/3/1997

INSTITUTIONS AND ORGANIZATIONS—INCLUDES ALL CITIES AND TOWNS, ESPECIALLY PROVIDENCE

Topic	Author	Vol./No./Year
ACLU and Church-State Issues	Milton Stanzler	12/4/1998
B'nai B'rith Judah Touro Lodge	Bernard Kusinitz	7/1/1975
B'nai Israel, Woonsocket	Geraldine Foster	11/3/1993
Bureau of Jewish Education	Geraldine Foster	11/3/1993
Chartered Organizations		2/1/1956
		2/2/1957
Congregation of the Sons of Israel and David (Temple Beth-El)		
Early Years	David Adelman	3/4/1962
Percival Goodman/Beth-El	George Goodwin	11/4/1994
Recollections	William Braude	8/4/1982
Congregation Sons of Zion		
Congregation Sons of Zion	Beryl Segal	4/3/1965
Sons of Zion Synagogue	Melvin Zurier	11/2/1992
Hebrew Free Loan Association	Benton Rosen	5/3/1969
		5/4/1970

Topic	Author	Vol./No./Year

IV. Demographic and Statistical Studies

Demographic studies of the Rhode Island Jewish community have been exceptionally strong. Sidney Goldstein, Alice Goldstein, and Calvin Goldscheider, world-renowned demographers and social scientists on the Brown faculty, have been commissioned to investigate the Rhode Island Jewish population by the Jewish Federation of Rhode Island. This was one of the first federations in North America to sponsor such research.

Many of the key articles on demography published in *Rhode Island Jewish Historical Notes* are listed below.

Aronson, Stanley M. and Betty E. Aronson. "'Thy Name Shall be Abraham': A Survey of First Names in the Jewish Population of Rhode Island." Volume 12, Number 2 (1996): 1990–204.

———. "A Population in Transition: The Role of Demographic Data." Volume 13, Number 3 (2001): 403–420.

Babin, Nehama Ella. "Residential Mobility of Jews in Rhode Island." Volume 6, Number 3 (1973): 390–453.

Goldscheider, Calvin. "A Century of Jewish Fertility in Rhode Island." Volume 10, Number 3, Part B (1989): 335–349.

Goldstein, Alice. "Mobility of Natives and Jews in Providence, 1900–1920." Volume 8, Number 1 (1979): 63–93.

Goldstein, Sidney. "A Social Profile of the Jewish Population of Greater Providence, 1963." Volume 4, Number 2 (1964): 91–111.

———. "Number and Distribution of Jewish Households in Rhode Island, 1970." Volume 6, Number 1 (1971): 36–48.

———. "A Further Assessment of the Use of Yiddish in Rhode Island Households," Volume 9, Number 3 (1985): 209–219.

———. "Migration and the Jewish Community of Rhode Island." Volume 12, Number 2 (1996): 217–232.

Goldstein, Sidney, Calvin Goldscheider, and Alice Goldstein. "A Quarter Century of Change in Rhode Island Jewry, 1963–1987." Volume 10, Number 2 (1987): 93–114.

Goldstein, Sidney and Alice Goldstein. "The Declining Use of Yiddish in Rhode Island." Volume 7, Number 3 (1977): 401–409.

Kempner, Brian. "Jewish Immigration into Providence: A Comparison of the Settlement of Soviet Jews, 1970–1982 with that of Russian Jews, 1881–1924." Volume 9, Number 1 (1983): 5–29.

Perlmann, Joel. "Beyond New York, A Second Look: The Occupations of Russian Jewish Immigrants in Providence, R.I., and in Other Small Jewish Communities, 1900–1915." Volume 10, Number 3, Part B (1989): 374–387.

Additional demographic studies of the Rhode Island Jewish community, not appearing in *The Notes*, are listed below.

American Jewish Yearbook. Philadelphia: Jewish Publication Society. (Detailed population statistics for American and world Jewry.)

Goldscheider, Calvin. *American Jewish Fertility: Trends and Differentials in the Providence Metropolitan Area*. Providence: Brown University, 1986.

Goldscheider, Calvin and Sidney Goldstein. *The Jewish Community of Rhode Island: A Social and Demographic Study, 1987*. Providence: Jewish Federation of Rhode Island, 1988.

Goldstein, Sidney. *The Greater Providence Jewish Community: A Population Study*. Providence: General Jewish Committee of Greater Providence, Inc. 1964.

Goldstein, Sidney and Calvin Goldscheider. *Jewish Americans: Three Generations in a Jewish Community*. Englewood Cliffs, N.J.: Prentice-Hall, Inc., 1968.

Goldstein, Sidney and Alice Goldstein. *Jews on the Move: Implications for Jewish Identity*. New York: State University Press of New York, 1996.

Marcus, Jacob Rader. *To Count a People: American Jewish Population Data, 1595–1984*. Lanham, Md.: University Press of America, 1990.

Rosenwaike, Ira. *On the Edge of Greatness: A Portrait of American Jewry in the Early National Period*. Cincinnati: American Jewish Archives, 1985.

Sheskin, Ira. M. *The 2002 Rhode Island Jewish Community Study: Major Themes Report*. Providence: Jewish Federation of Rhode Island, 2003.

INDEX

Page numbers in bold indicate illustrations.

266

Index